Reading Success in the Early Primary Years

Reading Success in the Early Primary Years is a step-by-step guide to structured literacy instruction for teachers working in the early years of primary school. Written by a teacher, for teachers, this book supports teachers to understand the evidence base of reading instruction and how to successfully implement it.

Structured in three parts, the book breaks down complex concepts in a concise, accessible manner, guiding teachers on eight key actions to take to get every child on the path to reading proficiency. These include instruction in phonics, phonological and phonemic awareness, integrated reading and spelling opportunities, and the use of decodable texts. Highly practical, *Reading Success in the Early Primary Years* offers over 20 explicit instructional routines that teachers can implement in their classrooms and guidance on how to get the most out of instructional time. These practical elements are further supported by a summary of relevant research and theories about how reading develops, including an outline of high impact, explicit teaching that draws on cognitive load theory.

Rich with sample lesson plans, tools, and examples from real classrooms, this book allows teachers to get on with the business of teaching reading. This is a must-have resource for all who are responsible for children's reading instruction in the first three years of school.

Jocelyn Seamer is a teacher and former school leader who provides simple, practical solutions to help teachers implement structured literacy instruction. She can be reached at www.jocelynseamereducation.com

Reading Success in the Early Primary Years

A Teacher's Guide to Implementing Systematic Instruction

Jocelyn Seamer

LONDON AND NEW YORK

Cover image: © Jocelyn Seamer

First published 2023
by Routledge
4 Park Square, Milton Park, Abingdon, Oxon OX14 4RN

and by Routledge
605 Third Avenue, New York, NY 10158

Routledge is an imprint of the Taylor & Francis Group, an informa business

© 2023 Jocelyn Seamer

The right of Jocelyn Seamer to be identified as author of this work has been asserted in accordance with sections 77 and 78 of the Copyright, Designs and Patents Act 1988.

All rights reserved. No part of this book may be reprinted or reproduced or utilised in any form or by any electronic, mechanical, or other means, now known or hereafter invented, including photocopying and recording, or in any information storage or retrieval system, without permission in writing from the publishers.

Trademark notice: Product or corporate names may be trademarks or registered trademarks, and are used only for identification and explanation without intent to infringe.

British Library Cataloguing-in-Publication Data
A catalogue record for this book is available from the British Library

Library of Congress Cataloging-in-Publication Data
Names: Seamer, Jocelyn, author.
Title: Reading success in the early primary years : a teacher's guide to implementing systematic instruction / Jocelyn Seamer.
Description: First Edition. | New York : Routledge, 2023. | Includes bibliographical references and index.
Identifiers: LCCN 2022022732 (print) | LCCN 2022022733 (ebook) | ISBN 9781032154442 (Hardback) | ISBN 9781032154459 (Paperback) | ISBN 9781003244189 (eBook)
Subjects: LCSH: Language arts (Primary) | Literacy. | Reading. | Vocabulary.
Classification: LCC LB1528 .S36 2023 (print) | LCC LB1528 (ebook) | DDC 372.6--dc23/eng/20220727
LC record available at https://lccn.loc.gov/2022022732
LC ebook record available at https://lccn.loc.gov/2022022733

ISBN: 978-1-032-15444-2 (hbk)
ISBN: 978-1-032-15445-9 (pbk)
ISBN: 978-1-003-24418-9 (ebk)

DOI: 10.4324/9781003244189

Typeset in Bembo
by KnowledgeWorks Global Ltd.

We all stand on the shoulders of those who have come before and pave the way for those who are still to come. I dedicate this book to my own teachers who devoted their professional lives to the well-being of children, to my mother who taught me to love words and aim high, and to the teachers everywhere who strive to ensure Reading Success for every child in their care. Lastly, but in no way least, I dedicate this book to my husband and children, without whose support, love, and encouragement it would not have come to be.

Contents

List of figures ix
List of tables xi
Foreword xiii
Acknowledgements xv
Terms and Abbreviations xvi

Introduction 1

PART I
Setting up for Success 5

1 The Theoretical Underpinnings of the Big Six 7
2 What to Teach 24
3 Bang for Your Buck Teaching 34
4 Differentiation and Supporting Students with Reading Difficulty 40

PART II
The 8 Key Actions 53

5 8 Key Actions One, Two, Three, and Four 55
6 Key Actions Five, Six, Seven, and Eight 69

PART III
Structured Literacy Practices 79

7 High Impact Teaching 81

8	Organising the Literacy Block	93
9	Oral Language and Vocabulary	106
10	Phonological and Phonemic Awareness	121
11	Phonics	136
12	Using Decodable Texts	150
13	Irregular High Frequency Words	161
14	Text Level Reading	171
15	Skills-Based Assessment	183
	Appendix 1	191
	Glossary	192
	More from Jocelyn	194
	Index	195

Figures

1.1	The Simple View of Reading (Gough & Tunmer, 1986)	7
1.2	The Many Strands That Make up Skilled Reading (Hollis Scarborough, 2001)	8
1.3	The Big Six of Reading Instruction	10
1.4	The Language House. Professor Pamela Snow	11
2.1	Ratio of Decoding to Comprehension Instruction	30
2.2	The Lower Primary Literacy Block	31
5.1	Suggested Sequence of Learning for Sentence Structure	56
5.2	Suggested Sequence of Learning for Parts of Speech (Based on English Sequence of Content - Australian Curriculum, ACARA, 2015)	57
5.3	Semantic Networks - Every Word Has Other Words and Concepts Associated with It	58
5.4	Suggested Time Frame for Acquiring Phonological and Phonemic Skills	62
6.1	Decision-Making Framework When Moving on From Decodable Texts	77
7.1	Mariani's High Challenge, High Support Environment	81
7.2	A Visual Timetable. Photo Courtesy of Liz Foley. *Used with Permission*	85
7.3	Visuals on a Lanyard	85
7.4	Instructional Routine Visual	86
7.5	The Gradual Increase of Context Model. Copyright - Jocelyn Seamer Education.	87
8.1	Intersection of Scarborough's Reading Rope with the Literacy Block	94
8.2	Tub Time Set up. Photo Courtesy of Mikalya Luxton. *Used with Permission*	96
8.3	Framework to Develop Skills for Independent Tasks	98
8.4	Daily Shared Writing Routine	100
9.1	Subject and Verb Pictures to Support Oral Sentence Instruction	112
13.1	Sight Word Boxes	161

13.2 Map the Word   165
13.3 Write in the Regular Part   166
13.4 Write in the Irregular Part   166
13.5 Rewrite the Word   166

Tables

2.1	The English Alphabetic Code	25
2.2	Scope and Sequence of Phonics and Morphology Instruction	28
2.3	Connecting the Strands of Scarborough's Reading Rope with the Literacy Block	32
4.1	Options for Differentiation in the Literacy Block	43
7.1	Establishing Learning Behaviours	84
9.1	BICS Versus CALP, Developed by Jim Cummins (1981)	107
9.2	Partner Talk Lesson Plan	107
9.3	Vocabulary Introduction Lesson Plan (Beck et al., 2013)	109
9.4	Timeline of Teaching Sentence Structure Across the Early Years 'At Least' Points	111
9.5	Teaching Compound Sentences Lesson Plan	114
10.1	'Jump it Out' Lesson Steps	122
10.2	Syllable Blending in Instructions Lesson Steps	122
10.3	Syllable Segmenting During Transitions Lesson Steps	123
10.4	Rhyming During Transitions Lesson Steps	124
10.5	Early Phoneme Identification Lesson Steps	125
10.6	Beginning Blending (I Do) Lesson Steps	127
10.7	Beginning Blending (We Do) Lesson Steps	128
10.8	Beginning Blending (You Do) Lesson Steps	129
10.9	Beginning Segmenting (I Do) Lesson Sequence	130
10.10	Beginning Segmenting (We Do) Lesson Steps	130
10.11	Beginning Segmenting (You Do) Lesson Steps	131
11.1	Steps to a Basic Code Phonics Lesson	139
11.2	Complex Code Phonics Lesson Steps	143
12.1	Alternatives to Guided Reading Practices	150
12.2	Sentence Level Transcription Lesson Steps	157
13.1	Sight Words Versus IHFW	162
13.2	IHFW Arranged According to Letter Sound/Spelling Patterns	164

13.3 Teaching Irregular High Frequency Words Lesson Steps 165
14.1 Responding to Student Needs in Text Use across the
    Curriculum 173
14.2 A Lesson with Mostly Decodable Texts 176
14.3 National Assessment of Educational Progress Fluency Scale
    (Pinnell, 1995) 179

Foreword

There is no way to sugar-coat the fact that one of the persisting and most frustrating aspects of the decades-old reading wars has been the dumbing down of teacher pre-service preparation for the task of teaching young children to read. In the pre-electronic era, the shelves of university libraries were groaning with volumes upon volumes of scientific journals whose pages detailed the nature of the reading process and how best to teach it. International inquiries in the United States (2000), Australia (2005), and England (2006) were convened in an effort to call 'time' on the perpetuation of practices that were not embedded in sound theoretical understandings of the reading process and not supported by robust research. But still, the symbiotic relationship between so-called "balanced literacy" and teacher pre-service preparation has persisted, with minimal disruption, even at the time of my writing this Foreword in April 2022.

The good news in this otherwise sometimes bleak landscape is that teachers themselves are increasingly seizing the reigns and becoming impactful agents of classroom and system-level change. One such teacher is Jocelyn Seamer, whose odyssey away from balanced literacy has culminated in her writing this book.

Seamer shares here what she herself has had to learn the long and circuitous way about what the reading process really is and how best to teach it. In so doing, she lifts the veil on some of the apparent mysteries of the English language from a historical perspective, so that teachers no longer need to resort to an unsatisfactory and uncomfortable "that's just the way English is" shrug in response to students' questions about spelling and pronunciation patterns.

Seamer has written a book that strikes a "just right" balance between enough theoretical content and practical applications that support teachers to transform their classroom practice. It is one thing to emphasise the need for teachers to teach using a scope and sequence, but something else altogether for an author to guide readers on what that looks like and how to use it in practice. Seamer supports teachers to know what to look for in a scope and sequence, in order to make optimal use of a literacy block. It is easy for any teacher to create busy work that looks like students are "engaged" in the most general of ways. It is something else altogether, however, for teachers to take responsibility for students' learning through their own rigorous application of explicit instruction principles and robust monitoring of student progress.

Seamer approaches explicit instruction at two levels throughout the book: firstly, in her presentation of what in many cases will be new information for practising teachers about the science of learning (the *what*), and secondly in her guidelines for implementing this in classrooms (the *how*) with respect to reading instruction. Far too many teachers, even those who are recent graduates, look blankly when concepts such as biologically primary and secondary skills, cognitive load, data-based differentiation, and explicit instruction are mentioned in the context of professional learning.

Coverage of explicit instruction is often avoided in teacher preparation and is not uncommonly given a "bad rap" in such circles. Yet when teachers fully understand what explicit instruction is and is not, and how it enables them to support the learning of *all* students in their classrooms, they are keen to embrace it and promote its use. Results speak for themselves and there is no turning back. When those results occur for early reading achievement, students are given the keys to the academic success treasure chest and to the life opportunities this affords.

Mainstream classroom reading instruction should be successful for the vast majority (95%) of students, regardless of their starting point. Seamer's book will be a strong addition to the libraries of teachers who have turned their backs on balanced literacy and are determined, as our friends at The Reading League urge us, to know better and do better.

Professor Pamela Snow, School of Education,
La Trobe University, Australia

Acknowledgements

Firstly, I wish to thank Professor Pamela Snow for her generosity and guidance as I prepared this work.

I would like the take the opportunity to acknowledge and thank the amazing teachers who have generously agreed to share their experiences with you all in the snapshots of practice and photographs presented throughout the book.

- Alison Fahey
- April Brown
- Brynell Francis
- Charlene Stewart
- Dan Colquhoun
- Diane Herman
- Jo Dick
- Karen Lane
- Eldon Jenkin
- Xanthi Rice
- Liz Foley
- Larissa Marchant
- Karen Michell
- Kathryn Thorburn
- Nadine MacAninch
- Suzanne Powell
- Mikalya Luxton

I would also like to acknowledge the wonderful teachers who have participated in the Reading Success in the Early Primary Years Teach Along course. Your commitment to improving your practice is a constant inspiration.

Finally, I wish to thank the teachers and students at Montello Primary School, Tasmania, for allowing me the opportunity to support you in your structured literacy journey.

Terms and Abbreviations

References to Phonemes and Graphemes

Throughout the book, I have referred to 'sounds' 'phonemes'. These have been represented by the use of slashes and the most simple grapheme that represents these phonemes. For example, the 'sound' at the start of snake is written as /s/, and the sound at the start of chair is written /ch/. The long A sound is written as /ai/ and the long i sound as /igh/ because these graphemes do not commonly represent any other phoneme. While the international phonetic alphabet is more precise, it is not generally familiar to classroom teachers, and I felt that a simpler approach would serve you better. I have also referred to specific graphemes or letters. These are represented by the use of apostrophes. For example, 'ai' or 'sh'. So, the phoneme /w/ can be written down as 'w' or 'wh'.

Should We Say 'Phonemes and Graphemes' or 'Sounds and Letters'?

The technical word for the sounds we say when we speak is 'phonemes'; however, in practice we very often use this interchangeably with the word 'sounds'. Each school will have its own preference regarding this and it is my view that children are neither advantaged nor disadvantaged by this choice. This book uses both words interchangeably, and teachers and schools should use terminology that makes the most sense to them. Similarly, the word graphemes may or may not be used directly with students. I believe that children are more capable than we often give them credit for in their ability to learn this terminology; however, if you refer to graphemes differently, that is fine too. In my experience, it is more important to achieve consistency in the terminology used across classrooms than it is to use a particular phrase.

Programs

There are two ways that I refer to programs.

1 The body of work a teacher produces in preparation for teaching
2 A commercially available, off-the-shelf tool used to structure content and teaching

Introduction

Dear Colleagues

I have been compelled to write this book for you after many conversations, emails, training sessions, and social media posts with teachers all asking the same question, 'What does the science of reading look like in my classroom?'

In my role as a school leader and now teacher trainer and consultant, I have one goal: to make the teaching of reading simpler, more effective, and aligned with the evidence about reading instruction. For far too long teachers have struggled along, doing the best they could with the knowledge and strategies available to them only to end each school year feeling like a failure because some (or many) of their students were still not reading at an appropriate level. This book aims to bring to life the evidence around structured literacy for you in a manner that is easy to implement, draws on the evidence base of the science of language and reading, and supports your cognitive load. After all, nothing is accomplished when we feel overloaded and overwhelmed. This is true for both children and adults alike.

It is time to let go of professional learning that yields no professional development. It is time to let go of teaching methods that require children to 'put it together' themselves and are built on the misinformed, outdated, and often damaging assumptions of a time before we knew what was happening in our brains when we read.

With this book, I hope to equip you with knowledge, skills, and guidance that allows you to gain (or recapture) a love of reading instruction and to help you build the feelings of success in your students that light the spark of a love of learning. To be a good teacher, it is necessary to be a good learner. I am here to walk alongside you in your learning journey, to give you a flotation device if you feel like you are drowning and support you to learn what structured literacy looks, feels, and sounds like in your classroom. Together, I know that we can help every one of your students achieve Reading Success in the Early Primary Years.

DOI: 10.4324/9781003244189-1

What You Can Expect From This Book

To truly possess a skill, we need understanding. If you are looking for an academic text full of dense language and discussions of the finer points of research, this is not the text for you. If, however, you are looking for plain language outlines of research, practical overviews, and a guide full of strategies and techniques that you can use in your classroom right away, then welcome!

The book is structured as follows:

> Part I – Setting up for Success. An outline of the Big Six of reading instruction and an explanation of other key ideas such as cognitive load, differentiation, supporting students with reading difficulty, and high impact teaching strategies.
>
> Part II – A discussion of Eight Key Actions of Structured Literacy.
>
> Part III – Structured Literacy Practices. Specific guidance and teaching routines across the literacy block. The teaching routines and structures shared have not all been rigorously studied; however, they reflect the findings of the research described in Parts I and II.

I have structured Reading Success in the Early Primary Years so that you can use it in the way that makes the most sense for you. If you wish to start at Chapter 1, reading about the research supporting structured literacy, you can do so. If you are looking for a teaching routine for any point across the literacy block that you can implement tomorrow, then you can do that too. When it comes to implementing what you find in this book, I fully expect that you will tweak and change the routines I have provided. You are, after all, a teacher with experience. You are also responding to the needs of your students, which requires changes and adjustments to meet them where they are up to. If you are concerned that your changes might reduce the effectiveness of the lesson outlines provided, refer to Part II (8 Key Actions) and review the features of explicit instruction and recommendations grounded in the research. With one eye on your students and the other eye on the research, you will be in a good place to support the needs of every student in your class.

A Word on Terminology

You can't visit the 'Science of Reading' faculty at your local university or enrol in a course that will teach you how to become a reading scientist. What you can do is access, literally, thousands of research papers that have been published by researchers from a range of disciplines that tell us what works best for the largest number of children in reading instruction. The term 'Science of Reading' has become so pervasive in our profession that this term, and all that it stands for, is in danger of taking on the status of a fad or 'next shiny thing' in education. It is for this reason that I will refer to the approach to reading instruction described in this book as 'systematic reading instruction' or 'structured literacy'.

I hope that you gain as much enjoyment reading this book and implementing what you find within its pages as I did in writing it. Happy teaching.

All my best
Jocelyn

Part I
Setting up for Success

1 The Theoretical Underpinnings of the Big Six

Frameworks That Underpin Our Understanding of Reading

There are several key frameworks that help shape our understanding of reading: The Simple View of Reading (Gough & Tunmer, 1986), Scarborough's Reading Rope (2001), Linnea Ehri's Phase Theory, and The Big Six Ideas of Reading (NICHD, 2000).

The Simple View of Reading

Gough and Tunmer's Simple View of Reading (1986) has stood the test of time and remains one of the central ways that teachers can understand the skills students require to be competent and efficient readers. Gough and Tunmer argued that effortless, automatic word reading combined with strong language comprehension results in reading comprehension. They expressed this as the formula $R = D \times C$, where each part of the formula is represented by a number from 0 (not present) to 1 (perfection). The 'C' in the equation relates to oral/linguistic comprehension and the 'D' to decoding. The Simple View of Reading is often represented with the image below (see Figure 1.1), although this is not part of Gough and Tunmer's original paper.

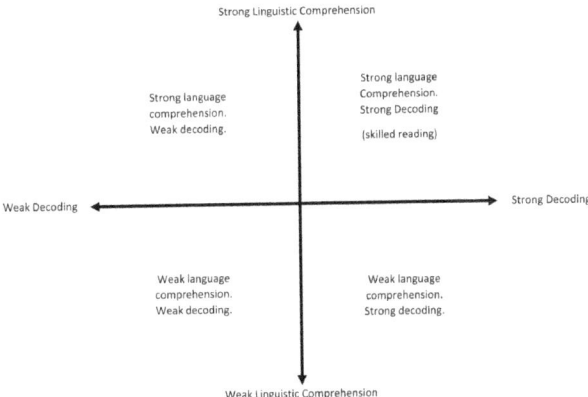

Figure 1.1 The Simple View of Reading (Gough & Tunmer, 1986)

DOI: 10.4324/9781003244189-3

8 *Setting up for Success*

Scarborough's Reading Rope

Dr Hollis Scarborough produced the infographic, 'The Many Strands that Make up Skilled Reading' as a workshop handout (see Figure 1.2). It has since become one of the most recognisable infographics in the structured literacy world. Dr Scarborough used the strands of the rope to indicate the many skills and areas of knowledge that need to be developed in order for skilled reading to occur. The top of the rope relates to the linguistic components that teachers must focus on and the bottom of the rope to the 'decoding' components. While it appears that the top and bottom strands of the rope relate to Gough and Tunmer's Simple View of Reading, this is a coincidence and not Dr Scarborough's intention. This connection does however make it easier for teachers to understand the framework of their literacy teaching and plan for teaching accordingly.

Linnea Ehri's Phase Theory

Linnea Ehri proposed four phases of development in learning to read words by sight (Ehri, 2005).

- Pre-alphabetic phase
- Partial alphabetic phase
- Full alphabetic phase
- Consolidated alphabetic phase

THE MANY STRANDS THAT ARE WOVEN INTO SKILLED READING

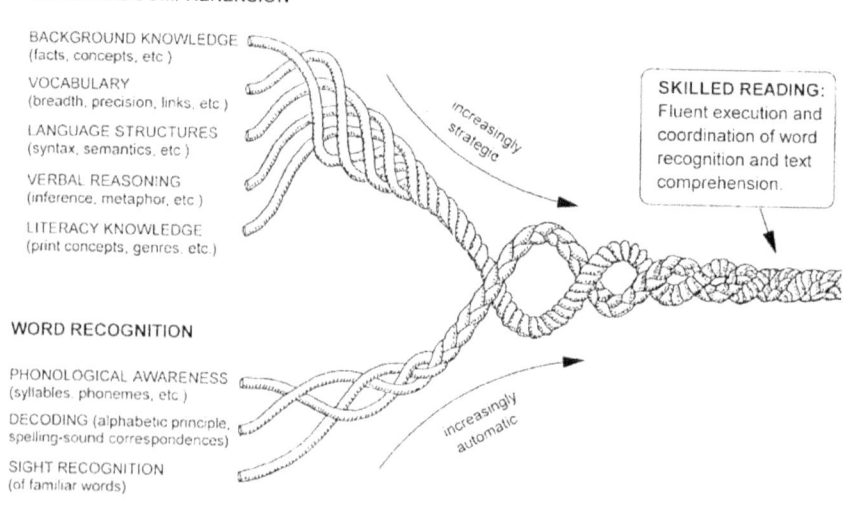

Figure 1.2 The Many Strands That Make up Skilled Reading (Hollis Scarborough, 2001)

Ehri's phases are characterised by differences that develop in the way that children access the alphabetic code as they make connections between the way a word looks, the way it sounds, and what it means.

Pre-alphabetic phase – children do not attend to the alphabetic features of a word, but rather to visual cues such as the 'oo' resembling eyes in the word look. In this phase, children rely on the visual features of the image or shape that accompanies the text and are not connecting the text with the pronunciation of the word at all.

Partial alphabetic phase – children create connections between some of the letters in the word and the way the word is said. For example, a student may remember the 't' and 'n' in the word 'train', and this helps them to remember the word when they see it again. However, the remainder of the letters are not attended to, which makes it difficult to distinguish between the words 'train' and 'town' in reading.

Full alphabetic phase – children connect all of the graphemes in a word to the way the word is said, making it much easier to bond the written word with its pronunciation. It is this attention to the internal structure of whole word that promotes orthographic mapping, the bonding of a word's spelling, pronunciation, and meaning in memory (Ehri, 2014). This is also a more reliable way to read words than the approach of the partial alphabetic phase as it eliminates the confusion between *train* and *town* or *spoon* and *soon*. Further, the full alphabetic phase enables children to read words they have never seen before, which is an important step in becoming a skilled reader.

Consolidated alphabetic phase – through repeated reading of words that contain similar patterns, children commit these patterns into long-term memory as units. These units can be graphemes, syllables, morphemes, or word parts such as onsets and rimes. This makes the task of reading longer words easier because there are fewer elements to process than in the full alphabetic phase.

It is important to know that these phases are not a continuum of instruction, but rather a way to understand what happens in our brains when we read. Orthographic mapping is not an activity we do in the classroom, but a cognitive process whereby children make connections between the way a word looks, the way it sounds, and what it means. As we will explore, instruction should focus on building understanding and fluency with the alphabetic principle and helping children develop strong word recognition skills.

The Big Six Ideas in Reading Instruction

The Big Six is a framework that has become synonymous with an evidence-informed approach to reading instruction. In 2000, the U.S. National Reading Panel released a report of its findings on the evidence base of reading instruction. This report outlined five key areas to be addressed in order to provide comprehensive literacy instruction (NICHD, 2000):

phonological and phonemic awareness, phonics, vocabulary, fluency, and comprehension. These became known as the 'Big Five'. In 2014, Deslea Konza published a paper called *Teaching Reading: Why the 'Fab Five' should be the 'Big Six'* (Konza, 2014) in which she made the case for oral language to be included as the sixth key component due to its impact on every aspect of reading development. Considering the critical role of oral language in early childhood and in literacy development, I will refer to the 'Big Six' in this book.

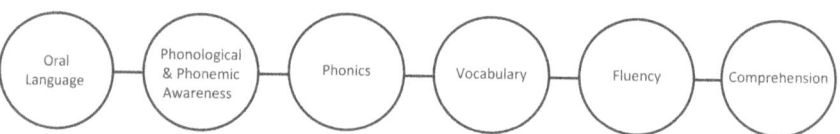

Figure 1.3 The Big Six of Reading Instruction

The Theoretical Basis of the Big Six

Oral Language

Oral language is the ability to speak and to listen. As vocabulary and phonological and phonemic awareness are dealt with in their own categories in the Big Six, we will talk about other elements of language here such as semantics (meaning), syntax (sentence structure and parts of speech – teachers often call this grammar), and morphology (the study of the smallest units of meaning in words) (Gambrell, 2004). We can also add phonology (the sounds in words), the ability to say them (articulation), and pragmatics (knowing which language is appropriate in different social situations) to the mix (Hulme & Snowling, 2014). We can see from this list that oral language is a complex mix of interdependent skills. In her Language House infographic (see Figure 1.4), Professor Pamela Snow provides a conceptual framework highlighting the interactions between oral language, literacy development, well-being, and later life outcomes (Snow, 2020).

Professor Snow highlights the importance of both home and school environment and their roles in promoting oral language development as well as the role of oral language in reading acquisition. Acquiring solid foundations in oral language is critical, not just for reading but also for social and emotional well-being. Professor Snow describes the development of early language as a 'metaphorical slab of granite' on which other skills can be built.

Oral language skills develop quite naturally for most children (Seidenberg, 2017), and unlike reading, we are hard-wired to develop them. You may ask, 'If most students are going to develop oral language, why include it in

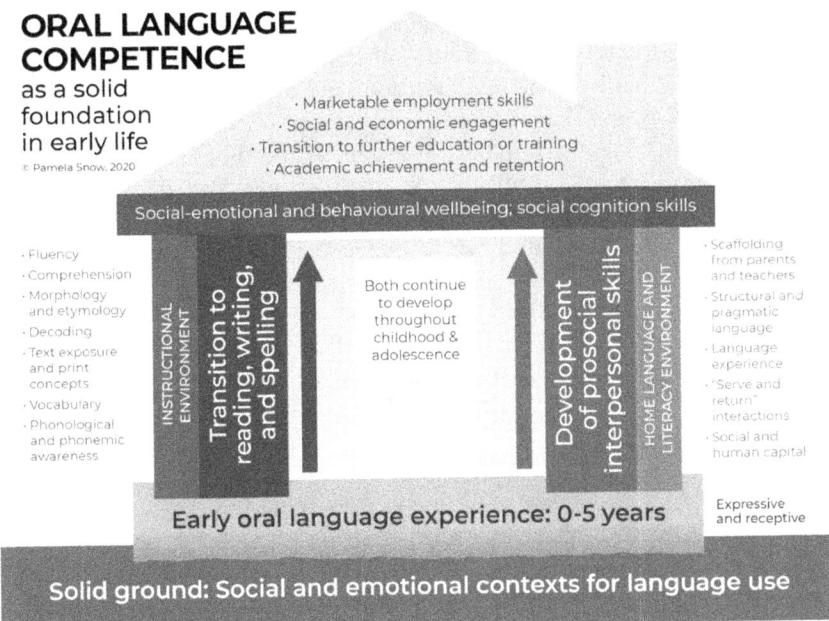

Figure 1.4 The Language House. Professor Pamela Snow

our programs at all?' The answer is twofold. First, oral language skills play a significant part in a student's developing capacity to comprehend what they read. This, of course, is the ultimate goal of reading instruction (Dickinson & Porche, 2011; Hulme & Snowling, 2014; Lepola, 2016; Lervåg et al., 2018; Moats, 2020). In fact, oral language skills are a strong predictor of future reading achievement (Seidenberg, 2017). In terms of early decoding skills, there is a positive 'knock-on' effect. The development of language skills supports phonemic awareness development, which then supports early decoding development (Dickinson et al., 2010). The second reason to address oral language skills in our teaching is that students who struggle in some way in this area are prime candidates for reading difficulty. Kilpatrick's (2015) text 'Essentials of Assessing, Preventing and Overcoming Reading Difficulties' discusses the link between challenges with grammar (syntax and parts of speech) and oral comprehension, which in turn leads to difficulties with reading comprehension. For students experiencing this difficulty, it is critical that we identify and support them early to build the necessary skills for language development and reading (Goldfeld et al., 2021). Challenges in oral language skills make it difficult for students to acquire phonemic awareness skills (and therefore decode) and to monitor their own comprehension while reading. This particularly affects students with developmental language disorder and other language challenges (such as experienced by students on the autism spectrum) (Moats, 2020). However, challenges can also come about because of neglect or disruptions to the home environment in the early years of life (Snow, 2020). What we do in our classrooms matters. Teachers are not speech pathologists or counsellors, but we can support all students by creating a classroom environment rich in oral language. This can be as simple as choosing rich picture books and non-fiction text to read with students and then facilitating structured shared reading experiences. A meta-analysis conducted by Swanson et al. (2011) found that language and literature-rich teaching led to moderate to high gains in reading outcomes, especially when the storytelling aspects were transferred to the children during instruction. We will examine high-quality oral language instruction and its impacts on literacy development in greater detail in the following chapters.

Phonological and Phonemic Awareness

Phonological and phonemic awareness (PA) is the bridge between oral language and decoding. Kilpatrick (2015) describes three broad levels of PA:

1 Early phonological awareness – rhyming, alliteration, and syllable segmentation.
2 Basic phonemic awareness – identifying the initial phoneme, phoneme blending, and segmenting. Blending occurs when children combine the phonemes /c/ - /a/ - /t/ into the word 'cat'. Every time we utter a word, we are engaging in oral blending. Taking the separate phonemes in a word and blending them is the vehicle by which we lift unfamiliar words from the page. Segmenting occurs when we separate and isolate the phonemes in a word, such as being able to separate the word 'dog' into /d/ /o/ /g/. Spelling is what happens when we represent those phonemes with a written symbol.
3 Automatic and more developed awareness – automaticity in phonemic awareness that enables students to delete, add, and substitute phonemes in words. This develops once students are familiar with how words work, have acquired the fundamentals of blending and segmenting, and have a firm understanding of the alphabetic code.

Phonological and phonemic awareness is an integral part of early oral language development and can be developed before reading instruction commences. There is ample evidence of the positive effects of this on later reading development (Anthony & Francis, 2005; Ayres, 1995; Kilpatrick, 2015; Lundberg et al., 1988). A lack of these skills is one of the primary predictors of reading difficulty (Stone, 2013). Students with dyslexia very often have core phonological deficits which significantly impact their reading development (Kilpatrick, 2015) in all aspects of word-level reading. As many children develop phonological and phonemic awareness skills without difficulty, the role of explicit teaching in this area is easy to overlook. A recent surge in prepared, whole class oral programs has resulted in an increased awareness of phonological and phonemic awareness in our classrooms; however, the role of graphemes in this work has been difficult for some classroom teachers to establish in practice. This is made more challenging when we consider that the matter is still hotly contested by reading researchers. While phonological and phonemic awareness tasks can be performed 'with your eyes closed', when it comes to instruction, phonemic awareness is most effective when combined with phoneme/grapheme correspondence (Kilpatrick, 2015). Further, while children can learn to blend and segment orally, the National Reading Panel found that the effects of phonemic awareness instruction were greater when graphemes were used than when they were not. The meta-analysis described in this report showed that all students benefit from explicit instruction in phonemic awareness including typically developing readers and those at risk of reading failure (NICHD, 2000). Finally, it is important to note that phonemic awareness is a means to enable reading and spelling, not an end in itself. That is, it is not a separate, stand-alone activity done for the entire time a student is in primary school. An important take-home message from the National Reading Panel's report was that more PA instruction isn't necessarily better. Approaches that focused on teaching a small number of skills for a shorter period of time yielded better results than those that addressed a large number of skills and ran for longer. Most children will not require explicit phonological and phonemic awareness instruction beyond the second year of school; however, continuing to provide support to older students who require it is important (NICHD, 2000).

Phonics

It is important to state that reading experts do not agree on one definition of phonics. For the purpose of this book, I will adopt the following definition: 'Phonics is a body of knowledge about the relationship between the sounds of spoken language and the letters used to represent them in writing' (Buckingham et al., 2019, p. 50). The issue of phonics instruction is one that has been a 'hot topic' in recent decades. Just about everyone will agree that building connections between phonemes (the speech sounds of our language) and graphemes (the letter or combination of letters that represent them) is important in learning to read. However, there are some wildly diverging opinions about the role of phonics in the overall process of acquiring literacy and how best to teach it. This section is not focused on critiquing opinion, but on presenting evidence and findings. Let's start with an exploration of how English works. English is one of the most orthographically deep languages of the world (Petscher et al., 2020). That is, we have a complex alphabetic code system in which one grapheme can represent multiple phonemes and a single phoneme can be represented by multiple graphemes. Our language has for over more than 1000 years and has been heavily influenced by languages such as German, Scandinavian tongues, Latin, Greek, and French. In addition, words aren't only constructed based on phonemes, but also on morphemes (the smallest units of meaning in a word). There is a pervasive myth in our profession that the English language is too complex and too devoid of logic to be taught explicitly and systematically and, therefore, beginning readers need to memorise words as whole units. This is simply not true. Ninety-six per cent of words in English can be decoded using knowledge of phonics, morphology, and etymology (the origins of words) (Moats, 2020).

Phonics is, in essence, the development of phoneme/grapheme correspondence and while a quality phonics lesson will include so much more than this, the development of this essential knowledge is critical to reading development. It is necessary to keep in mind that phonics instruction needs to continue beyond the first year of school so that students acquire automatic recognition and recall of multiple representations of all 44 phonemes of English (although the number of phonemes recognised can depend on dialect). Maintaining a robust, yet responsive pace in this learning will take most children up to three years to acquire the code knowledge they need for automatic word recognition and fluent reading (Moats, 2020).

To understand the important role of phonics instruction in overall reading instruction, we need look no further than the findings of the inquiries of three nations into the evidence base of reading instruction. The United States of America, Australia, and England all convened national inquiry panels between 1995 and 2006 to examine the best way to teach reading to young children. The three reports produced by these panels outlined the need for the systematic teaching of reading in the early years of school. The word 'systematic' is important here. Australia's National Inquiry into the Teaching of Literacy found that reading instruction that did not include a systematic phonics instruction or, indeed, did not include phonics instruction at all not only underperformed in equipping students for reading, but also impeded the students' ability to read, spell, and comprehend (Rowe, 2005). There is some conjecture about how best to implement systematic phonics instruction. Synthetic phonics instruction explicitly teaches the connections between graphemes and phonemes (letters and sounds) and how to blend them together to read words. Analytic phonics instruction, on the other hand, approaches word-level reading through the larger units of onset and rime (word families), so children would learn the 'at' family r-at, s-at, f-at, etc. While there is evidence for both systems of teaching phonics, the synthetic approach is the most direct and systematic approach (Buckingham, 2020). It contains far fewer conceptual units for students to learn and effectively represents current evidence around the benefit of learning to map sounds to letters (Dehaene, 2009). While there are few research studies comparing the two approaches (Wheldale & Buckingham, 2020), one large study can be considered. In the 2004 Clackmannanshire study,

Johnston and Watson compared the reading and spelling progress of 300 students in the first years of school who were divided into instructional groupings including both synthetic and analytical approaches to teaching phonics and word-level decoding. They then followed the progress of these students for seven years to assess the long-term impacts of the approaches. Students who had experienced systematic, synthetic phonics instruction in their first years of reading instruction were three years, six months ahead of their chronological age in word-level reading by the end of their seventh year of school (Johnston et al., 2011). It is important to acknowledge that the original Clackmannanshire study did not contain a control (one criterion for robust research).

Despite these results and the anecdotal evidence from schools, there are those in education who argue that there is no evidence that systematic synthetic phonics is superior to other types of phonics instruction. However, this is not reflected in the research. The National Reading Panel defined systematic instruction as involving

> …explicitly teaching students a prespecified set of letter-sound relations and having students read text that provides practice using these relations to decode words.
> (NICHD, 2000, p. 2–92)

This is the essence of systematic synthetic phonics. The panel also reported:

> 'Findings provided solid support for the conclusion that systematic phonics instruction makes a bigger contribution to children's growth in reading than alternative programs providing unsystematic or no phonics instruction'.
> (NICHD, 2000, p. 2–132)

Linnea Ehri, who has been studying reading and reading instruction for decades, states that the ability to decode new words is necessary to move to the full alphabetic phase of reading. Further, the key to this development is knowledge of phoneme/grapheme correspondences and the ability to blend phonemes together to decode unfamiliar words. She and her team worked with teachers to implement a reading program where students learned key words containing common spelling patterns and were then taught to read new words by comparing them to the key words (an analytical approach). Ehri's team found that some students had difficulty committing the core patterns to memory, but when instruction shifted to teaching phoneme/grapheme correspondences (via a synthetic phonics instructional approach), learning was much stronger (Ehri, 2020).

From this, we can see that current indications are that the most efficient way to teach decoding is by using a systematic, synthetic approach rather than an analytic phonics instructional approach.

Vocabulary

Vocabulary forms a significant part of our oral language development and is equally important as decoding for beginning readers (Dehaene, 2009), as it is the means by which children compare a decoded word to words in their oral language lexicon to make sense of the text. Some of the most influential work on vocabulary development in the school years has been done by Beck et al. (2013). In their well-known text 'Bringing Words to Life' (2013), they describe three tiers of vocabulary to assist teachers to think about instruction that builds this part of students' language skills.

Tier 1 – common, everyday words that we use in conversation.
Tier 2 – high utility words that are more formal and are more likely to appear in academic writing. These words often appear in different contexts and genres. Learning about these words can be transferred across learning situations.
Tier 3 – subject-specific words used when a specific need arises such as when learning about biology or politics.

In the sentence 'The plant performs photosynthesis', the word *plant* would be regarded as Tier 1, the word *performs* as Tier 2, and the word *photosynthesis* as Tier 3.

Far from being solely a school-based undertaking, the learning of specialised vocabulary begins long before children learn to read, often by having stories read to them by adults (Seidenberg, 2017). Vocabulary development, in general, begins in infancy and the level of vocabulary achieved by the first year of school is one of the predictors of later reading ability (Moats, 2020).

For Beck et al. (2013), the goal of vocabulary instruction is to 'enhance students' ability to participate in complex language situations' (p. 146). That is, we want students to be able to actually use language in meaningful ways, not just to copy out dictionary definitions and make an attempt to use a word in a contrived sentence. Beck et al. describe four stages of word knowledge on a continuum from never having seen the word before to knowing about several aspects of the word including meaning, relationships to other words, and metaphorical use (Beck et al., 2013). This richness of understanding supports a student's development in both reading and writing. In writing, it enables students to fully express their ideas and emotions. In reading, a two-way relationship exists. The development of a rich vocabulary makes it easier to learn to read and learning to read promotes vocabulary development as students interact with and experience more words in the written form (Seidenberg, 2017). Vocabulary development is critical for both oral and reading comprehension. When reading, a student must know what 90% of the content words mean in order to understand what they are (Moats, 2020). There is also a relationship between vocabulary knowledge and reading fluency that we will examine next.

Fluency

Reading fluency is not an activity or skill in and of itself. We don't 'do' fluency. Fluency is the product of strong development across a number of domains including decoding/word recognition, phonemic awareness, vocabulary acquisition, and background knowledge. As such, it tends to evolve as these skills emerge and can be improved by strengthening these sub-skills and/or through particular instructional processes such as repeated oral reading that is accompanied by guidance as needed (NICHD, 2000). Fluency comprises accuracy, automaticity, and prosody (Paige et al., 2012).

Kuhn et al. (2010) described these three components in the following way:

1 Accuracy – relates to correctly lifting the individual words from the page.
2 Automaticity – achieved when speed, effortlessness, autonomy, and lack of conscious awareness exist.
3 Prosody – describes smooth reading with expression.

So often, teachers focus on text-level reading rate to measure fluency; however, this is only part of the picture. In fact, simply measuring reading rate is unlikely to provide us with the information to know what the underlying challenges may be with a child's reading development (Kilpatrick, 2015).

The development of fluency begins with phoneme/grapheme correspondences and the ability to lift words from the page with increasing accuracy and speed via orthographic mapping. This word-level fluency is the gateway to overall reading fluency and, therefore, comprehension (Kilpatrick, 2015). In the early years of primary school, it is important to teach students *how* words work by ensuring that they have a comprehensive knowledge of the alphabetic principle and a beginning level of understanding of morphology.

The second area of fluency is automaticity. In general, automaticity exists when we can perform a skill without conscious thought, enabling us to focus on a second, higher order task. Automaticity in decoding enables us to focus on prosody and supports reading comprehension. Without automaticity, fluent reading and comprehension cannot develop (Kuhn et al., 2010).

For most students, reading fluency develops between Year 1 and Year 3 with the development of automatic decoding (Schwanenflugel et al., 2006). A broadening of vocabulary and oral language skill development further enhances reading fluency. Rather than thinking of automaticity as a 'yes' or 'no' proposition, it can be helpful to view it as a continuum; one that children will progress through as their reading skills develop (NICHD, 2000). This idea of a 'continuum' has important implications for expectations not only of reading speed, but also of the types of reading material we provide for students in reading instruction.

Finally, we need to consider prosody, the expression and phrasing we use during reading. Prosody is related to both fluency and comprehension. When we have well-developed prosody, our pauses are intentional as we respond to punctuation and phrasing rather than error-based, as we attempt to decode unknown words (Kuhn et al., 2010). When a student reads with accuracy and speed, but lacks prosody, this could indicate that the student's word-level decoding is not as automatic as it first appears or that the student is not fully comprehending the text (Kilpatrick, 2015).

All three components of fluency are critical to overall reading development. The ability to assess skills and knowledge and then provide instruction that responds to student needs is vital if we are to move students from simple decoding to fully comprehending the texts they read. Simply measuring reading rate is not going to provide the full picture of a student's learning needs.

Comprehension

Comprehension simply means understanding what we read. Far from being a passive exercise where words are lifted from the page and implanted in our heads, comprehension is an active interaction between the text and the skills and experiences of the reader (Schwanenflugel et al., 2006). Like fluency, comprehension is the confluence of a range of skills and knowledge. We don't 'do' comprehension activities. We learn skills and knowledge and undertake activities that require us to interact with the text. The Simple View of Reading (Gough & Tunmer, 1986) tells us that reading comprehension comes about when students have strong oral language comprehension and strong word recognition skills, and as such the instructional focus on decoding in the early years is critical (Hulme & Snowling, 2011; Moats, 2020; Seidenberg, 2018). As with vocabulary learning, the foundations of comprehension emerge before students start school (Stahl, 2014). They arrive on their first day of school with a range of oral language skills including the ability to infer, to integrate what they are hearing with their existing background knowledge, and to monitor comprehension. These are the foundation skills required for early reading comprehension and, as such, it is the development of strong decoding skills that most heavily influences reading comprehension in the early years (Moats, 2020). This focus shifts to language and text-based skills and knowledge in the middle and upper primary years once students are decoding proficiently and reading fluently.

While a novice reader's comprehension is heavily supported by their existing oral language and strong word recognition skills, it doesn't mean that the early years teacher doesn't have a part to play in supporting the development of reading comprehension. The ability to infer can be a critical difference between strong and weak readers (Stahl, 2014). The ability to infer is heavily influenced by a student's background knowledge and has been identified as a predictor of overall comprehension across all ages (Smith et al., 2021). We can support students' inferencing skills in a number of ways:

- Reading rich texts as part of classroom life and using those texts as the jumping-off point for great language teaching.
- Ensuring that we explicitly attend to oral language and vocabulary teaching.
- Embedding reading (this may be the teacher reading to the students until they can do so for themselves) across the curriculum and including a wide variety of text types including non-fiction for a range of purposes.
- Understanding the role of coherence and cohesion within and between texts. Coherence relates to the macro structures that provide text clues and links across the text. Cohesion, on the other hand, refers to links between text elements on a more local (micro) scale (Smith et al., 2021). These might include pronoun referents, inferring the meaning of unfamiliar words and filling in unstated information (Stahl, 2014). Texts may have high or low levels of cohesion and coherence, and this must be considered when we choose them for inclusion in our classroom work. Knowing where students may experience difficulty in comprehending a text enables us to focus instruction on important teaching to build this capacity.

One of the challenges of establishing effective instructional practices to support comprehension is that the words 'strategy' and 'skills' are often used interchangeably, which can lead to a misunderstanding of what each one is and its role in instruction. Comprehension skills usually relate to a set of supposedly transferable generic skills often taught in isolation week after week, year after year with the assumption that learning the skill (e.g. visualising or inferring) in the context of one text will improve overall reading comprehension. Comprehension strategies, on the other hand, are cognitive processes that can be focused on *briefly* to help children engage with texts (Such, 2021). While instruction in strategies such as comprehension monitoring and summarising is supported by research, particularly when more than one strategy is taught at a time (NICHD, 2000), the effectiveness of ongoing instruction in strategies is not established beyond their inclusion in initial reading instruction (Smith et al., 2021). McKeown et al. (2009) concluded that while strategies instruction has a place, it should not be the driver of reading comprehension instruction. They proposed that a 'content' model characterised by close reading, with strategically placed teacher-facilitated discussion during text reading, is a more effective approach. Their two-year study involving Year 5 students showed that students who had experienced a content model of instruction had higher levels of independent recall of a text than those who experienced a strategies instruction approach. They posited that content instruction guided by a teacher helps students take the most direct path to the important elements of a text. Despite the focus of this study being upper primary, the messages have important implications for our early primary classes.

Finally, our discussion of comprehension would not be complete without addressing the issue of students who experience comprehension challenges. Children with such difficulties may experience challenges in decoding, oral language, or in both domains (Hulme & Snowling, 2011). It is important that our assessment processes and tools help us identify the root cause of a student's comprehension challenges. Supporting the development of decoding is usually a straightforward endeavour but addressing the needs of those students with oral language deficits is more challenging for most teachers. A 2010 study by Clarke et al. found that weak comprehenders (who had better decoding than language skills) maintained the positive impacts of oral language training 11 months after a 20-week intervention program. These results seemed to be related to vocabulary instruction (Hulme & Snowling, 2011). This speaks to the importance of a focus on oral language across all areas of reading instruction and its impact on the development of reading comprehension.

The theoretical foundations of current recommendations about reading instruction is strong and well-established. For the early year's classroom teacher, having an understanding of the theoretical frameworks that underpin our work is critical if we are to create classroom environments that provide the most direct path to reading success for our students. While there is still much research to be conducted about the specifics of instruction, we can be confident that our path forward is built on solid ground.

References

Anthony, J. L., & Francis, D. J. (2005). Development of phonological awareness. *Current Directions in Psychological Science, 14*(5), 255–259. http://www.jstor.org/stable/20183039

Ayres, L. (1995). The efficacy of three training conditions on phonological awareness of kindergarten children and the longitudinal effect of each on later Reading acquisition. *Reading Research Quarterly, 30*(4), 604–606. doi: 10.2307/748191.

Beck, I., McKeown, M., & Kucan, L. (2013). *Bringing words to life* (2nd ed.). Guildford Publications.

Buckingham, J. (2020). Systematic phonics instruction belongs in evidence-based reading programs: A response to bowers. *The Educational and Developmental Psychologist, 37*(2), 105–113. doi: 10.1017/edp.2020.12.

Buckingham, J., Beaman Wheldall, R., & Wheldall, K. (2019). Systematic and explicit phonics instruction: A scientific, evidence-based approach to teaching the alphabetic principle. In R. Cox, S. Feez, & L. Beveridge (Eds.), *The alphabetic principle and beyond* (pp. 49–67). Primary English Teaching Association Australia.

Clarke, P. J., Snowling, M. J., Truelove, E., & Hulme, C. (2010). Ameliorating Children's Reading-Comprehension Difficulties: A Randomized Controlled Trial. *Psychological Science, 21*(8), 1106–1116. http://www.jstor.org/stable/41062341

Dehaene, S. (2009). *Reading in the brain: The new science of how we read*. Penguin Books.

Dickinson, D., & Porche, M. (2011). Relation between language experiences in preschool classrooms and children's kindergarten and fourth-grade language and reading abilities. *Child Development, 82*(3), 870–886. Retrieved June 15, 2021, from http://www.jstor.org/stable/29782878

Dickinson, D., Golinkoff, R., & Hirsh-Pasek, K. (2010). Speaking out for language: Why language is central to reading development. *Educational Researcher, 39*(4), 305–310. Retrieved June 15, 2021, from http://www.jstor.org/stable/27764601

Ehri, L. C. (2014). Orthographic mapping in the acquisition of sight word reading, spelling memory, and vocabulary learning. *Scientific Studies of Reading, 18*(1), 5–21. doi: 10.1080/10888438.2013.819356.

Ehri, L. C. (2020). The science of learning to read words: A case for systematic phonics instruction. *Reading Research Quarterly, 55*(S1), S45–S60. https://doi.org/10.1002/rrq.334

Ehri, L. C. (2005). Learning to read words: Theory findings and issues. *Scientific Studies of Reading, 9*(2), 167–188. Retrieved March 18, 2022, from https://mimtsstac.org/sites/default/files/Documents/Presentations/AnitaArcherWorkshops/January2014/LearningtoReadWords.pdf

Gambrell, L. (2004). Issues and trends in literacy: Exploring the connection between oral language and early reading. *The Reading Teacher, 57*(5), 490–492. Retrieved June 15, 2021, from http://www.jstor.org/stable/20205388

Goldfeld, S., Beatson, R., Watts, A., Snow, P., Gold, L., Ha ND, L., Edwards, S., Connell, J., Stark, H., Shingles, B., Barnett, T., Quach, J., & Eadie, P. (2021). Tier 2 oral language and early reading interventions for preschool to grade 2 children: A restricted systematic review. *Australian Journal of Learning Difficulties*. doi: 10.1080/19404158.2021.2011754.

Gough, P. B., & Tunmer, W. E. (1986). Decoding, reading, and reading disability. *Remedial and Special Education, 7*(1), 6–10. https://doi.org/10.1177/074193258600700104

Hulme, C., & Snowling, M. (2011). Children's reading comprehension difficulties: Nature, causes, and treatments. *Current Directions in Psychological Science, 20*(3), 139–142. Retrieved August 24, 2021, from http://www.jstor.org/stable/23045722

Hulme, C., & Snowling, M. (2014). The interface between spoken and written language: Developmental disorders. *Philosophical Transactions: Biological Sciences, 369*(1634), 1–8. Retrieved June 22, 2021, from http://www.jstor.org/stable/24499216

Johnston, R., Mcgeown, S., & Watson, J. (2011). Long-term effects of synthetic versus analytic phonics teaching on the reading and spelling ability of 10 year old boys and girls. *Reading and Writing - READ WRIT*, 25. 10.1007/s11145-011-9323-x.

Kilpatrick, D. (2015). *Essentials of assessing, preventing and overcoming Reading difficulties*. John Wiley and Sons.

Konza, D. (2014). Teaching reading: Why the "Fab five" should be the "Big six". *Australian Journal of Teacher Education, 39*(12). http://dx.doi.org/10.14221/ajte.2014v39n12.10

Kuhn, M. R., Schwanenflugel, P. J., Meisinger, E. B., Levy, B. A., & Rasinski, T. V. (2010). Aligning theory and assessment of reading fluency: Automaticity, prosody, and definitions of fluency. *Reading Research Quarterly, 45*(2), 230–251. http://www.jstor.org/stable/20697184

Lepola, J., Lynch, J., Kiuru, N., Laakkonen, E., & Niemi, P. (2016). Early oral language comprehension, task orientation, and foundational reading skills as predictors of grade 3 reading comprehension. *Reading Research Quarterly, 51*(4), 373–390. Retrieved June 15, 2021, from http://www.jstor.org/stable/43999168

Lervåg, A., Hulme, C., Melby, & Lervåg, M. (2018). Unpicking the developmental relationship between oral language skills and reading comprehension: It's simple, but complex. *Child Development, 89*(5), 1821–1838. https://doi.org/10.1111/cdev.12861

Lundberg, I., Frost, J., & Petersen, O.-P. (1988). Effects of an extensive program for stimulating phonological awareness in preschool children. *Reading Research Quarterly, 23*(3), 263–284. http://www.jstor.org/stable/748042

McKeown, M., Beck, I., & Blake, R. (2009). Rethinking reading comprehension instruction: A comparison of instruction for strategies and content approaches. *Reading Research Quarterly, 44*(3), 218–253. Retrieved August 24, 2021, from http://www.jstor.org/stable/25655454

Moats, L. C. (2020) *Speech to print* (3rd ed.). Paul Brooks Publishing.

(NICHD) Eunice Kennedy Shriver National Institute of Child Health and Human Development, NIH, DHHS. (2000). Report of the national reading panel: Teaching children to read: Reports of the subgroups (00-4754). Government Printing Office.

Paige, D. D., Rasinski, T. V., & Magpuri-Lavell, T. (2012). Is fluent, expressive reading important for high school readers? *Journal of Adolescent & Adult Literacy, 56*(1), 67–76. http://www.jstor.org/stable/23367761

Petscher, Y., Cabell, S. Q., Catts, H. W., Compton, D. L., Foorman, B. R., Hart, S. A., Lonigan, C. J., Phillips, B. M., Schatschneider, C., Steacy, L. M., Terry, N. P., & Wagner, R. K. (2020). How the science of reading informs 21st-century education. *Reading Research Quarterly, 55*(S1), S267–S282. https://doi.org/10.1002/rrq.352

Rowe, K., & National Inquiry into the Teaching of Literacy (Australia). (2005). Teaching reading: Report and recommendations. Department of Education, Science and Training. https://research.acer.edu.au/tll_misc/5

Scarborough, H. S. (2001). Connecting early language and literacy to later reading (dis)abilities: Evidence, theory, and practice. In S. Neuman, & D. Dickinson (Eds.), *Handbook for research in early literacy* (pp. 97–110). Guilford Publications Incorporated.

Schwanenflugel, P., Meisinger, E., Wisenbaker, J., Kuhn, M., Strauss, G., & Morris, R. (2006). Becoming a fluent and automatic reader in the early elementary school years. *Reading Research Quarterly, 41*(4), 496–522. Retrieved August 3, 2021, from http://www.jstor.org/stable/4151815

Seidenberg, M. (2018). *Language at the speed of sight: How we read, why so many can't, and what can be done about it.* Basic Books.

Smith, R., Pamela Snow, P., Serry, T., & Hammond, L. (2021). The role of background knowledge in reading comprehension: A critical review. *Reading Psychology, 42*(3), 214–240. doi: 10.1080/02702711.2021.1888348.

Snow, P. (2020). SOLAR: The science of language and Reading. *Child Language Teaching and Therapy, 37*(3), 222–233. https://doi.org/10.1177/0265659020947817

Stahl, K. (2014). Fostering inference generation with emergent and novice readers. *The Reading Teacher, 67*(5), 384–388. Retrieved August 24, 2021, from http://www.jstor.org/stable/24573634

Stone, L. (2013) Reading for Life: High Quality Literacy Instruction for All. Routledge.

Such, C. (2021). *The art and science of teaching primary reading.* Sage Publications Ltd.

Swanson, E., Wanzek, J., Petscher, Y., Vaughn, S., Heckert, J., Cavanaugh, C., Kraft, G., & Tackett, K. (2011). A synthesis of read-aloud interventions on early reading outcomes among preschool through third graders at risk for reading difficulties. *Journal of Learning Disabilities, 44*, 258–275. 10.1177/0022219410378444.

Wheldale, K., & Buckingham, J. (2020). Nomanis Notes. Retrieved January 11, 2021, from https://57ebb165-ef00-4738-9d6e-3933f283bdb1.filesusr.com/ugd/81f204_f8c0bc6c48f84da59fddb28e9b391282.pdf

2 What to Teach

How the Code Works

Of all of the languages in the world, English is one of the most complex in terms of its orthography (Eide, 2012). It is generally accepted that there are 44 phonemes in Standard Australian English, although even this point is sometimes contested among linguists (Moats, 2020) and can depend on accent and dialect as much as professional viewpoint. Denise Eide, the author of Uncovering the Logic of English, asserts that there are 75 of the most common graphemes for us to teach (letter or letters that represent the 44 phonemes) and that 27 of these graphemes represent more than one phoneme. Table 2.1 demonstrates some of this complexity.

To accompany this, there are 31 spelling generalisations (often called rules) that can be used to explain how spelling works for most of the words in English.

You may have been told that English is too complex to teach explicitly and needs to be simply memorised through exposure and practice, but this view reflects a lack of understanding of just how English works. We may have one of the most complex orthographies in the world, but 50% of words can be spelled when we consider phoneme/grapheme correspondence alone. A further 36% of words can be spelled with just one 'irregularity'. Finally, 10% of words can be spelled easily if we understand the word origin, meaning or morphological structure. This means that less than 4% of words in English are truly irregular (Moats, 2020).

As teachers, it is important that we have the foundational knowledge of our language so that we can help provide the most direct path for students to unlock the code of English. But exactly what do we need to know? Let's start with the history.

The English language has been developing for over 1000 years and has been influenced by a range of cultures and languages, including Latin, French, Celtic, Norse, Anglo-Saxon, and German (Eide, 2011). As one army after another invaded England, cultural and linguistic shifts occurred that altered and added to the language we call English. The way that language was written down also shifted, meaning that our English orthography is now as influenced by those invaders as the spoken language. Writing systems became widespread

DOI: 10.4324/9781003244189-4

Table 2.1 The English Alphabetic Code

Vowels		Consonants	
Phoneme	Grapheme/s	Phoneme	Grapheme/s
'short' a	a	b	b bb
'short' e	e ea	d	d dd ed
'short' i	i y	f	f ph gh
'short' o	o a	g	g gg gh gu
'short' u	u ou oo	h	h wh
'long' a	a ay ai a_e ey ea	j	j g dge ge
'long' e	e ee ea y ey ei	k	k c ck ch qu
'long' i	i igh i_e y ie	l	l ll le
'long' o	o oa ow oe	m	m mm mb
'long' u	oo ew u u_e	n	n nn kn
ar (as in car)	ar a	p	p pp
or (as in for)	or aw a our oar au ore	r	r wr rh
air (as in chair)	air are ear	s	s c ss sc
er (as in fern)	er ir ur ear (w)or	t	t tt ed
ou (as in loud)	ou ow	v	v ve
oy (as in toy)	oy oi	w	w qu wh
ew (as in stew)	ew u_e	y	y
ear (as in hear)	ear eer	z	z zz s x es
oo (as in look)	oo ou u	ch	ch tch tu
Unstressed vowel (schwa) as in the 'i' in pilot		sh	sh ci ti ch
		th (voiced as in this)	th
		th (unvoiced as in thin)	th
		zh (as in treasure)	si s
		ng	ng n̲k

approximately 500 years ago, which is a relatively short period of time in our evolutionary history. As such, we are not biologically programmed to read and spell. This is an entirely human-made invention (Moats, 2020).

Helping children unravel the complex world of English orthography can be made more difficult by two factors. First, while we use phonemes every time we speak, these phonemes overlap and run into each other, which changes them slightly (Moats, 2020). Learning to isolate and understand phonemes separately is one of the fundamental skills that early readers must develop. The second factor that can impact the ease at which children unlock the English code is that English is a morpho-phonemic language, meaning that it is just as influenced by morphemes (smallest units of meaning) as it is by phonemes (smallest units of sound).

Very often, the method of instruction provided in classrooms makes it even harder for students to learn the foundational knowledge of reading and spelling. 'Hangover' techniques such as sight word programs, spelling lists that require children to memorise words, predictable texts that take students' focus away from the structure of words, and the assumption that children will learn by 'exposure' all contribute to students experiencing an increased level of difficulty in learning to read and spell.

To become proficient readers and spellers, we must have an equal understanding of the role of both phonemes and morphemes.

Let's begin with phonemes. To begin with, we must help students build a strong understanding of the alphabetic principle, the connection between phonemes and graphemes, and how words 'work' at the phonological level.

What do teachers need to know to make this happen?

- There are 44 phonemes (speech sounds) in Standard Australian English (although the exact number can be influenced by dialect).
- There are over 150 graphemes (letter or letters) used to represent those phonemes and 75 basic graphemes that are the core of instruction (Eade, 2012).
- Some phonemes are represented by more than one grapheme.
- Some graphemes represent more than one phoneme.
- Words can have a different number of phonemes and graphemes.

Consider the words below:

    cat   blow   patched   bellowing

How many phonemes can you hear in each word?

    Cat – three phonemes
    Blow – three phonemes
    Patched – four phonemes
    Bellowing – six phonemes

How can this be? Graphemes can have more than one letter.

    Graph – one letter representing one phoneme – 'a' as in cat, 'b' as in bob
    Digraph – two letters representing one phoneme – 'sh' as in shop and 'ay' as in play
    Trigraph – three letters representing one phoneme – 'igh' as in light and 'tch' as in match
    Quadgraph – four letters representing one phoneme – 'eigh' as in eight and 'ough' as in though

To make this visible to students, we teach them to 'map' words. This is done by:

1. Counting the number of phonemes we can hear in words
2. Representing the number of phonemes we can hear (counting on our fingers, writing lines)
3. Adding in the graphemes that represent the phonemes

Consider the word **blow**.

1 Count the phonemes /b/ /l/ /ow/
2 Represent the number of phonemes _ _ _
3 Add in the graphemes <u>b</u> <u>l</u> <u>ow</u>

Now consider **patched**.

1 Count the phonemes /p/ /a/ /ch/ /t/
2 Represent the number of phonemes _ _ _ _
3 Add in the graphemes <u>p</u> <u>a</u> <u>tch</u> <u>ed</u>

Now here's where things get tricky. You might be thinking that 'ed' is not a digraph and you would generally be right. But this is where morphology comes in. The suffix 'ed' indicates past tense (meaning), but it also has three different pronunciations (phonology). In the word 'patched', the 'ed' is said using the phoneme /t/. Say the following three words carefully and listen for the sounds:

    landed   helped   lagged

Each of these words has a different sound at the end, even though the morpheme 'ed' is consistent across all three words and changes the meaning of the word in the same way. This brings us to the second job of early years teachers: introducing the concept of morphology and word origins.

As stated, English is a morpho-phonemic language. As such, it is important to ensure sufficient explicit instruction in both phonics and morphology. In the early years, the major focus is on phonics. Instruction in read with a variety of morphemes can be managed in the context of phonics instruction and text-level reading from pictured books. Morphemes are the smallest unit of meaning in words (Moats, 2020) and we often understand these to be prefixes and suffixes. However, there is more to morphology than this.

Let's explore some concepts around morphology.

- Morphemes can be bound (must be used in conjunction with other morphemes). For example, -tion, -un, and situ (as in situation).
- Morphemes can also be free. That is, they can stand on their own as a complete word. Free morphemes can contain one or more than one syllable. For example, chair, ocean, or table.
- There are three layers of language origin to consider that are related to those invasions mentioned earlier: Anglo-Saxon, Latin, and Greek. These layers contribute to how words 'work' and our expectations of how we use them. For example, words that use the grapheme 'ch' for the phoneme /k/ are most likely of Greek origin. For example, chemist, chord and chaos.

The important thing is that we know that morphology instruction can (and should) begin in the early years of school alongside phonics. Table 2.2 provides a suggested scope and sequence for phonics and morphology. This is not an exhaustive list and there will be other ways to arrange the content across the three years, but as long as the concepts are covered (particularly across Year 1 and 2), your students will be set up for success.

It is not within the scope of this book to provide you with all of the knowledge you need to understand how our language works, but the above guidelines will get you started.

Table 2.2 Scope and Sequence of Phonics and Morphology Instruction

	Phonics (for reading)	*Morphology (for reading)*
Foundation (first year of school)	The basic code – alphabetic sounds and the most common consonant digraphs (sh, th, ch, ng)	Oral opportunities to explore plurals, -ing, un Once students can read words with four or five phonemes, add -s and -ing to phonics lessons (presuming that they know these graphemes) and address them in shared reading and writing opportunities
Year 1	Semester 1 – the early complex code (one representation of the remaining phonemes of English - ay, ee, igh, oa, oo, are, or, air, er, ou, oy) Semester 2 – begin to teach alternate spellings of all phonemes of English including: - ow (snow), oi, ir - 'split digraphs' for long vowels – a_e, i_e, o_e, u_e, e_e - Other representations of long vowels ea, ai, ie and other phonemes aw, ur, ear, ew	Concept of base words Inflections – bound morphemes that indicate tense, gender, number, or mood (s, er, ed, ing, est) Common prefixes – un, dis, in, re, pre, mis, non Compound words – free morphemes that combine to create a new word (hilltop, rainbow, birdcage)
Year 2	Build flexibility with the full complexity of the code. Extend knowledge of alternate spellings including the ability to identify the multiple spellings of phonemes and the multiple phonemes represented by graphemes	Some less common prefixes – pro, inter, non, mid, anti, post, ex Common derivational suffixes – morphemes that create a new word – y, ly, ful, ment, hood, less, ness

Some suggestions for further reading are listed below.

> Louise Moats (2020), Speech to Print (Third Edition). Paul Brookes Publishing Co.
> Lyn Stone (2022), Spelling for Life (Second Edition). Routledge.
> Lyn Stone (2015), Language for Life. Routledge.
> Denise Eide (2012), Uncovering the Logic of English.

The Literacy Block

There may be six fundamental areas of literacy instruction (the Big Six) and eight strands of Scarborough's Reading Rope, but that does not mean that our literacy block follows these frameworks with discrete, stand-alone sections. The key to developing a strong literacy block lies in the following:

- Understanding the components of literacy we need to teach
- Knowing how much of what is required at different ages
- Knowing what kind of instruction and activities will develop key skills and knowledge
- Having knowledge of how the different aspects of literacy instruction interact with and impact each other

Even having this knowledge doesn't get us to the finish line, however. We then need to work out how to meet the needs of students at various stages of reading development in a teacher-led, explicit manner that is responsive to the research about how we learn and to the developmental and social needs of our students. Sounds easy right?

If you are thinking 'No!', you are not alone. One of the reasons that it is so challenging to work out what to do with our literacy blocks is that no two classrooms will look alike. Just as no two teachers come to the classroom with exactly the same levels of skill, knowledge, and strengths, children are all different. What might work beautifully in one classroom may need tweaking for the classroom next door. It is important to note that I am not suggesting that one classroom follow a structured literacy approach and the next classroom a whole language one. All teachers need to be working within an evidence-informed framework, but meeting the needs of students might mean that implementation is handled slightly differently in response to student data and need. The below information is intended to provide you with a guide about the 'what' of the literacy block. The 'how' of instruction is fleshed out for you in subsequent chapters.

What Do We Need to Include in the Block?

We have seen that early reading comprehension is heavily dependent on the word recognition strands of Scarborough's Reading Rope. As such, we are going to focus much of our literacy block on helping students develop the foundational skills necessary to lift the words from the page and put them on the page with increasing fluency. Now, I am not saying that the language comprehension strands are not attended to (quite the opposite), but that the ratio of decoding to comprehension work will depend on the students' level of reading development (Figure 2.1).

A typical 120 minutes structured literacy block might include the following:

- Daily review of previously learned skills and knowledge (15 minutes)
- Explicit phonics and phonemic awareness instruction (20–30 minutes)
- Decoding and reading (20 minutes)
- Sentence level transcription instruction (15 minutes)
- Shared writing (an opportunity to promote partner talk idea generation and participation in the practice of segmenting while reviewing key, previously learned skills and knowledge) (15 minutes)
- Language and literature-based lessons such as text-based unit including syntax, concepts from the top of the rope such as character development, text structure and 'grammar', and writing (30–40 minutes)

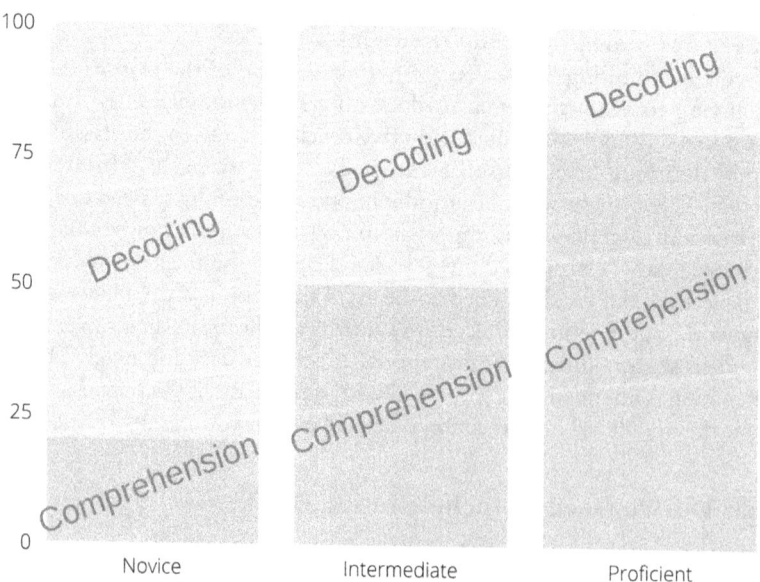

Figure 2.1 Ratio of Decoding to Comprehension Instruction

The Literacy Block

Lower Primary

Daily review (whole class) – 15 minutes
Quick-fire practice of concepts and skills previously learned. Phonological and phonemic awareness, phonics, sentence structure, grammar, etc.

Explicit Phonics and PA Instruction (differentiated) – 20–30 minutes
Phoneme/grapheme correspondences with word level reading and spelling. Including review of previously learned graphemes. Explicit teaching of phonemic skills to meet the needs of the students.

Decoding and Reading (differentiated) – 20–30 minutes
Reading decodable texts or more complex texts. Partner work at grapheme / word / and text level. Phonics and word-level Tier 2 intervention, small group lessons as necessary, depending on staff availability.

Sentence level Transcription (whole class) – 10–15 minutes
Explicit sentence level transcription work, jointly constructed and then differentiated for supported practice.

Shared Writing (whole class) –10 minutes
Joint construction at sentence-level, reinforcing concepts, skills, and content from previous lessons.

Language and Literature-Based Lesson – 30 minutes
Whole-class lesson covering an aspect of reading or writing in the context of a rich text (picture book, short story, letter, persuasive piece, or information report)

Instruction uses the same stimulus for both language and literature experiences and writing to teach and engage in supported practice in concepts at the top of the Reading Rope as appropriate to the grade. Adjustments are provided to support students who require assistance.

© Jocelyn Seamer Education

Figure 2.2 The Lower Primary Literacy Block

We can see from Figure 2.2 that most of the literacy block is focused on the development of foundational skills and knowledge with approximately 25% focused on the 'top of the rope' concepts and skills. We can also see that 'group rotations' are not included. This is intentional. In order to help every child learn, we seek to minimise (or preferably eliminate) the time in the block when students are not experiencing fully guided instruction. Group rotations are not a 'must do' of early literacy and much is to be gained when we prioritise fully guided instruction.

But how do we do this? Table 2.3 outlines the interactions between Scarborough's Reading Rope (Scarborough, 2001) and the components of the lower primary literacy block.

Table 2.3 Connecting the Strands of Scarborough's Reading Rope with the Literacy Block

Strand of the rope	Activity or section of the literacy block where instruction occurs
Background knowledge	Daily review
	Other subject areas (science, HASS, etc.)
	Intentional selection of non-fiction texts paired with fiction text
Vocabulary	Daily review
	Language and literature-based lessons
	Review of key words in shared writing
Language structures	Language and literature-based lessons
	Review of concepts in daily shared writing
	(Potentially in daily review)
Verbal reasoning	Through exploration of texts in language and literature-based lessons
	Review of concepts such as pronoun referents in share writing and decodable text reading
Literacy knowledge	Decodable text reading, language, and literature-based lessons
Phonological and phonemic awareness	Phonological sensitivity activities embedded in regular classroom activities as in transitions between lessons or exit tickets before recess and lunch
	Phonemic awareness – major focus on blending and segmenting using graphemes, embedded in phonics lessons. Utilised in context in decodable text reading and daily sentence-level transcription lessons
Decoding	Core phoneme/grapheme correspondences taught in explicit phonics lessons, reinforced by daily review, utilised in context in decodable text reading, sentence-level transcription lessons and shared daily writing
Sight recognition	Developed through systematic phonics lessons and careful selection of decodable texts

Being clear about what is important, aiming for fully guided instruction, and understanding the impact on learning of each section of the literacy block means that we can make the shift away from balanced literacy activities (such as guided reading with levelled texts and sight word programs) and provide the chance for every student to develop strong foundational skills.

References

Eide, D. (2012). *Uncovering the logic of English*. Logic of English Inc.

Moats, L. C. (2020). *Speech to print* (3rd ed.). Paul Brooks Publishing.

Scarborough, H. S. (2001). Connecting early language and literacy to later reading (dis)abilities: Evidence, theory, and practice. In S. Neuman, & D. Dickinson (Eds.), *Handbook for research in early literacy* (pp. 97–110). Guilford Publications Incorporated.

3 Bang for Your Buck Teaching

Cognitive Load Theory

Cognitive load theory provides us with a framework to understand how memory works and our role in supporting student learning. This important theory developed by educational psychologists, John Sweller and others, outlines key factors for teachers to consider when teaching students to read.

The first thing we need to know is that memory comes in two forms: working memory and long-term memory. Working memory is extremely limited in nature. On average, we can only work with seven pieces of information and process (manipulate and relate to other things), three or four of them at any one time (Sweller, 2021). Working memory is the part of our cognitive architecture where we process novel (new) material. It is also where thinking happens (Lovell, 2020). Being asked to process too many novel items results in cognitive overload (Archer & Hughes, 2011), a situation that can significantly impede our students' ability to learn. Material that we have rehearsed or revised resides in our long-term memory. This part of our cognitive architecture is unlimited in nature (Lovell, 2020) and once knowledge is learned well enough to become automatic, we can retrieve it from this mental treasure chest with ease.

However, not all skills and information are learned the same way. Biologically primary skills and information are those that are developed automatically and effortlessly simply because we are human (Sweller, 2020). Sweller argues that these skills and knowledge do not usually need to be taught in schools because they are learned automatically. Examples of this are speaking and listening in your home language or regulating basic cognitive processes such as simple problem solving. Biologically secondary skills and knowledge, on the other hand, are unlikely to develop without conscious effort, very often involving instruction from someone else (Sweller, 2021). Examples of biologically secondary skills are reading and writing or learning about the complex inner workings of our own bodies. We have not evolved to acquire these skills or knowledge and so they will not be learned unless culturally necessary and explicitly attended to (Lovell, 2020).

Put simply, cognitive load refers to the amount of content we are being asked to attend to at any given time. Too little cognitive load can negatively impact learning as can too much cognitive load (Paas et al., 2004). In the reading classroom, tasks that do not require students to actually think about reading and writing (e.g. craft-oriented tasks disguised as phonics) result in very little learning. On the other end of the cognitive load continuum, tasks that are overly complicated (e.g. texts that contain graphemes and vocabulary that the student has not yet learned) take the students' attention away from the core skills and knowledge that are supposed to be in development.

How do we know whether a task is of sufficient complexity to result in learning? We can start to tailor our teaching to student needs by categorising load as either intrinsic or extraneous. Intrinsic load is the actual material that we want students to learn. We don't want to eliminate this load. Instead, we want to optimise it (Lovell, 2020). We can optimise intrinsic load by comparing the level of skills/knowledge required to complete the task with what the student currently holds in long-term memory. If there are too many novel pieces of information involved, the intrinsic load of the task may be too high and confuse the student. We can also consider the level of interactivity between the elements of a task. A high level of element interactivity (Sweller, 2020) will result in a more complex task and a greater risk of a student becoming cognitively overloaded. However, this is not the end of the story. Not all students will find the same task equally as challenging. Students who have more background knowledge and experience, that is, they already have elements of the task in their long-term memory, will likely find the task less demanding. However, those for whom all elements of the task (or even most of them) are effortful can very quickly become overloaded. In our early years students, this can result in an emotional outburst that may be labelled as 'bad behaviour'.

We often see this when we ask our young students to write. Those students who have developed handwriting, phonemic segmenting, and basic sentence structure to the point of automaticity can focus their energies on thinking about what they would like to write. However, those students who have not yet developed these prerequisite skills will likely find the act of writing a single sentence a cognitively overloading task.

Overly complex task design, confusing instruction, poor acoustics, presentations that are too busy, and anything that takes focus away from the core learning at hand are categorised as extraneous load (Lovell, 2020). As we seek to support our young learners, we should always have the goal of reducing extraneous load in mind.

Novice learners lack the background knowledge and experience to be able to solve problems by discovering learning solutions for themselves (Archer & Hughes, 2011). Asking them to do so only serves to push their cognitive load limits past the point where learning can occur. They need to be guided through the learning process, working from simple to more complex concepts and tasks (Dehaene, 2021). Understanding the part that teachers play in supporting students' cognitive load will help us to teach in a way that helps all learners to be successful.

High Impact Teaching Strategies

We all know that time in the classroom is limited. We might even say that there isn't a single minute to waste when it comes to helping students build strong foundations in literacy and numeracy. One of the ways we can get more 'bang for our buck' is to employ high impact teaching strategies. High impact teaching strategies are teaching techniques that we employ to have a maximum positive impact on student learning. Barak Rosenshine's Principles of Instruction provide us with a simple, highly effective framework we can use to build a strong teaching program. The origins of these principles lie in a combination of cognitive neuroscience, the instructional practices of the most effective teachers, and techniques developed during the course of researching how to support student learning (Rosehshine, 2012). These ten principles are outlined below:

1. Begin with a review
2. Present material in small steps with practice after each step
3. Ask questions and check responses of all students
4. Provide models and worked examples
5. Guide student practice
6. Check for understanding
7. Obtain a high success rate
8. Provide scaffolds for difficult tasks
9. Require and monitor independent practice
10. Weekly and monthly review

Tom Sherrington (2012) describes Rosenshine's principles as common-sense actions that bridge the gap between research, which so very often confounds us teachers, and the practices we need to employ to support all students. He divides the ten principles into the following four categories:

Sequencing concepts and modelling

- 2. Present material in small steps with practice after each step
- 4. Provide models and worked examples
- 8. Provide scaffolds for difficult tasks

Questioning

- 3. Ask questions
- 6. Check for student understanding

Reviewing material
- 1. Daily review
- 10. Weekly and monthly review

Stages of practice
- 5. Guide student practice
- 7. Obtain a high success rate
- 9. Independent practice

When we consider the way that we teach reading in the early years, particularly phonics and word-level decoding and encoding, we can see that being able to apply Rosenshine's ten principles is an achievable and effective goal to help every child achieve reading success.

A teacher-directed approach is also supported by Anita Archer and Charles Hughes in their 2011 book Explicit Instruction. Archer and Hughes outline their own principles of Effective Instruction:

1. Optimise time on task
2. Promote high levels of success
3. Increase content coverage
4. Have students spend more time in instructional groups
5. Scaffold instruction
6. Address different forms of knowledge (declarative, procedural, conditional)

The idea of optimising time on task is one that has been the subject of many a social media post. Exactly how to maximise instructional time while providing instruction at the appropriate 'level' to prevent student cognitive overload is one of the million-dollar questions of our profession. Throughout this book, I will provide suggestions for possible options to achieve this, but know that there is no one magical way to do this in all classrooms. Your school context, instructional history, development of students, and current goals will have a significant impact on the decisions you make in your school.

While there isn't a 'one size fits all' answer to this, there are certainly lessons to be learned about maximising student engagement in general. The Beginning Teacher Evaluation Study, published by Rosenshine in 2015, found significant differences in the amount of time students spent engaged in core learning tasks. This study focused on Grade Two and Grade Five and evaluated the time on task and level of engagement for 'average' students. The study found that higher performing teachers can spend half an hour more teaching academics each day than an average teacher and up to an hour more than a lower performing teacher. Not only did higher performing teachers spend more minutes teaching, but they also maximised the amount of time students were actively engaged during lessons. High performing Year 2 teachers taught for only 15 minutes more than average teachers but added 20 minutes to the amount of times students were actively engaged. When compared with lower performing teachers, these teachers engaged students for twice the amount of time each day (85 minutes compared with 43 minutes). It is staggering to add up these lost instructional minutes and know that two students in classrooms in the same school can be receiving very different amounts of time engaged in learning. Based on this research, over the course of a year, the average student in a higher performing classroom might receive 140 hours of instruction more than students in a lower performing teacher's class.

So, what leads to those high levels of engagement? The answer lies in 'substantive interactions' (Rosenshine, 2015) which involve questioning, answering, giving and receiving feedback, and providing explanations. Basically, involving students in the lesson and asking them to think. This idea of active engagement is echoed in the quotes below.

> 'Student engagement is created when the teacher asks the students to do something' – John Hollingsworth
>
> (Hollingsworth and Ybarra, 2012, p. 17)

> 'The brain that is not processing is not learning' – Sylvia Ybarra
>
> (Hollingsworth and Ybarra, 2012, p.17)

> 'The brain learns efficiently only if it is attentive, focused, and active in generating mental models'.
>
> (Dehaene, 2021, p. 178)

The Beginning Teacher's Evaluation Survey research was conducted on Year 2 and Year 5 classes, but it is reasonable to suggest that younger students or those with additional needs would likely have lower levels of engagement and time on task than their 'average' peers. This is a sobering thought when we think about the learning trajectory of our most vulnerable students.

The idea of high impact teaching strategies is not just a fad or next, bright, shiny thing of education, but rather a way for us to understand the actions that will result in the best learning possible for our students. All instructional routines and lessons suggested in this book are aimed at helping you to increase not only time on task, but also student level of active engagement in learning.

References

Archer, A., & Hughes, C. (2011). *Explicit instruction: Effective and efficient teaching*. Guildford Press.

Dehaene, S. (2021). *How we learn: Why brains learn better than any machine...for now.* Penguin Books.

Hollingsworth, J., & Ybarra, S. (2012). *Explicit direct instruction for English learners.* Corwin Press Inc.

Lovell, O. (2020). *Sweller's cognitive load theory in action.* John Catt Educational.

Paas, F., Renkl, A., & Sweller, J. (2004). Cognitive load theory: Instructional implications of the interaction between information structures and cognitive architecture. *Instructional Science, 32*(1/2), 1–8. Retrieved September 7, 2021, from http://www.jstor.org/stable/41953634

Rosehshine, B. (2012). Principles of instruction: Research based strategies that all teachers should know. *American Educator, 36*(1), 12–19, 39 Spr 2012. Retrieved September 7, 2021, from https://eric.ed.gov/?id=EJ971753

Rosenshine, B. V. (2015). How time is spent in elementary classrooms. *The Journal of Classroom Interaction, 50*(1), 41–53. http://www.jstor.org/stable/44735710

Sherrington, T. (2012). *Rosenshine's principles in action.* John Catt Educational.

Sweller, J. (2020). Cognitive load theory and educational technology. *Educational Technology Research & Development, 68*(1), 1–16. https://doi-org.rp.nla.gov.au/10.1007/s11423-019-09701-3

Sweller, J. (2021). Analysis paper 24 (AP24): Why inquiry-based approaches harm student learning. The Centre for Independent Studies Limited. Retrieved September 7, 2021, from https://www.cis.org.au/app/uploads/2021/08/ap24.pdf

4 Differentiation and Supporting Students with Reading Difficulty

Differentiation

The definition of differentiation is one that is tricky to establish with any consistency. We could ask 20 teachers what differentiation means to them and receive 20 different answers. At its core, differentiation is the idea of teaching in a way that responds to the needs of the variety of learners in our classrooms. It assumes that children are going to have different learning needs and that we will provide experiences that enable all of our students to learn (Watts-Taffe et al., 2012). In her 2001 text, 'How to Differentiate Instruction in Academically Diverse Classrooms', Carol Tomlinson (2017) reminds us that differentiation does not automatically assume the following:

- Students will be grouped for instruction.
- Small group work is preferable to large group work.
- Some children will learn and some will not.
- We need to design a different lesson for each student.
- We need to only differentiate for our struggling students.

It *does* ensure the following:

- Our decisions are grounded in assessment.
- We are responsive to our students' level of cognitive load and the evidence around how people learn.
- Our decisions are based on what is best for students, not what we prefer as a teacher.
- We consider content, process, and product in our instructional decision-making.
- Whole class, small group, and individual teaching respond to student learning needs thoughtfully and effectively.

Differentiation is not just about handing out different levels of worksheet but can occur across three domains:

1 Content
2 Instruction
3 Product

When it comes to early years literacy instruction, the messaging about how to support the learning needs of a range of students can be conflicting and confusing. On the one hand, we hear that we should be teaching everything whole class and that a 'good' teacher can do so in a way to meet everyone's needs. On the other hand, we hear that small group work is the best way to support student learning needs and just about every online search for literacy instruction results in suggestions for 'literacy centres' and 'reading groups'. There are challenges with both of these viewpoints. I'd much rather we approach this with the question, 'When is it most appropriate to...?' It is not that one way is better than the other in all circumstances or that every school will do things in the same way. School context, range of reading development, your own skill and experiences as a teacher, and the teaching approach you use are all going to influence what differentiation looks like. For me, there are many underlying principles to consider when making decisions about this in relation to reading instruction.

1. Sweller's cognitive load theory helps us understand that different children will have different capacities for processing and working with content and different learning processes (see Chapter 3 for more details).
2. This theory also helps us understand that some skills are biologically primary and some are biologically secondary. Biologically secondary skills need to be explicitly taught (Sweller, 2020).
3. Stanislas Dehaene's four pillars of learning (Dehaene, 2021) show us that learning is more effective when we direct student attention, ensure that they are fully engaged, provide corrective feedback, and help them consolidate learning.
4. A firm understanding of the alphabetic principle and the capacity to attend to the internal structure of the word is critical to building strong, fluent decoding skills (Dehaene, 2009; Ehri, 2005).
5. Different children will come to this understanding with different levels of ease and speed.
6. Some children (such as those with dyslexia) are more vulnerable to cognitive overload than others.
7. Reading instruction is not a one-size-fits-all proposition.
8. There are instructional practices that are fine for many of our students but negatively impact the development of our struggling students.
9. There are instructional practices that are critical for our students with difficulties but are beneficial for all. It is best to utilise these rather than the practices from point eight.
10. Not all students will need the same content or approach at the same time.

11 Never teach in a small group what you could teach in a large one. It is a waste of instructional time.
12 The way we teach something at the start of a school year may be different from the way we teach it towards the end.

Table 4.1 provides answers to the question, 'When is it most appropriate to...' around reading instruction and is borne from my own teaching experiences, the experiences of others, and my best interpretation of the evidence around how children learn in general and learn to read specifically.

Supporting Students with Reading Difficulty

There are varied reasons that a student might struggle with learning to read. Let's start by addressing dyslexia for which there are many definitions with differing criteria, presentations, and causes. Lack of common understanding of exactly what dyslexia is often causes confusion for parents and means that it is difficult for researchers to produce valid findings (because they aren't necessarily measuring apples with apples in studies) (Bowen & Snow, 2017). Difficulties in defining dyslexia and obtaining a reliable diagnosis can also interfere with a child receiving the help they need for their reading difficulty. Where one child, whose parents can afford to access outside of school consultation, may receive additional funding and support, another less advantaged student may well miss out. For this reason, I am going to refer to both dyslexia and 'reading difficulty' for the remainder of this section, but this in no way means that I am not sensitive and responsive to the struggles of the dyslexic community. Some of our students experience severe, persistent reading difficulty due to a neurological impairment (dyslexia), but while all children with a dyslexia diagnosis experience reading difficulty, not all children who experience reading difficulty have dyslexia (Seidenberg, 2017). Our job, as teachers, is not to try to diagnose students with anything (that's not our zone of professional experience), but to communicate openly and fully with parents about any concerns we have and then support all children, regardless of the presence of a diagnosis.

What Do We Need to Understand?

There are two distinct areas students may struggle with:

1 Difficulties lifting words from the page
   This occurs when children have difficulties in recoding (blending words to read them). For students who have a neurological foundation for their reading difficulty, this is usually related to a phonological impairment (Kilpatrick, 2015; Seidenberg, 2017; Snowling & Hulme, 2005).

Differentiation and Supporting Students with Reading Difficulty 43

Table 4.1 Options for Differentiation in the Literacy Block

Practice	Examples of application	Reasoning	Considerations
Teach in small groups	When teaching phonics – group students according to regular monitoring data. Ensure groups are flexible and enable all students to grow	The connections between phonemes and graphemes are abstract (until you learn them). It is important to include blending and segmenting in phonics lessons. To work cumulatively and respond to student cognitive load needs, we shouldn't be asking students to read words with unfamiliar graphemes in the initial phases of instruction	At the start of the Foundation year, teach the class together and then make changes as your data indicates that it is needed. Decide on the point at which staying in the 'same group' becomes difficult for children in terms of managing cognitive load. For all ages, base this decision on your knowledge of your students' learning profiles and your class data
	When the demands of a task exceed a student's current level of self-regulation and ability to attend in a whole group	A child's capacity to attend and learn in a whole group situation is dependent on their ability to self-regulate. At times, despite our best efforts, some children simply need the proximity of an adult to be able to attend to learning. This is particularly true for our students with additional needs	Actively promote self-regulation with predictable, repeatable instructional routines to enable students to move towards being able to participate in whole class experiences. Adopting high impact teaching strategies and low-variance routines is one way to engage the largest possible number of children in whole class lessons
Differentiate content across the class with a whole class lesson	Decodable text reading and partner practice – with a strong instructional routine, students can all be engaged in partner reading but be reading words and texts that match their stage of code knowledge and reading development	This short and sharp activity (—10 – 15 minutes) is a chance to practise decoding using graphemes and irregular high frequency words children have already learned. Partner students according to development so that each child has the chance for success and the support of their partner	It is possible to provide additional support for students who need it by having them complete this partner reading in a 'small group' guided by the classroom teacher or paraprofessional assistant. The teacher and assistant should swap roles throughout the week to enable the teacher to engage with all students

(Continued)

Table 4.1 Options for Differentiation in the Literacy Block (Continued)

Practice	Examples of application	Reasoning	Considerations
Differentiate content across the class with a whole class lesson	Daily review – a regular opportunity for rapid practice of previously learned content. Sit students in their 'groups' on the mat. Alternate content between groups. Aim for rapid answers to questions. All are exposed to the content, but only those who have learned it explicitly are expected to answer. This might be called 'exposure without expectation' for some children	Consolidation of content is an important part of learning. This requires repeated exposure to phoneme/grapheme correspondences and practice reading and spelling words. This differentiated session can be combined with whole class language-based content such as syntax and vocabulary lessons	Have predictable routines that students can learn and repeat. Teach students to manage materials such as whiteboards and markers and be firm in your expectations around this. The exposure that less developed students receive may be helpful but don't rely on it as the only means to 'catch them up'. Continually monitor growth and target lessons to cover knowledge and skills students do not yet know
Have small groups working with paraprofessional assistants	As part of daily lessons – train and support assistants to learn the same teaching routines that you use in the classroom so that all students receive the same high-quality instruction	This approach means that you can maximise instructional time and minimise the loss of time given to fully guided instruction that arises in a typical group rotation set-up. If you have three groups in your class, both the teacher and assistant can be teaching a high-quality phonics lesson with only one group doing independent work. The assistant can then provide additional guided practice to the 'lowest' group while the teacher teaches the phonics lesson to the rest of the class. Everyone receives their phonics instruction in 40 minutes rather than the 70 minutes it would take the teacher to do all the teaching themselves	It is critical to provide a high level of professional learning to paraprofessional assistants and foster their skill development. The situation may arise where an assistant is assigned to support one particular student. Both the teacher and the assistant should work with this student as much as possible (depending on the needs of the student). Small group time is a good time for this to happen

(Continued)

Table 4.1 Options for Differentiation in the Literacy Block (Continued)

Practice	Examples of application	Reasoning	Considerations
Teach the whole class the same lesson and differentiate expectations of student output.	Writing – when writing instruction begins from an oral foundation, all students can participate. The model & deconstruct and joint construction phases of a lesson can be conducted so that all students can access the content with student writing output expectations varied	Oral language is biologically primary. We are hard-wired to acquire and develop it. All children in a class can participate in language production and lessons that focus on sentence structure and sentence development. From there, we can adjust our expectations of student writing output depending on the level of transcription a student is ready for. Some students may label a picture, others might write a sentence and others might write a paragraph, but all will have received the same oral stimulus	When you use a rich text as the foundation for language-based writing lessons, you provide the context and background for all students to participate in the development of more sophisticated concepts such as sentence structure and parts of speech. Ensure that you continually work to build the transcription skills of all students through your explicit teaching, not just accommodate some students' lack of writing skills
Teach the whole class the same content, with the same expectations of output but vary the process	Vocabulary instruction – teach vocabulary in the context of a rich text, with full participation in explicit lessons to embed the understanding and use of the target words	Development of Tier 1 vocabulary usually occurs naturally through interactions with the story, information, and other people. Tier 2 vocabulary development often requires explicit teaching. Children with developmental language disorder and other language-based difficulties can learn the same content as other students but will need additional support to learn the target vocabulary. This might take the form of additional visuals or more highly scaffolded interactions with the help of an adult	Aim to create a language-rich classroom as well as plan for explicit vocabulary instruction. We can't teach all the words but we can make enthusiasm for words and the development of language a core part of our teaching

(Continued)

Table 4.1 Options for Differentiation in the Literacy Block (Continued)

Practice	Examples of application	Reasoning	Considerations
Group students across classrooms	To teach phonics and the foundations of decoding – when resources permit and the student need indicates it would be valuable, you might consider grouping students across classes in the same age range for 40–60 minutes of the day for phonics and decoding	There are times when the range of student learning needs makes it extremely difficult or unsustainable for one teacher to manage well. This choice results in whole class teaching and fully guided instruction aimed squarely at students' needs. This kind of grouping is based on a common assessment (a phonics and word level check-in assessment), is flexible (students move groups as they learn more), and is characterised by the same high-quality instruction in each group	Involve all teachers in examining student data and making decisions about this grouping. It is easy to 'lose track' of your own students, so teachers will need to build opportunities to listen to children read and monitor their growth. This can occur in quiet reading time after lunch or in whole class language and literature-based lessons

2   Difficulties with language processing and comprehension
    Children may present with intact decoding, but experience significant difficulty understanding and interacting with what they read. Owing to the language difficulties experienced by so many children with autism, many children on the autism spectrum experience difficulty in this area (Snowling & Hulme, 2005). These language-based difficulties may or may not be present in children diagnosed with dyslexia (Vellutino & Fletcher, 2005).

There can also be two primary causes of reading difficulty.

1   Related to the child's processing
2   Related to the child's environment or instruction

In order to determine the cause of a student's reading difficulty, it is important to provide strong, systematic, evidence-informed instruction for a period of time before concluding that a student may need formal assessment (e.g. 6 months). This means that we are not simply making assumptions about why a child might be experiencing a challenge learning to read (Vellutino & Fletcher, 2005). From this point, the student's progress can be investigated and some conclusions suggested.

How Do We Identify Students with Reading Difficulty?

The first thing to know is that most children will find learning to read challenging at some point. The difference for our students with a pervasive difficulty, such as dyslexia, is that they will continue to find it harder than their peers, despite quality instruction (Seidenberg, 2017). There are several key indicators that a student may be at risk of, or experiencing, a reading difficulty. Seidenberg (2017) suggests the following:

- Poor performance on phonological and phonemic tasks
- Slow, effortful, disjointed oral reading
- Difficulty sounding out pseudo words
- Slow processing in rapid automized naming tasks
- Limited knowledge of English spelling structures
- Working memory challenges
- Language-related difficulties such as limited spoken vocabulary, proficiency with only a small number of spoken sentence structures, and difficulty reading aloud with appropriate expression

It is important to note that the simple presence of these factors does not immediately indicate a reading difficulty (remember that previous instruction is a significant factor), but they can certainly be seen as 'red flags'.

Children with Oral Language Difficulties

The link between oral language and reading acquisition is well established. Language is biologically primary and most children develop oral language knowledge and skills naturally. However, not all children do so with ease. It is estimated that two children in every class of 30 will have a language difficulty severe enough to interfere with their academic progress (Norbury et al., 2016). The recommended term for children who have language difficulties that don't have a biomedical cause, such as autism spectrum disorder or foetal alcohol syndrome, is developmental language disorder (DLD) (Bishop et al., 2017). When a child has a language difficulty that arises from another condition such as an acquired brain injury, autism spectrum disorder, or foetal alcohol syndrome, the term used is language disorder (LD) (Snow et al., 2021). As teachers, it is not for us to decide what the root cause of a child's language difficulty is. Instead, we should base the support we provide on the recommendations of speech and language professionals.

For teachers, the first step is to identify students who may have a previously undiagnosed language difficulty. Keep an eye out for students who:

- Struggle with aspects of language learning (vocabulary and grammatical markers, such as plurals, tense, and sentence structure) (Reilly et al., 2015).
- Have weak verbal short-term memory. That is, they find it difficult to repeat back sentences and strings of words (Bishop, 2006).
- Have consistent difficulty following instructions in the classroom, particularly multi-step instructions that other students manage without difficulty.
- Have trouble retelling stories or verbally sharing information that you know they have experience with.
- Struggle with 'behaviour' such as aggression and acting out. A high percentage of children with behavioural challenges also test as having a language disorder (Snow, 2016).

If you suspect that a student has a language difficulty, it is important to communicate with families and refer the student to a speech and language pathologist for assessment.

Preventing Reading Difficulty

The first thing to do is examine our own practices. Most reading challenges can be prevented or have their impact reduced through systematic, quality instruction. This involves the practices described in this book. These practices need to be used from the very start of a child's schooling and carried on through the early primary years. Using these practices, 95% of students can learn to read. Effective instruction includes the skills and knowledge of both word recognition and language comprehension and use (Moats, 2020).

Response to Intervention

Response to intervention is a well-regarded approach to providing support for students experiencing difficulty. Tier 1 instruction is designed to provide the most robust, effective practices possible so that as many children as possible can achieve success within the everyday instruction of the classroom. Children who are not making the desired progress then receive additional support in Tier 2 small group situations. This support is usually a more intense and more frequent than what is delivered at Tier 1. Students with persistent, severe difficulties may progress to Tier 3 work, which is one on one, highly individualised, and highly intensive. Students requiring this level of support often attend special education settings (Seidenberg, 2017), although inclusive practices mean that students with complex needs are now often part of our mainstream classrooms and must be appropriately supported.

What Might Reading Intervention Look Like?

Reading intervention can take many forms. The best decoding focused reading interventions provide targeted instruction in both phonological and phonemic awareness, teach or reinforce phonic-based decoding, and include connected reading (reading passages with two or more sentences related to each other) when the student has the fundamental skills to engage in this (Kilpatrick, 2015). The optimal situation is that Tier 2 intervention is an extension or more intensive version of high-quality Tier 1 instruction with decisions and adjustments to instruction made based on data and the student's own response to the intervention. There are several high-quality programs and approaches for this, but there are also some approaches that are widely used but have no grounding in research or evidence. Some of these approaches include perceptual motor programs (PMP), sensory integration therapies, and tinted lenses or overlays. In their examination of these three practices, Hyatt et al. (2009) found that there is no evidence to support them. They are not included in the DSM (Diagnostic and Statistical Manual of Mental Disorders) and they are not consistent with current research evidence about how we learn to read. On the issue of coloured lenses and overlays, Dr Caroline Bowen and Professor Pamela Snow are equally as clear. There is no evidence that coloured lenses, overlays, or special glasses provide any benefit for students with reading difficulty (Bowen & Snow, 2017).

How Can Teachers Support Students and Families?

Besides learning about evidence-informed instruction and intervention and developing proficiency in teaching through structured practices, teachers can connect with organisations such as Learning Difficulties Australia (https://www.ldaustralia.org/) and the Code Read Dyslexia Network (https://codereadnetwork.org/). These two sites contain a wealth of information. Teachers can also develop the unwavering belief that all students can learn and grow and have high expectations for student development. The very best thing you can do is be your students' biggest champion, never giving up on them, no matter how slow or difficult progress might be.

Snapshot of Practice 1 – Supporting Students Who Require Tier 3 Intervention

Kathryn Thorburn, Speech Therapist and Teacher

It's a controversial thing to discuss but not all children do well with a standard phonics approach. These children are often those students who, in your universal screening, have poor rapid automatic naming (RAN) and phonemic skills. Often these students have no diagnosis when they come to your class, but equally they may have a complex early childhood medical profile such as prematurity, apraxia (known to be clumsy), or a severe speech disorder.

The alternative to standard phonics for students with additional needs (SWAN) in Foundation to Year 3 is dropping back to an onset-rime approach to blending that matches the phonological skills the student has. This may be effective because there are fewer pieces of information for the student to have to deal with. This involves learning phoneme/grapheme correspondences as they do with the mainstream program; however, when it comes to blending and segmenting, the focus is on onset-rime rather than individual phonemes. This continues only as long as the student needs it. Some students' blending will progress to the phoneme level as with their peers. (In my experience, these children do not often have a language disorder.) However, other children will go on to require additional support such as assistive technology.

Students often need many more repetitions than their peers. Online tools and apps can be a part of this and maintain inclusion in the mainstream classroom. Be cautious that your choice of tool matches your phonics sequence and is grounded in evidence.

Creating an individual program is about customising the approach for the student. Start with the research for the mainstream classroom and then consider the tool bag of approaches that research indicates may be beneficial for 'outliers'. From there, work with the child, parents, and practitioners to decide on a plan of action. Even though the end result may look a bit different from what the rest of the class is doing, you will still be working with the 'Science of Reading' because the evidence informs your decision-making.

Advice for Teachers

- When working with students with additional needs, it is not about trying to fit the students in a box of 'normal'. It's about knowing and valuing who the student is and what they need from you (and the school team) to be successful in a way that is meaningful for them.

- When responding to the needs of SWANs, it is important to remember that there is no cookie cutter approach that is suitable for every child you encounter.
- When you are reading reports and the student has skill levels at the 1st and 2nd percentile, that's a red flag for disability. If, after 6–12 months of quality, evidence-informed intervention, those skills are still at the low end, that's when we see that those skills are unlikely to develop further and it's time to think differently for those children.
- SWANs need the support of the classroom teacher. It is fine to have a paraprofessional staff member work with the students, but the teacher must own and drive instruction. This should involve input from knowledgeable practitioners.
- There is no hard and fast rule for identifying when a child becomes a 'Tier 3' student. Universal, whole school screening and a clear understanding of progress and intervention points are needed. Essentially, when the Tier 2 intervention is not working or is not suitable for the student, different approaches are required.

Further Reading and Information

Bowen, C., & Snow, P. (2017). *Making sense of interventions for children with developmental disorders: A guide for parents and professionals.* J&R Press Limited.
Code REaD Dyslexia Network (https://codereadnetwork.org/)
Language and Learning Wesbite – Kathryn Thorburn (https://www.languageandlearning.com.au/)
Learning Difficulties Australia (https://www.ldaustralia.org/)
Read3 Tier 3 intervention website (https://read3.com.au/)
Various SPELD organisations around Australia

References

Bishop, D. V. M. (2006). What Causes Specific Language Impairment in Children? *Current Directions in Psychological Science, 15*(5), 217–221. http://www.jstor.org/stable/20183118
Bishop, D. V. M., Snowling, M. J., Thompson, P. A., Greenhalgh, T., & the CATALISE Consortium. (2017). CATALISE: A multinational and multidisciplinary Delphi consensus study of problems with language development. Phase 2. Terminology. Retrieved April 17, 2022, from https://peerj.com/preprints/2484/
Bowen, C., & Snow, P. (2017). *Making sense of interventions for children with developmental disorders: A guide for parents and professionals.* J&R Press Limited.
Dehaene, S. (2009). *Reading in the brain: The new science of how we read.* Penguin Books.
Dehaene, S. (2021). *How we learn: Why brains learn better than any machine...for now.* Penguin Books.
Ehri, L. (2005). Learning to read words: Theory findings and issues. *Scientific Studies of Reading, 9*(2), 167–188. Retrieved March 18, 2022, from https://mimtsstac.org/sites/default/files/Documents/Presentations/AnitaArcherWorkshops/January2014/LearningtoReadWords.pdf

Goldfeld, S., Beatson, R., Watts, A., Snow, P., Gold, L., Le, H. N. D., Edwards, S., Connell, J., Stark, H., Shingles, B., Barnett, T., Quach, J., & Eadie, P. (2021). Tier 2 oral language and early reading interventions for preschool to grade 2 children: A restricted systematic review. *Australian Journal of Learning Difficulties*. doi: 10.1080/19404158.2021.2011754.

Hyatt, K. J., Stephenson, J., & Carter, M. (2009). A review of three controversial educational practices: Perceptual motor programs, sensory integration, and tinted lenses. *Education and Treatment of Children*, 32(2), 313–342. http://www.jstor.org/stable/42900024

Kilpatrick, D. (2015). *Essentials of assessing, preventing and overcoming reading difficulties*. John Wiley and Sons.

Moats, L.C. (2020) *Speech to Print* (3rd edition). Paul Brooks Publishing, Baltimore.

Norbury, C. F., Gooch, D., Wray, C., Baird, G., Charman, T., Simonoff, E., Vamvakas, G., & Pickles, A. (2016). The impact of nonverbal ability on prevalence and clinical presentation of language disorder: Evidence from a population study. *Journal of Child Psychology and Psychiatry and Allied Disciplines*, 57(11), 1247–1257. doi: https://doi.org/10.1111/jcpp.12573.

Reilly, S., McKean, C., Morgan, A., & Wake, M. (2015). Identifying and managing common childhood language and speech impairments. *BMJ: British Medical Journal*, 350. https://www.jstor.org/stable/26519832

Seidenberg, M. (2017). *Language at the speed of sight: How we read, why so many can't, and what can be done about it*. Basic Books.

Snow, P. C. (2016). Elizabeth usher memorial lecture: Language is literacy is language - positioning speech-language pathology in education policy, practice, paradigms and polemics. *International Journal of Speech-Language Pathology*, 18(3), 216–228. doi: 10.3109/17549507.2015.1112837.

Snow, P. C., Leitão, S., & Kippin, N. (2021). Language and literacy in the context of early life adversity. In M. Ball, J. Damico, & N. Müller (Eds.), *Wiley-Blackwell handbook of language and speech disorders* (pp. 266–285). Wiley-Blackwell.

Snowling., M., & Hulme, C. (2005). Learning to read with a language impairment. In M. Snowling, & C. Hulme (Eds.), *The science of reading: A handbook* (pp. 397–412). Blackwell Publishing Limited.

Sweller, J. (2020). Cognitive load theory and educational technology. *Educational Technology Research & Development*, 68(1), 1–16. https://doi-org.rp.nla.gov.au/10.1007/s11423-019-09701-3

Tomlinson, C. A. (2017). How to Differentiate Instruction in Academically Diverse Classrooms. Office of Educational Research and Improvement. Retrieved September 14, 2021, from https://eric.ed.gov/?id=ED443572

Vellutino, F. R., & Fletcher, J. M. (2005). Developmental dyslexia. In M. Snowling, & C. Hulme (Eds.), *The science of reading: A handbook* (pp. 362–378). Blackwell Publishing Limited.

Watts-Taffe, S., Laster, B. P. B., Broach, L., Marinak, B., Connor, C. M., & Walker-Dalhouse, D. (2012). DIFFERENTIATED INSTRUCTION: Making informed teacher decisions. *The Reading Teacher*, 66(4), 303–314. http://www.jstor.org/stable/23321311

Part II
The 8 Key Actions

5 8 Key Actions One, Two, Three, and Four

The Simple View of Reading and the Big Six ideas of reading instruction provide us with a solid overview of the practices that best serve the greatest number of students in reading instruction. It is now time to drill down further into the key actions that teachers need to take to put all of this into practice. While I am presenting eight separate actions here, this doesn't mean that these eight actions are done sequentially or separately. They exist as part of the overall framework of evidence-informed reading instruction and are performed every day in your teaching. In this section, I am providing a suggestion for a progression of skills across the first three years of school. Some of the items and timings come from researchers, some from documents such as the Australian Curriculum, and some from my own observations and expectations developed through my own teaching. Your students' skill and knowledge development through these years will depend greatly on their starting point when they entered school, their individual learning needs, and the context of your school community. Use the suggested progressions as a guide, knowing that we serve children best when we find where they are up to and meet them there. The key actions described here will be further expanded on with the practical 'how to' and snapshots of teacher practice in Part III.

Key Action 1 – Prioritise General Oral Language Development

Oral language is critical for the development of both reading and writing. A saying that helps bring this home is,

> 'If you can't say it, you can't read it and you can't write it'.

We have seen that oral language is made up of several interconnected areas including semantics, syntax, vocabulary, morphology, and articulation. As vocabulary has a particular part to play in reading comprehension, it is addressed as a separate key action. Regardless of which aspects of oral

DOI: 10.4324/9781003244189-8

language you are trying to help your students develop, it is important to approach instruction with two questions in mind:

1. How am I explicitly, intentionally, and systematically teaching the various aspects of oral language?
2. How am I creating a language-rich environment for my students to be immersed in?

We are biologically primed to acquire language and are uniquely positioned as a species to learn it from each other (Moats, 2020). As such, it makes sense to create a classroom environment that is rich in vocabulary and sophisticated sentence structures and facilitates interactions between student and student and between teacher and student.

The quality of the interactions we facilitate in our classrooms is critical to our students' engagement in learning. These interactions do not only have to occur between people but can also come about through interactions with books. In the early years, while children are still developing the ability to decode and recognise words, careful choices about the books we read *to* children are just as important as the books they read for themselves. Until children have the ability to lift the words from the pages of rich text with ease, teachers take on the role of the decoder. It is through this facilitation that we help children develop a relationship with the story and provide them with the exposure to language that comes about from beautiful, rich picture books.

Rich stories and non-fiction texts can also be the jumping-off point for explicit instruction in syntax (sentence structure), parts of speech (grammar), oral and written morphology, descriptive language development, and, of course, vocabulary. Rich texts provide the context required for effective language learning. Explicit teaching, contextualised through story and included right from the earliest years of school, ensures that children have their attention drawn to precisely the content we want them to learn. From there, we can scaffold their experiences and help them build proficiency in a safe, structured environment.

A breakdown of sentence structure and parts of speech is provided in Figures 5.1 and 5.2.

Foundation (First year of school) Simple sentences oral and written. Compound sentences oral (written by advanced students)

Year 1 (Second year of school) Simple sentences oral and written. Compound sentences oral and written

Year 2 (Third year of school) Simple sentences oral and written. Compound sentences oral and written. Complex sentences oral (written by advanced students)

Figure 5.1 Suggested Sequence of Learning for Sentence Structure

Foundation (First Year of School) Understanding that different words in a sentence have a different function (action, person/place/thing/, where and how the action takes place)

Year 1 (Second Year of School) Understand the concepts of nouns and pronouns, verbs, adjectives, and adverbs and use these word classes in their own writing. Students understand that words can change class depending on the context of a sentence. For example, the word birthday can be a noun (your birthday) or an adjective (a birthday party).

Year 2 (Third Year of School) Nouns can represent concrete and abstract concepts. There are three types of nouns (common, proper, and pronouns). Students can expand a noun phrase to add detail to their writing.

Figure 5.2 Suggested Sequence of Learning for Parts of Speech (Based on English Sequence of Content – Australian Curriculum, ACARA, 2015)

Considerations for Planning and Teaching

- All students can be engaged in the development of the key oral language concepts listed above, regardless of reading and writing ability. Design all explicit lessons so that every student has the opportunity to 'talk to a partner' to produce oral responses before asking them to write. Provide appropriate scaffolding for students whose reading and writing skills are not in line with their oral skills. Most students will be able to produce something in writing with support, even if it is identifying the first letter of the words they wish to write.
- Include an 'I say, you say' component in your lessons. Say the target words, phrases, and sentences aloud and ask your students to repeat you. Do this several times to allow students to keep up with the flow of the lesson. This repetition is particularly important for those students who have weak working memories, developmental language disorder, or who require extra support to focus their attention.
- While copying is great for oral work, it is not ideal for written work. It is much better to engage students in a fully guided, full participation joint construction of a phrase or sentence and then have them write it themselves (after you have covered the example) rather than ask them to simply copy. Copying is the enemy of active engagement! Lesson plans for sentence transcription work are provided in Chapter 12.
- Remember that you are the model for language in your classroom. Use Tier 2 vocabulary, ask higher order questions, make your thinking explicit through 'think alouds', and demonstrate a general enthusiasm for the English language. Teach your students to ask when they don't understand something and to seek answers to their questions. This oral comprehension monitoring forms the basis of the reading comprehension monitoring we want children to develop all through their primary years.
- Remember to provide opportunities for students to both speak and listen. Both paths of communication are important.

Key Action 2 – Explicitly Build Vocabulary and Background Knowledge

In order to read the words that have been read, a reader must know what those words mean. It is not, however, always enough to just know the surface meaning of a word. We need to have a deeper understanding of it (Oakhill et al., 2015) and this is where background knowledge comes in. If we read the words 'plant respiration', we might know that respiration relates to breathing. However, it is our understanding of the way a plant 'breathes' through its leaves with the help of sunlight that helps us fully comprehend the importance of the number of daylight hours a plant receives. It is important to note that strong background knowledge can provide some compensation for poor decoding, but knowledge cannot compensate for poor decoding completely (Smith et al., 2021). Therefore, it is necessary to continue to provide instruction in basic decoding skills for as long as a student requires it.

Vocabulary and background knowledge are closely related to reading comprehension for students of all ages (Beck et al., 2013). Explicit, structured, and systematic vocabulary development must be a feature of literacy instruction across the school. This not only involves teaching children about the meaning of words, but also about how to use those words. We do this through explicit teaching followed by engaging, meaningful interactions with the words and each other (Beck et al., 2013).

What Do We Teach?

Teach Word Relationships

Words don't exist in our minds in isolation, but as part of semantic networks (Moats, 2020). Every word has other words and concepts associated with it. The more awareness we can raise of these networks, the more students will be able to comprehend. This is demonstrated in Figure 5.3.

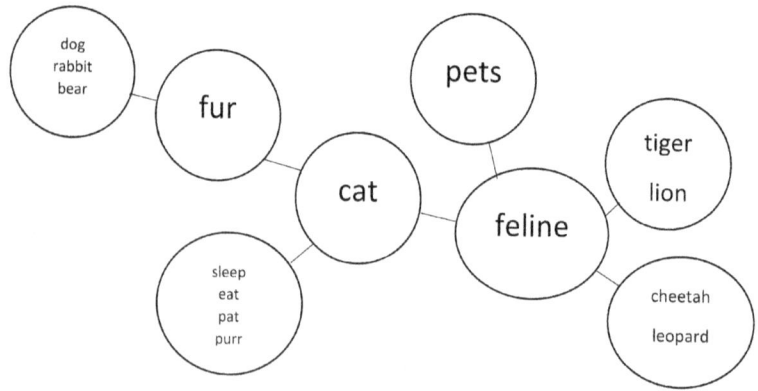

Figure 5.3 Semantic Networks – Every Word Has Other Words and Concepts Associated with It

Teach the Multiple Meanings of Words

A large number of content words have multiple meanings. Teaching and drawing attention to the multiple meanings of words supports comprehension because when a student comes across the word, they can quickly consider those multiple meanings to make a connection to the author's message. For example, the word cream can mean the following:

- The part of the milk we remove to make skim milk
- Thickened cream that we whip and put on a pavlova
- A thick, white substance we rub into our skin (sun cream, moisturising cream)
- An informal word that means to 'beat' another team in sports
- The very best of a group – 'The cream of the crop'
- An off-white colour

It isn't necessary to teach every word in great detail, but it is important to raise children's awareness of these multiple meanings during word work/ exploration (Figure 5.3).

Include Non-Fiction Texts Related to The Stories You Are Reading

One of the ways you can help children build background knowledge and appropriate vocabulary is by including both fiction and non-fiction texts in your teaching, right from the start of the Foundation year. Choose short texts that unpack some aspect of the fiction text that children are unlikely to be familiar with. For example, if you were reading a story that contained a well, you might read non-fiction texts or view short video clips about real-life wells to help children understand the deeper meaning of the story. If you were reading '"Slowly, Slowly, Slowly," said the Sloth' by Eric Carle, you might watch a clip about sloths to build knowledge of how a sloth moves in the forest.

Of course, you can't do this for every single concept that might appear in a book. There simply isn't the time and it isn't necessary. Choose to build knowledge around the parts of the text where it will make the most difference to the students' overall understanding and the concepts that students are most likely to have difficulty developing for themselves.

Include Simple, Fast-Paced Vocabulary Practice and Knowledge Building in Your Morning Routine

There is also a place for decontextualised review of background knowledge and vocabulary. Including a review of previously learned words or words you are currently teaching can be valuable for all students, but particularly those students who may experience memory lapses or have trouble making connections themselves. Asking questions such as 'What do these two words have in common?' or 'If you were hungry would you look forward to a feast or a famine?' can provide the needed repetition and multiple interactions needed for long-term learning.

Use Picture Books as A Source of Tier 2 Vocabulary

Picture books have an important part to play in vocabulary development. Children's picture books contain more unique words and more words overall than are present in a child's natural speech (Montag et al., 2015). As such, they are an accessible and valuable source of language modelling for children. When we read rich texts to our students, we are exposing them to a broader and richer vocabulary than we ourselves would ever use. Reading to children several times each day (even into the upper primary years) is a great habit to establish. It not only provides a relaxing, engaging brain break, but also provides a stimulus for vocabulary learning.

Considerations for Teaching

- You can't teach all of the words or all of the knowledge. Don't worry so much about teaching the 'right' words that you don't teach any. Simply choose the words and knowledge that you think will be the most valuable for the students.
- While most students won't need explicit teaching in Tier 1 vocabulary (everyday words), children with English as an Additional Language or Dialect may need this instruction.
- Remember that teaching a word isn't a one-time deal. We must provide follow-up opportunities to practice using words and revisit them regularly.
- As with other aspects of oral language, a teacher's enthusiasm for words will set the tone for vocabulary learning. Express delight and enjoyment when you encounter interesting or useful words and praise children for using new vocabulary.
- When helping children make connections with background knowledge, ask them, 'Where have you heard of this thing before?', 'What do we already know about this?', or 'Is this the same or different from what we've seen before?' and then 'How is it different?'

Key Action 3 – Explicitly Teach Phonological and Phonemic Skills

The National Reading Panel (NICHD, 2000) concluded that phonological and phonemic skills are critical for students to read and spell. Phonological skills relate to a sensitivity of linguistic units larger than the phoneme level (words, syllables, onset, and rime). Phonemic awareness, on the other hand, refers to the awareness that words are made up of individual phonemes (speech sounds) and the capacity to manipulate them by blending, segmenting, adding, deleting, and substituting those phonemes. The development of phonemic awareness is not necessarily automatic (Dehaene, 2009; Moats, 2020; Seidenberg, 2017). Many children, particularly those who are at risk of reading difficulty, require explicit instruction to develop this awareness.

The National Reading Panel's (NICHD, 2000) examinations of 52 studies about phonemic awareness found the following:

- Instruction in one or two skills at a time yielded better results than teaching a larger range of skills at once.
- Instruction that included graphemes was more effective than instruction that was purely oral in nature.
- Phonemic awareness instruction that included graphemes had a much larger impact on spelling than oral only instruction.
- Instructional programs that lasted between 5 and 20 hours yielded the best results. Longer programs were less effective.
- Instruction in blending and segmenting had a larger impact than instruction involving multiple skills.
- Phonemic awareness training was found to be beneficial for all students in the first year of school; however, its inclusion in Year 1 and 2 should be provided on an as-needed basis to those students still working to develop these skills.

The panel also identified that phonemic awareness instruction in small groups appeared to be more beneficial than in whole class or individual lessons; however, it also identified this as a point requiring further research. More recent studies have indicated that phonemic awareness instruction can be effective at the whole class level (Kilpatrick, 2015).

This list of recommendations paints a clear picture of the most important elements of teaching phonemic awareness. When it comes to phonological awareness (the sensitivity to linguistic units bigger than phonemes), the research is equally clear. Introducing an oral phonological awareness program to preschool children provides significant benefits that persist well into the primary grades (Lundberg et al., 1988). This instruction can include:

- Games
- Nursery rhymes
- Rhyming stories
- Dance and movement
- Syllable games

While some may express concern about bringing academic instruction into the preschool years, the benefits of the activities described above should not be underestimated. Instruction can be provided in these early skills (moving on to phoneme level when students are ready) in a developmentally appropriate way.

Figure 5.4 shows a suggested time frame for learning phonological and phonemic awareness.

Preschool – phonological sensitivity including the ability to blend and segment syllables, identify how many words are in a sentence, and identify words that rhyme. Some preschool children will develop early phonemic awareness at this stage; however, many won't.

Foundation – development of general phonemic awareness and blending and segmenting (CVC words). Note that a student's ability to do this with graphemes is heavily influenced by the automaticity of their phoneme/grapheme correspondence. Some sources indicate the development of this skill by the end of Year 1; however, this means that children won't be reading until then. My view is that you should expect oral blending by the end of Term 1 of Foundation and blending with graphemes to develop by the middle of the year as an 'at least' indicator.

Year 1 – Substituting, deleting, adding phonemes. This develops once students have a grasp on the fundamentals of spelling with the basic code and strengthens as they develop proficiency with more complex words. You can expect students to acquire these higher order skills by the end of Year 1 and into Year 2.

Figure 5.4 Suggested Time Frame for Acquiring Phonological and Phonemic Skills

Considerations for Teaching

In addition to the guidelines above, when deciding on the teaching program for phonological and phonemic awareness, keep the following in mind:

- Monitor skill development throughout the year to identify those students whose progress indicates that there may be a learning difficulty. A failure to develop adequate phonemic skills in the presence of strong instruction is a red flag.
- Follow-up lessons may need to be delivered in a small group situation for additional support or if the rest of the class does not require this content to be taught.
- Assessment need not be by way of a norm-referenced, formal assessment. An informal assessment is highly effective when determining the next steps for teaching.
- Embed phonological sensitivity activities into daily transitions between activities rather than spending large amounts of instructional time on this. Some students may require Tier 2 support in this area, but that doesn't mean that all students will need it, particularly in Year 1 and 2.
- Embed phonemic awareness tasks in your phonics and shared writing lessons each day. The development of phonemic awareness is important for the function that it serves in reading and spelling, rather than as an activity in and of itself.

- Once students can perform a particular skill with ease, stop focusing on it.
- Do not wait for phonological sensitivity to be fully developed before introducing phonemic awareness. They can be developed at the same time.

Key Action 4 – Teach Phonics Explicitly and Systematically

Phoneme/grapheme correspondence (letter-sound relationships) is critical for students to be able to lift the words from the page and develop strong reading skills (Dehaene, 2009). In terms of exactly how to teach the relationships between sounds and letters, the United States National Reading Panel concluded that explicit, systematic instruction yields the best results (NICHD, 2000). But exactly what does that mean?

The answer lies in Rosenshine's 10 principles of explicit instruction (Rosenhshine, 2012) outlined below:

1. Begin with a review
2. Present material in small steps with practice after each step
3. Ask questions and check responses of all students
4. Provide models and worked examples
5. Guide student practice
6. Check for understanding
7. Obtain a high success rate
8. Provide scaffolds for difficult tasks
9. Require and monitor independent practice
10. Weekly and monthly review

In a balanced literacy approach, our phonics instruction may have been 'light touch' with students singing a song, doing craft, watching YouTube clips, and having the phoneme/grapheme correspondences pointed out to them in the context of big book reading. While this may be sufficient for some students, for most it simply won't be enough to help them embed these correspondences into their long-term memory for easy retrieval. There is clear evidence that novices (just about every single student who will enter our early years classrooms) do much better with fully guided instruction than with an inquiry or constructivist approach to learning. Fully-guided, or explicit, instruction is more direct and efficient for all and better supports at-risk students than other approaches (Clark et al., 2012). Further, a synthetic approach that directly teaches the phoneme/grapheme correspondences and how to blend them together is regarded as the most efficient method of phonics instruction to support student cognitive load (Buckingham, 2020) and recent research evidence indicates that children make strong gains when it is used (Ehri, 2020).

When we are learning about implementing an explicit, systematic synthetic phonics lesson, it can be helpful to discuss what explicit instruction in phonics is not, so let's start there.

Explicit, systematic, synthetic phonics does not include the following:

1 Independent or group work conducted without teacher guidance or direction – we do not rely on small group rotation activities to teach content and skills.
2 Discovery or incidental opportunities within play-based learning (it might be engaging for some students if you include these in your play-based lessons, but it is not a replacement for teacher-led instruction).
3 The expectation that 'exposure' to content alone will result in learning. We know that explicit teaching is required.
4 Learning whole words and then 'analysing' them to make the phoneme/grapheme correspondences visible.
5 Singing songs or doing craft as a core part of the instruction (include this after lunch or in the 'down time' before recess, lunch, or home time, but do not mistake these activities for explicit instruction).
6 Exposing the children to the whole alphabet all at once (even just as 'exposure') and then noticing what they do and do not pick up. This approach can compromise working memory for many students.
7 Teaching word families (-at, -it, -on) or blends (st, pl, nt) as units.
8 Spending hours each day focusing on learning phoneme/grapheme correspondence. A 20–30 minutes daily lesson gets the job done.
9 Having a multitude of teaching routines that are changed regularly to 'keep it fun'.
10 Working your way through the scope and sequence with the time frames guided by the program or approach, rather than the response of the students.

This list might leave you scratching your head and wondering exactly what you are supposed to do. It's possible that many of the items above form the core part of your phonics approach. If that's the case, fear not. Shifting practice to a systematic, explicit one can be simple and quick and can ease your cognitive load.

Let's examine the features of a systematic, synthetic phonics approach.

1 Low variance teaching routines that are repeated each day. Rather than adjusting the lesson steps or routine, it is the content that is changed. This enables students to simply focus on what it is you want them to learn instead of spending their cognitive energy working out what they are supposed to do. Time on task is maximised.
2 Focus on a carefully considered amount of content at any one time. To support cognitive load, content is delivered in small, manageable chunks with students given the opportunity to learn to mastery before moving on.

3 Phoneme/grapheme correspondence is contextualised through word-level reading and spelling in each lesson (more on that later).
4 Every student is actively thinking about and working with the content being learned. No student is passive in the learning process.
5 Content is intentionally and tightly targeted at the point of learning appropriate for each student. Not too easy, not too hard.
6 Lessons involve the opportunity for review and consolidation.
7 Formative assessment is conducted each and every lesson and a recorded monitoring assessment is completed at regular intervals (six to eight weeks).
8 The pace of learning and the amount of content covered are determined by the response of students to the teaching, not the timings of a commercial program.
9 Lessons are designed to enable and facilitate a high rate of success. Scaffolds provide support but do not 'take over' the thinking for students. These scaffolds are removed as soon as possible so that students are actively engaged and thinking for themselves.
10 Lessons utilise an 'I do', 'We do', 'You do' structure.
11 The complexity of the English language system is made visible to students.
12 Simple to complex format – basic code and then complex.
13 Feedback is provided immediately in all activities so that students can learn from their errors.
14 Adjustments in the approach or lessons are driven by data and the learning needs of students, not the desire for novelty, fun, or entertainment. When learning is aimed at the right level, children who are experiencing success and can see the difference their learning is making do not become bored by predictable routines. They thrive in them.
15 Lessons keep a brisk pace.

Considerations for Teaching

The most obvious question to arise from the above lists is, 'How do we manage the diversity of student need in our classroom?' If small group rotations are not recommended, exactly how are we supposed to meet students where they are up to? My response is a multifaceted one.

First, dividing students into small groups to target learning specifically at their point of need isn't the enemy. It is the loss of instructional time when children are working 'independently' that we seek to avoid. When we take an honest look at our students working in small group rotations, how likely is it that they will be on task, focusing on exactly what we want them to learn if we are not there to guide them? For most of the young children I have taught in my career, the answer is, 'Not very.' Sure, they might not be running around the classroom or building towers with the magnetic letters, but that doesn't mean that learning will be as direct and effective as if we were there guiding them, providing feedback throughout the lesson. Dehaene (2021) outlines four conditions for effective learning.

Attention: children require adults to help them attend to the important content and skills in lessons. Our most important job as teachers is to focus student attention. We can only focus on one piece of content or skill at a time. Split attention leads to a loss of focus. Multitasking is a myth.

Active engagement: children must actively create mental models of what we want them to learn. They need to be thinking and working with content and skills. Many children adults to help them focus their attention to facilitate active engagement. Further, our brains do not attend to what is occurring around us if we don't perceive that there is something to be learned or gain. Lessons must be aimed at the right 'point' for students to properly engage.

Feedback: without signals that we have made an error, we will not learn.

Consolidation: children must have the opportunity to practise, review and revise if learning is to become embedded in long term memory.

When we apply the lens of Stanislas Dehaene's 4 Pillars (Dehaene, 2021) to our classroom structure, it is clear that children need us in order to learn well.

Second, we need to rethink how we recruit, train, and support the paraprofessionals in our schools. We must train and support every paraprofessional in our schools to deliver the same high-quality phonics lessons that teachers do. Low variance routines make this not only manageable, but highly effective.

Finally, if we are going to meet students where they are up to for the 20–30 minutes each day it takes to teach phonics well, we are going to need to embrace some 'out of the box' thinking. There are several options for arranging students and/or human resources to meet student needs.

1. Rather than having one paraprofessional in each classroom for the whole literacy block, have them rotate through the classes. Having three trained adults in a room for half an hour means that you can divide your class into three groups. Each group is taught the same type of lesson at the same time, but with the content that meets the students where they are up. No loss of instructional time. The remainder of the literacy block is then managed whole class. This can take a shift in thinking from staff who are used to working with 'my TA' or 'my class'.

2. Conduct one, consistent assessment for all students in a cohort and then arrange those students in flexible groupings across classes. For a certain period of time each day (50–60 minutes), students go to their 'reading group' to receive instruction with the exact content they need. Each adult uses the same routines and materials so that no matter who is teaching, the children have consistency and access to learning. Groupings are changed each time assessment is conducted so that those learning at a faster pace can receive instruction that responds to their needs and those students who need more time to embed learning can have it.

3. Assessment may show that your classrooms contain fairly homogeneous learners in terms of the content they are ready to learn, but that there

are a few 'outliers' in each class. Rather than having every student move, perhaps your 'spotlight' learners go to your learning support teacher for the hour and your 'fast lane' learners go to another group for that time.

4 Small schools are not without choices in this area. Being very clear about what does and does not need to be taught in groups will help minimise the amount of time students spend without adult guidance. In reality, the phonics lesson (20–30 minutes per day) is the only part of the literacy block that may need to be managed in groups. The rest of the block can be differentiated so that each student gets what they need while maximising time on task. We will cover this more in the following chapters.

5 You may be fortunate in that your class comes to you all at a similar 'level' of reading development. Depending on your students' profiles, you may find that you can teach phonics to the whole class and then provide further consolidation in a small follow-up group for those students who need it. This represents the ideal situation. You might even be able to have your students with knowledge gaps fill these gaps in that small group follow-up, eliminating the need for core small group instruction. This is most likely to be possible and beneficial when a student can learn at the same pace as their peers but has missed out on content for some reason. However, if a student has difficulty embedding new content into long-term memory or becomes quickly cognitively overloaded, this approach may do more harm than good. The key to getting this right is to know your students well and monitor data carefully. If the student is making progress and your data supports your current approach, continue with it. However, if things are not progressing as you had hoped, make adjustments as needed.

There will be as many solutions to the differentiation conundrum as there are schools. Your school context, staffing, student learning profiles, and stage in moving towards structured literacy will all influence how this is managed. Be prepared to adopt one approach and then adjust it over time as your school processes and teaching approaches mature and develop.

References

Australian Curriculum, Assessment and Reporting Authority (ACARA) 2010 to present, unless otherwise indicated. This material was downloaded (www.australiancurriculum.edu.au) (accessed 19 March, 2022) and was modified. The material is licensed under CC BY 4.0 (https://creativecommons.org/licenses/by/4.0).

Beck, I., McKeown, M., & Kucan, L. (2013). *Bringing words to life* (2nd ed.). Guildford Publications.

Buckingham, J. (2020). Systematic phonics instruction belongs in evidence-based reading programs: A response to Bowers. *The Educational and Developmental Psychologist*, 37(2), 105–113. doi: 10.1017/edp.2020.12.

Clark, R. E., Kirschner, P. A., & Sweller, J. (2012). Putting students on the path to learning: The case for fully guided instruction. *American Educator, 36*(1), 6–11, Spr 2012. https://eric.ed.gov/?id=EJ971752

Dehaene, S. (2021). *How we learn: Why brains learn better than any machine…for now.* Penguin Books.

Dehaene., S. (2009). *Reading in the brain: The new science of how we read.* Penguin Books.

Ehri, L. C. (2020). The science of learning to read words: A case for systematic phonics instruction. *Reading Research Quarterly, 55*(S1), S45–S60. doi: https://doi.org/10.1002/rrq.334.

Kilpatrick, D. (2015). *Essentials of assessing, preventing and overcoming reading difficulties.* John Wiley and Sons.

Lundberg, I., Frost, J., & Petersen, O.-P. (1988). Effects of an extensive program for stimulating phonological awareness in preschool children. *Reading Research Quarterly, 23*(3), 263–284. http://www.jstor.org/stable/748042

Moats, L. C. (2020). *Speech to print* (3rd ed.). Paul Brooks Publishing.

Montag, J. L., Jones, M. N., & Smith, L. B. (2015). The words children hear: Picture books and the statistics for language learning. *Psychological Science, 26*(9), 1489–1496. http://www.jstor.org/stable/24544089

(NICHD) Eunice Kennedy Shriver National Institute of Child Health and Human Development, NIH, DHHS. (2000). *Report of the national reading panel: Teaching children to read: Reports of the subgroups (00-4754).* Government Printing Office.

Oakhill, J., Cain, K., & Elbro, C. (2015). *Understanding and teaching reading comprehension – A handbook.* Routledge.

Rosehshine, B. (2012). Principles of instruction: Research based strategies that all teachers should know. *American Educator, 36*(1), 12–19, 39 Spr 2012. Retrieved September 7, 2021, from https://eric.ed.gov/?id=EJ971753

Seidenberg, M. (2017). *Language at the speed of sight: How we read, why so many can't, and what can be done about it.* Basic Books.

Smith, R., Pamela Snow, P., Serry, T., & Hammond, L. (2021). The role of background knowledge in reading comprehension: A critical review. *Reading Psychology, 42*(3), 214–240. doi: 10.1080/02702711.2021.1888348.

6 Key Actions Five, Six, Seven, and Eight

Key Action 5 – Teach Phonics and Reading Using a Set Sequence

As we have seen, systematic synthetic phonics is regarded as the most direct way to teach the fundamental skills of phonics and decoding. This approach begins by teaching a small number of phoneme/grapheme correspondences, enabling students to learn them to mastery before moving on. A key feature of this approach is the utilisation of a set scope and sequence that is followed by all teachers in a school as a road map to instruction (Moats, 2020). There are several reasons why a sequence is recommended.

1. Using a scope and sequence enables all teachers to work from the same 'play book'. This consistency allows teachers to work collaboratively, share common assessment tools and resources, and support each other in their teaching.
2. The scope and sequence enables learning to continue as teachers and students move from one school year to the next. Coupling the sequence with a common assessment tool means that teachers aren't required to go on a 'journey of discovery' at the start of each new school year but can pick up where the previous teacher left off.
3. Having a set sequence facilitates a cumulative approach. A cumulative arrangement of content means that each part of the teaching program builds on the one before (Moats, 2020). This means that words and texts contain only graphemes and irregular high frequency words that students have already learned.
4. A cumulative approach also keeps students focused on the internal structure of the word and out of the 'guessing zone'.
   For example, once you have learned s, a, t, p, i, n
   - you can read the words sat, pin, pat, nip, at, in, sit, tin, and sap
   - When you have learned r, m, o, and h
   - you can read the words rat, map, pot, not, rip, and rap

   There is no looking at pictures or guessing required because you will know the phoneme/grapheme correspondences in the words you are being asked to read and spell. Your eyes can remain on the words you are reading.

5   Once you know the sequence of teaching the code, you can then link that sequence with decodable texts. These texts might contain words that students haven't encountered before, but they will not contain graphemes and irregular high frequency words they don't know. From a cognitive load perspective, this is great news. It means that students can focus on what is important – using code knowledge and phonemic skills to lift words from the page quickly and efficiently.

Considerations for Teaching

When considering which scope and sequence to use, there are several to choose from. There is no one, proven sequence and all will have strengths and limitations depending on your focus. There are, however, some suggested features for a strong scope and sequence for phonics.

1   Code knowledge instruction extends beyond the 'basic code' (alphabet sounds and most common consonant digraphs – sh, th, ch, ng). It is recommended that a core group of graphemes should be taught (between 75 and 90 depending on the program) over a period of two or three years (Moats, 2020). The length of time it takes to learn these core graphemes will depend heavily on the student's starting point upon entering school, the student's learning profile, and how consistently and directly teaching occurs during the early years of school. Some students will be ready for the complex code in the first year of school and others will not. Let student responses and data drive the pace, not the program you may be using.
2   Teach the orthographic patterns and spelling guidelines that relate to particular graphemes when you teach the grapheme. This is particularly relevant in Year 1 and 2, and then revisit and review as needed. In this way, your phonics lessons then also act as your spelling program. For example, if you are teaching that 'ck' is used after a single, short vowel (as in tick, lock, muck, neck andback), there is no need to have a separate spelling program in the early years of school.
3   Begin teaching phonics with continuous sounds in the early Foundation lessons as these are the easiest for children to learn to blend with.
4   Teach graphemes that look or sound similar separately to avoid confusion. Many children will cope well with teaching them together, but those with speech challenges, phonological deficits, language processing difficulties, or poor memories may well be confused by teaching 'm and n' or 'ou and oa' close together.
5   A scope and sequence should consider which graphemes are the most common in written English and teach them first. Our brains automatically engage in a process called statistical sampling (Seidenberg, 2017).

This involves unconsciously taking note of which graphemes appear more frequently and developing an expectation of which phoneme a particular grapheme will be representing. We then use this to make choices about how to decode words. For example, the grapheme 'ea' can be used for the phoneme /e/ as in the head or /ee/ as in bead. 'ea' for the long e/ee/ (bead) is twice as likely to appear as if used for the /e/ phoneme (head). When we encounter the word 'dream', we will know that /ee/ is the most common sound associated with that grapheme and be able to produce an approximate pronunciation. It is our knowledge of the context of the sentence that provides the final confirmation.

However, word length also comes into play when choosing which graphemes to teach first. Some very common patterns (single e for the long sound /ee/ such as in recall and detail) may be left until later in the sequence because they appear in multisyllable words that children may not be ready to decode in the early stages of instruction.

The good news for us teachers is that we don't have to devise our own scope and sequence for teaching phonics. In fact, I wouldn't recommend that you try. Instead, defer to the scope and sequence included in a program if you are using one or connect your teaching to the main decodable text sequence you have in your school.

Key Action 6 – Closely Monitor Progress and Reteach as Needed

The inclusion of assessment in all phonics and reading instructional approaches is necessary to ensure that teaching focuses on meeting students where they are up to. There is little point in having a scope and sequence, strong phonics routines, tightly aligned decodable texts, and all of the other components of a strong phonics and decoding approach if we don't find where students are up to and meet them there. In order for students to be fully engaged in learning, content and pace must be matched to the needs of the students (Dehaene, 2021). The children in our classes may differ greatly in their knowledge, skills, and processing, and common sense tells us that trying to treat them as if they were all the same is sure to over or underwhelm at least part of the class.

In order to choose and use assessment effectively, we need to answer the question, 'What questions are we trying to answer with this assessment?' It is necessary that all members of the team can articulate the answer to that question so that each teacher can have full buy-in with the assessment tools available.

Assessment can take several forms and answer several questions.

How Have the Students Engaged with My Lesson? (Informal, Daily)

In-lesson formative assessment to 'check for understanding' – The concept of 'checking understanding' is a central one in explicit instruction (Archer &

Hughes, 2011). It involves questioning students during and at the end of a lesson to ask them to demonstrate that they are understanding what they are learning.

In a phonics lesson where you are teaching a new grapheme/phoneme correspondence – It might involve asking the children to write the target grapheme after a period of focusing on something else.

In a vocabulary lesson – This might mean asking a question such as 'If you were really hungry, would you rather have a feast or a famine?' and (without prompting) asking the children to share their answer.

The beauty of this kind of informal, in the moment assessment is that you can tell very quickly whether what you have taught has made sense and how likely it is to 'stick'. When you include content from the previous lesson and the previous week, you are able to determine what you need to reteach to keep all students on track. It isn't necessary to wait until the end of a teaching cycle to reteach. If you notice that something is 'wobbly', reteach it the very next day.

How Is the Student Keeping up with the Instruction Overall? What Have They Learned So Far? What Do They Need to Learn Next? (Informal, Every Six to Eight Weeks)

Informal, one-to-one assessment is also necessary to capture a data set for each student. This might involve assessing the following:

- A student's knowledge of phoneme/grapheme correspondence.
- A student's ability to blend 'real' words – examining whether this blending is sound by sound or automatic.
- A student's ability to blend 'nonsense' or 'pseudo' words. The purpose of this is to determine whether the student is blending with a given grapheme or just remembering the word from their long-term memory.
- A student's text-level reading rate, once the student reaches the point where this is useful.
- Whether a student is able to recall the details of what they have just read.

This assessment does not need to be norm-referenced. Its purpose is not to compare the student with other students across Australia, but to determine how much and to what degree the student has learned what you have taught and enable you to make a plan for the learning that is to come.

This kind of assessment can be created by your school or drawn from a program or set of decodable texts that you might be using. There are also free assessments available online.

How Does This Student Compare With Other Students Across Australia? (Formal, Once, or Twice per Year)

This kind of assessment is usually only completed once or twice each year. A norm-referenced, interview style reading assessment where an adult listens to a child read might only be available to speech therapists or those teachers with advanced qualifications, although there are options available to schools. You might also consider having students participate in a computerised, multiple-choice reading assessment that is used by many schools. This doesn't give you the diagnostic observations in terms of a student's reading 'behaviours', but does provide scores that can tell you reasonably reliably how your students compare with other children across the country. Of course, there are limitations to any multiple-choice assessment. However, if anomalies appear in your data, you will be able to triangulate the data (compare the various forms of assessment used in the school to make a judgement about the student's current point of development).

Considerations for Choosing and Conducting Assessment

- Is the assessment you are using going to give you the information you need to truly determine a student's current point of development?
- How are you ensuring consistency between the people conducting the assessments?
- How often will you conduct the assessment? How often is too often?
- How will the assessment inform your next steps in teaching?
- How will you ensure that students are an active part of the process and understand the purpose of the assessment?
- What kind of data conversation is going to be of benefit to the students?
- Do you need a one-to-one assessment or can you answer your questions through a targeted assessment of classroom-level work? This question is particularly pertinent when it comes to assessing comprehension.
- How will you help your teachers and paraprofessional colleagues build proficiency in conducting assessment and using the data to ensure maximum impact in teaching?

Key Action 7 – Teach Reading and Spelling Together

Reading and spelling enhance each other (Weiser & Mathes, 2011) with positive effects seen when we have young students learn to read and spell using their phonics knowledge. In fact, it has been suggested that the inclusion of encoding practice in phonics lessons might be the missing link when working to prevent reading difficulty for some students (Weiser, 2013). Research indicates that we are able to recognise words that are in our long-term memories because we have mapped them both from speech to print and print to speech (Moats, 2020). As such, when helping students build the fundamental skills of reading and writing, it is advisable to include both decoding (reading) and encoding (spelling) in each lesson.

In practice, this is a simple thing to achieve. Your phonics lesson will include word-level reading that enables children to practice reading with the graphemes that have been taught. Simply take these same words and ask the children to spell them, providing feedback as you go so that they may 'tick it or fix it'.

The terrific thing about taking this approach is that it isn't necessary to provide stand-alone spelling instruction in the early years because spelling lessons are incorporated into your daily phonics lessons. No spelling lists or weekly tests are required because you will be providing daily review and revisiting words that contain graphemes the children are having difficulty with.

Considerations for Teaching

- While learning the basic code, only include words containing graphemes that children are already familiar with, not the correspondences they just learned in that day's lesson. This enables them to focus on blending and segmenting; skill that may not yet be automatic. If we ask children to blend and segment with phoneme/grapheme correspondences they have learned in the current lesson or are 'wobbly' on, the task can become too cognitively demanding.
- This 'instructional lag' is largely unnecessary once children are learning the extended or complex code because their ability to blend and segment is well developed.
- Include words with three, four, and five phonemes as children become more proficient in phonemic processing.
- Introduce morphology through this portion of your phonics lesson by adding plural 's' as soon as children can blend words with four phonemes. Be careful to do this with words that end in an unvoiced consonant 't', 'p', 'c', 'f' to maintain the /s/ sound at first (tops, cats, pots, etc.). Once students are aware that a single letter can be used for more than one phoneme (usually after they have learned a few irregular high frequency words such as 'is' and 'was'), you can include plurals or present tense verbs that have any final phoneme (runs, grabs, dogs).
- Have students map words with their fingers, on their arms, or with lines for spelling only. For reading, simply have them say the 'sounds' they can see.
- Don't shy away from words that students may be unfamiliar with. For example, including the word 'toil' in your lesson about 'oi' is an opportunity to expand vocabulary. Be mindful of not having too many unfamiliar words, but remember that vocabulary knowledge is critical if children are to move beyond reading simple texts.

Key Action 8 – Use Decodable Texts Matched to Your Sequence of Teaching

Decodable texts are temporary reading instruction tools designed to help children practice reading words with the graphemes and irregular high frequency words they have learned. They introduce novice readers to the experience of reading at sentence and text level and assist in the development of fluency. Further, being able to use phoneme/grapheme correspondences in the context of stories allows the way a word is spelled, the way it is said, and what it means to become 'bonded' and committed to long-term memory (Ehri, 2020). While decodable texts have become a core part of many teachers' structured literacy instruction, their use isn't what we can call directly 'research informed' in that we don't have firm peer-reviewed, randomised control research evidence that they work. This is partly because it is difficult to isolate the effect of decodable texts in amongst all of the other tools and techniques we use in teaching reading (Snow, 2021) and also because there hasn't actually been as much research done on their use as has been done for phonics, phonemic awareness, and vocabulary instruction (Petscher et al., 2020). That doesn't mean that we shouldn't use decodable texts, but we do need to be aware that there is more research needed in this area.

However, the provision of texts that control the number of phoneme/grapheme correspondences, sentence structures, and vocabulary need not be controversial. In the absence of comprehensive research about the matter directly, there are several areas of theory for us to draw on as we consider the use of these controlled texts.

1. Research shows us that the route to sight reading (effortlessly lifting words from the page) is through phoneme/grapheme correspondence and word-level decoding (sounding out) (Dehaene, 2009; Ehri, 2020; Moats, 2020; Seidenberg, 2017). Decodable texts provide practice in critical decoding skills as well as the repetitions necessary for the connections to form that help students develop a strong sight vocabulary; that is, they can effortlessly recall words from long-term memory (Ehri, 2005).
2. Unlike 'natural' or 'predictable' texts that contain a large number of phoneme/grapheme correspondences that children have not yet learned, decodable texts allow novice readers to keep their focus on the internal structure of the word and use their phonics knowledge to identify the words rather than guessing words from pictures or context, which is a lost opportunity when it comes to committing words to long-term memory (Petscher et al., 2020).
3. Cognitive load theory can also inform what we do here. We have seen from this theory that if a task is too hard (because the person doesn't have sufficient background knowledge of the task to engage well), the learner may well become overwhelmed (Archer & Hughes, 2011).

4 David Share's self-teaching hypothesis posits that children use their phonics knowledge to decode or partially decode unknown words before 'problem solving' the identification of that word (Share, 1999). In order for this to occur, children must be able to attend to the sounds within the word. They cannot do this if they do not have knowledge of the phoneme/grapheme correspondences in the words they are reading.

Decodable texts provide a useful tool for students to practise lifting words from the page, and in my own teaching practice, they have been particularly useful for struggling or at-risk readers. Students, who had struggled to decode even simple texts, were able to successfully read by applying their knowledge of phonics and decoding, often for the first time since starting school. But decodable texts are not the end of the story. Students must be moved on to further reading opportunities to enable them to move onto full reading competence. The question is when?

For typically developing readers, students will need decodable texts until about grade 2 (Moats, 2020); however, the age of the student isn't the only consideration. As we have seen from David Share's self-teaching hypothesis, a child's ability to have a 'good go' at sounding out words they aren't familiar with relies on them having:

1 Phonics knowledge (including the fundamentals of the extended code)
2 The ability to blend phonemes together with ease
3 The ability to think about the context that the word appears in a sentence

You might be wondering about the inclusion of thinking about context. This is not a return to three-cueing that asks children to guess at words, but a recognition that there does come a point when context and syntactic cues come into play. However, this is **after** students have developed an understanding of the alphabetic principle and after the student has begun to develop a sight vocabulary.

The next thing I encourage you to consider when deciding if a child is ready for mostly decodable texts, is what you observe when they come across an unfamiliar word. Do they say the first sound and guess? Do they look at the picture? Do they say any other word except the one that is actually on the page? If you observe these reading behaviours in your students, they are **not** ready to move on to less controlled/mostly decodable texts. The challenge is that, for many of our students, these behaviours are exactly what they have been told to do and reframing the way that these children interact with text may take some time. Figure 6.1 provides a suggestion for the milestones children reach in order to move on to less controlled texts. It is based on the self-teaching hypothesis, the advice of respected academics and researchers, and my own observations of working with many students.

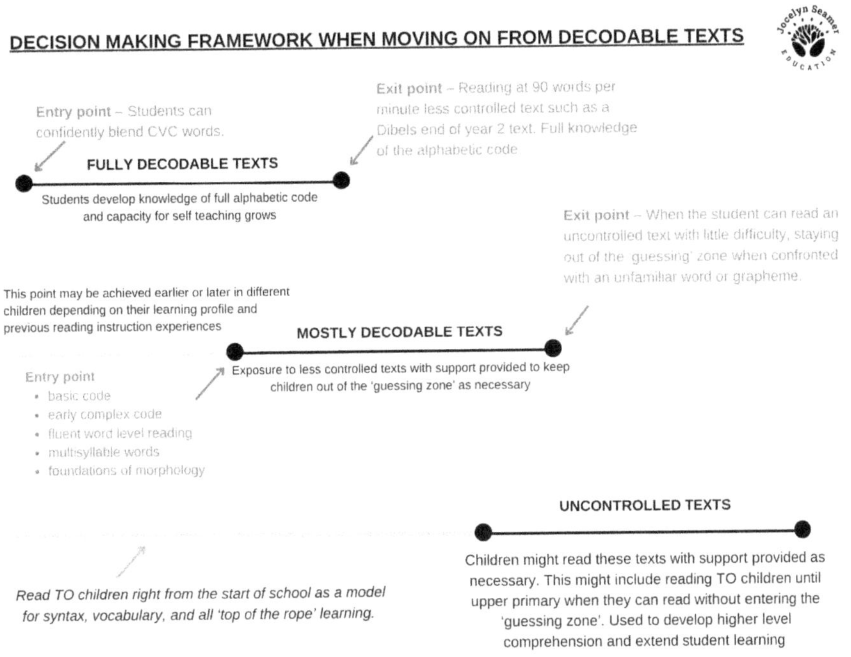

DECISION MAKING FRAMEWORK WHEN MOVING ON FROM DECODABLE TEXTS

Entry point – Students can confidently blend CVC words.

Exit point – Reading at 90 words per minute less controlled text such as a Dibels end of year 2 text. Full knowledge of the alphabetic code.

FULLY DECODABLE TEXTS

Students develop knowledge of full alphabetic code and capacity for self teaching grows

Exit point – When the student can read an uncontrolled text with little difficulty, staying out of the 'guessing' zone when confronted with an unfamiliar word or grapheme.

This point may be achieved earlier or later in different children depending on their learning profile and previous reading instruction experiences

MOSTLY DECODABLE TEXTS

Exposure to less controlled texts with support provided to keep children out of the 'guessing zone' as necessary

Entry point
- basic code
- early complex code
- fluent word level reading
- multisyllable words
- foundations of morphology

UNCONTROLLED TEXTS

Read TO children right from the start of school as a model for syntax, vocabulary, and all 'top of the rope' learning.

Children might read these texts with support provided as necessary. This might include reading TO children until upper primary when they can read without entering the 'guessing zone'. Used to develop higher level comprehension and extend student learning

Figure 6.1 Decision-Making Framework When Moving on From Decodable Texts

Considerations for Teaching

- Align your decodable text resources with your phonics scope and sequence.
- Remember that a decodable text can be a few lines of text on a piece of A4 paper. It doesn't have to be a glossy book. Don't let a lack of resources prevent you from introducing these important texts.
- Repeated reading has been shown to improve student fluency (NICHD, 2000) and provides opportunities for repeated exposures to words.
- Different children have a different need for decodables. Some will move on from them very quickly, while others will need them beyond Year 2. Use Figure 6.1 as a guide to your decision-making.
- In order to simplify instruction, ensure that core texts for teaching are fully decodable for all students. This means that everyone gets what they need. However, recognise when students are ready to be introduced to 'mostly decodable' texts and provide supported opportunities for this critical practice. This can be provided across the curriculum as you embed reading into science or history lessons. See Chapter 14 for further details.
- Decodable and 'predictable' texts are not books that exist on a continuum. Replace predictables with decodables for all students and supplement students' reading materials as appropriate. Remember, we cannot make assumptions about a child's reading development based on their age.

References

Archer, A., & Hughes, C. (2011). *Explicit instruction: Effective and efficient teaching.* Guildford Press.

Dehaene, S. (2021). *How we learn: Why brains learn better than any machine…for now.* Penguin Books.

Ehri, L. C. (2020). The science of learning to read words: A case for systematic phonics instruction. *Reading Research Quarterly, 55*(S1), S45–S60. doi: https://doi.org/10.1002/rrq.334.

Ehri, L. (2005). Learning to read words: Theory findings and issues. *Scientific Studies of Reading, 9*(2), 167–188. Retrieved 18 March, 2022, from https://mimtsstac.org/sites/default/files/Documents/Presentations/AnitaArcherWorkshops/January2014/LearningtoReadWords.pdf

Moats, L. C. (2020). Speech to print (3rd ed.). Paul Brooks Publishing.

(NICHD) Eunice Kennedy Shriver National Institute of Child Health and Human Development, NIH, DHHS. (2000). *Report of the National Reading Panel: Teaching children to read: Reports of the subgroups (00-4754).* Government Printing Office.

Petscher, Y., Cabell, S. Q., Catts, H. W., Compton, D. L., Foorman, B. R., Hart, S. A., Lonigan, C. J., Phillips, B. M., Schatschneider, C., Steacy, L. M., Terry, N. P., & Wagner, R. K. (2020). How the science of reading informs 21st-century education. *Reading Research Quarterly, 55*(S1), S267–S282. doi: https://doi.org/10.1002/rrq.352.

Seidenberg, M. (2017). *Language at the speed of sight: How we read, why so many can't, and what can be done about it.* Basic Books.

Share, D. (1999). Phonological recoding and orthographic learning: A direct test of the self teaching hypothesis. *Journal of Experimental Child Psychology, 72,* 95–129. Retrieved May 11, 2021, from https://citeseerx.ist.psu.edu/viewdoc/download?doi=10.1.1.540.6045&rep=rep1&type=pdf

Snow, P. (2021). Masking up in a pandemic and decodable texts for beginning readers: What's the link? Retrieved May 11, 2021, from http://pamelasnow.blogspot.com/2021/07/masking-up-in-pandemic-and-decodable.html

Weiser, B. L. (2013). Ameliorating reading disabilities early: Examining an effective encoding and decoding prevention instruction model. *Learning Disability Quarterly, 36*(3), 161–177. http://www.jstor.org/stable/24570120

Weiser, B., & Mathes, P. (2011). Using encoding instruction to improve the reading and spelling performances of elementary students at risk for literacy difficulties: A best-evidence synthesis. *Review of Educational Research, 81*(2), 170–200. http://www.jstor.org/stable/23014367

Part III
Structured Literacy Practices

7 High Impact Teaching

High impact teaching is about meeting students where they are up to and providing 'bang for your buck' learning experiences so that learning can occur in the shortest time possible with the greatest level of ease. It isn't about making everything 'easy', but about supporting students to work through challenges in such a way that they are successful and engaged.

Luciano Mariani's model of a high challenge, high support environment (Mariani, 1997) dovetails nicely with cognitive load theory (Sweller, 2021) and Dehaene's four pillars (Dehaene, 2021). In this model, Mariani describes four quadrants as illustrated in Figure 7.1.

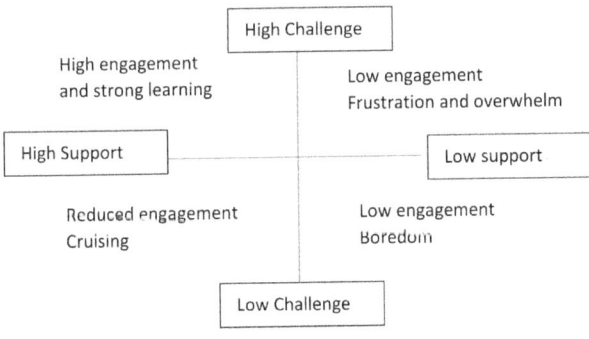

Figure 7.1 Mariani's High Challenge, High Support Environment

While it isn't possible to have students in the high challenge, high support quadrant all the time (there is only one of you and learning challenging things is tiring!), we can look at how best to manage the learning needs and demands of the range of students in our class.

Low Variance Routines

One of the secrets to being a calm, organised, and confident teacher and having a calm, organised, and focused classroom is low variance routines. I refer to these as 'same thing, different day' or 'sustainable' routines. Essentially, you decide on and teach according to a set routine each day (or each time you teach something), simply changing out the content as students learn. Low variance routines enable us to reduce student extraneous cognitive load as we eliminate the redundant presentation of information, cut down the unnecessary teacher talk (aka waffle that confuses students), and prevent students' attention from being 'split' by overly busy presentations (Lovell, 2020). This all sounds simple enough, but many teachers find it tricky to keep things simple. Trying to do this differently each and every day in different ways for different things results in exhausted teachers and distracted students. It is much more productive to have core instructional routines that carry you through the weeks and months of the teaching year and adjust them as necessary to respond to the needs of your students.

The good news is that, while you can design your own routines, to teach reading you don't have to. The remainder of this book will outline a number of low variance routines that are simple to use in your classroom. A common feature of these routines is that they follow an explicit or gradual release of responsibility model as follows.

Building the Field

An opportunity to 'tune students in' to the learning that's to come, building the vocabulary, and background knowledge students will need to engage with learning.

Model and Deconstruct (I Do)

Tell and show students what to do, breaking concepts down into small chunks. The teacher's role is to model thought processes and key skills of the content being learned.

Joint Construction (We Do)

The opportunity for students to 'dip their toe in the water' of the learning or task. Traditionally, joint construction involves the teacher calling on a small number of students who have raised their hands and recording their responses. A more effective way to do this is with a 'full participation' joint construction, which might follow the process below:

1 Teacher poses a question or provides a stimulus.
2 Students talk with a partner about the question or stimulus.
3 Students record responses (either on a shared board or piece of paper) or individually (followed by sharing their responses with their partners). While this occurs, the teacher circulates through the group supporting where necessary and noticing responses that they would like to bring to the attention of the group.
4 Teacher calls on their chosen students, selected either at random or to highlight responses that will be useful for the whole group. They record the students' contributions on the board at the front, modelling how to

produce a complete response. This step is an excellent opportunity to draw out shy students or those who require additional support and enable them to participate in the lesson. By providing advance notice that you are going to call on these students, you make sure that they are not caught off guard and are set up to experience success.

Supported Practice

Students engage with the learning in a scaffolded task. We might think of scaffolding as the traditional small group of students sitting with the teacher or paraprofessional staff member. This may, indeed, be the support that is provided, but there are other ways to ensure that students are supported to practise skills. For example, by following the steps in the 'joint construction' above, you are setting all students up for success, not only those who have a diagnosis or recognised difficulty. Supported practice can be further strengthened by the following:

- Differentiating the expectation of what the students do in this phase of the explicit teaching model. Students who struggle to do things on their own can simply repeat the task they undertook in the joint construction. The difference is that they are doing it on their own and this may be a significant step for our most vulnerable students on their journey to independent work. High-flying students can complete the core task and then be given the opportunity to extend their response.
- Having students work in partners.
- Asking most students to complete just one section of the task before coming back to the larger group to have the next section modelled, explained, and jointly constructed. High-flying students, who may well be bored or frustrated with this level of scaffolding, can complete the whole task on their own or with the assistance of a paraprofessional staff member while you support those students who benefit from a more structured approach. This is particularly relevant for writing tasks in which students can become overwhelmed with the task of putting pencil to paper while considering ideas and overall text structure.

Independent Practice

Students undertake tasks on their own, with feedback provided to help them refine their skills and knowledge. The role of feedback throughout each step of the explicit teaching model cannot be underestimated. Children learn when they have strong guidance and feedback that helps them to get and stay on track with tasks. Being able to 'tick it or fix it' word by word in a phonics lesson is a powerful way to support student learning. Instead of submitting their work to be corrected later, self-marking is a core part of the lesson engages students in thinking about their learning.

The gradual release of responsibility model is not new in education and we have all been exposed to it in one form or another in our classroom teaching. Like all things, the model is only as good as the way it is used.

The key to getting the most from your low variance routines is full participation from all students, a targeted focus on exactly what you want your students to learn, and a clear road map to how you will help your students move from where they are now to where they are going.

Establishing Learning Behaviours

It is necessary to support the development of learning behaviours in the same explicit way that we build academic skills. Some children will come to our classrooms having had a range of experiences that support their participation in school and others will not. Different children have different levels of self-regulation and, of course, our young learners' executive functioning skills are in the beginning stages of development. To teach any kind of learning behaviour, you could follow the steps given in Table 7.1.

Table 7.1 Establishing Learning Behaviours

Steps	Teacher actions
Build the field (tune students in)	
Briefly explain the need for the behaviour and discuss when it will be used	'Class, when we move from the mat to our tables, we need to be sensible, silent and careful. We do this so that we can get into our learning nice and quickly and so that everyone is safe.'
Model and Deconstruct (I do)	
Ask two children to come to the front of the group. Show them what you want them to do and then ask the two children who are modelling to copy what you have done. (This is a great opportunity for your students with a lower level of self-regulation to have a one-on-one lesson on the desired behaviour.) Provide feedback to the students and explain to the group what the children are doing 'right'.	'Molly and John, can you please come to the front? Now, I am going to show you how to move from the mat to our tables.' *(model the behaviour)* 'I walked silently and was really careful not to trip over Amanda's foot on my way. When I got to my desk, I stood behind my chair and folded my arms. Molly and John, can you please copy what I did?' *(Molly and John copy you)* 'I really like how Molly walked around the whole group of children instead of walking through the middle so that she didn't stand on anyone. I love how John stood behind his desk and folded his arms without me even reminding him. Well done Molly and John.'
Joint Construction (We do)	Have all students practise the desired behaviour, providing feedback until the whole group is demonstrating the behaviour appropriately
Supported practice (You do, with support) moving to Independent practice (You do with less support)	For **however long it takes**, you will support students by reminding them of your expectations before you want them to move from the mat to the tables. Different children will require a different number of 'learning trials' involving this kind of reminding, feedback, and support

High Impact Teaching 85

Using Visuals

Visuals are a powerful tool for learning in both academic and behavioural contexts. They help to deliver instructions and concepts better than spoken utterances for all students. Students with additional needs are not the only ones who find it easier to keep up in the classroom when visuals are used. Four ways you can include visuals in your classroom are as follows:

1 *Use a visual timetable.*
   Many teachers have one (Figure 7.2), but the way to take things to the next level is to remove each item as it's completed and place it in a 'finished' box. Our young learners have no real concept of time passing and you will find that they are more on track and focused when they can see the day 'counting down'.
2 *Instructional visuals on a lanyard.*
   Have you ever been in the position of wanting your students to be quiet (Figure 7.3), but the more times you told them to be quiet, the louder they got? (I think we've all done that) A more effective way to provide simple classroom instructions is to have a variety of visuals on a lanyard

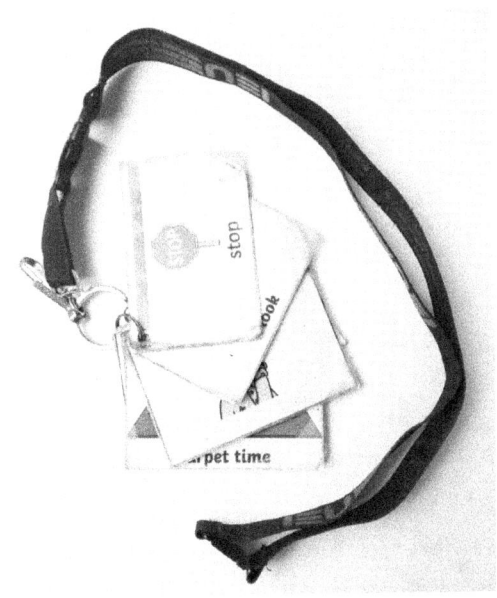

Figure 7.2 A Visual Timetable. Photo Courtesy of Liz Foley. *Used with Permission*

Figure 7.3 Visuals on a Lanyard

that you wear around your neck all day. Including things such as 'legs crossed', 'lining up', 'Ssssh!', 'arms folded', 'eyes looking' can help you to deliver 'silent instructions' using the visuals and body language. This not only saves your voice but seems to help children adjust behaviour much more quickly than when we use our voices alone.

3 *Visual countdown timers.*

Many teachers use a countdown timer of some sort to keep to time in their classrooms. To make this even more effective, make it a visual countdown timer such as a digital hourglass that you display on your smart board or a physical countdown timer where the red part gets smaller and smaller until the timer goes off.

4 *Instructional routine visuals.*

We assume that students know how long learning will take (Figure 7.4). When they are very young, they often don't. This makes it difficult to keep them focused. Displaying your instructional routines on A3 pieces of laminated paper on the board and moving a magnet along the display as you complete each step has two purposes. It helps you stay on track with your lessons and also helps children see how long there is to go in the lesson. Children who struggle to maintain focus will find it easier to stay on track with this countdown type of approach.

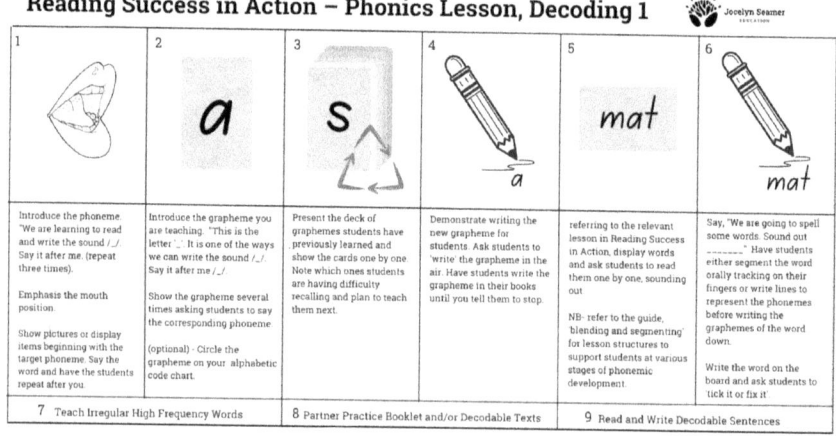

Figure 7.4 Instructional Routine Visual

Differentiation

Low variance routines keep students fully engaged when the content is directed at the optimal 'level' for students. It doesn't matter if you have the best routine available if the content is either too easy or too hard for the students. While we want to keep the students together as much as possible, there are times when it is necessary to make arrangements for more targeted teaching. If you are unsure about when it's appropriate to split the students into groups and have them work with a paraprofessional, refer to Chapter 4 for a guide. In order to differentiate effectively, we need to know where our students currently are in their learning and what their next steps need to be. We also need to know how they best learn in regard to environment, structures and degree of adult support. Armed with this information, you can make the plans to provide what students need.

One of the additional ways that we can differentiate the experiences of students is by considering the role of context in managing student cognitive load. Figure 7.5 is the gradual increase of the context model that I developed as a way to think about student learning and the role of context in our classrooms.

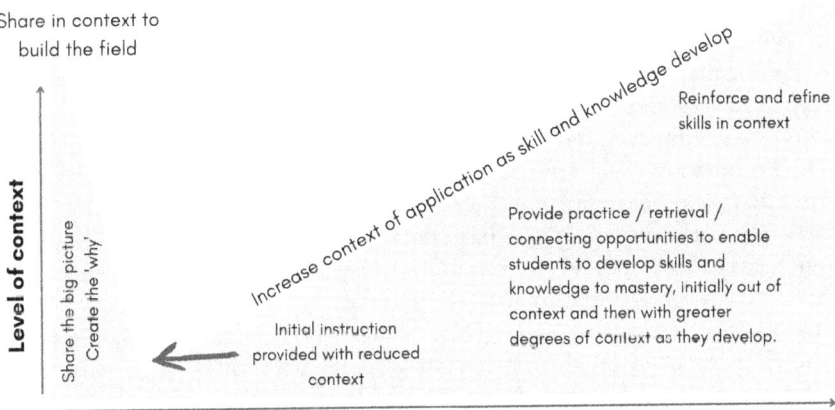

Figure 7.5 The Gradual Increase of Context Model. Copyright – Jocelyn Seamer Education.

Starting at the left-hand side of the model, we see that context is important in sharing the bigger picture and creating the model of what good performance looks like. In reading, this is what happens when we read stories and information texts to students. Moving to the right, we see that we can support student cognitive load by teaching individual skills and knowledge in a context reduced way. As students develop automaticity with particular skills and knowledge, we can increase the context until they are working in a fully contextualised way. This is reflected in the progression of teaching across the early years. We begin by teaching phoneme/grapheme correspondence, using those correspondences to read words and then simple decodable texts. As phonemic skills and phonics knowledge increases, the books become more complex until students can eventually read uncontrolled texts of their choosing. We can apply this idea to any learning experience. For some students, this gradual increase of context model is critical, and for others it is simply beneficial. The rate at which we can increase the context of a task is different for different students and we need to be sensitive to that.

Considerations for Foundation Teachers

The first year of school sets our students up for success, or it doesn't. Our youngest students' capacity to manage themselves in a formal learning environment is dependent on many factors including general development, the quality of the preschool learning environment, home factors, general language skills, interpersonal skills, and the level of executive functioning that a student has when they arrive in our classrooms. Routines help our students to feel safe. The transition to school is that much easier when the classroom is predictable, ordered, and safe. That doesn't mean that there isn't room for play or developmentally appropriate early childhood experiences. Those are a necessity. However, it does mean that we need to be organised and focused. The Foundation classroom can be surprising for those who have not taught this age group before for no other reason than our students' attention spans are often very limited. If you have taught an older grade, it will have been much easier to plan a 40–50 minute activity because older children usually have more cognitive stamina. At the start of the Foundation year, however, you may find yourself needing to have a new activity every 20 minutes. Many a teacher has been caught out having prepared an activity only to have the little people around them call out 'Finished!' in half the time they expected. If this is you right now, there is no need to despair. With intentional teaching and learning experiences that carefully meet students where they are up to, stamina will develop over time and your classroom will settle into a rhythm. It is, however, important to realise that not all students will develop this stamina naturally. In fact, it's not a bad idea to over-plan instruction in 'how to learn in our classroom'. You can do this by:

- Being willing to model and teach your expectations for routines and classroom transitions as many times as necessary. The ability to be persistent, insistent, and consistent is particularly important in the Foundation classroom.

- Using visuals as described in this chapter for all students and continuing to do so for the whole school year. Many of your students may reach the point where they no longer require the 'legs folded' visual on the mat, but you will have those who continue to need this each and every day for all four terms of Foundation. If they need support, provide it for them.

- Remember to have clear routines for entering the classroom to support both your students and their parents. Sending a little person off to school for the first time can be difficult for many parents, but having clearly communicated expectations around this for both students and parents can help you avoid uncomfortable conversations. Encourage independence in all things as soon as possible.

Considerations for Year 1 and 2 Teachers

By Year 1 and 2, most students are starting to develop independence in classroom routines; however, there is always a range of development to consider. It's important to remember that six- and seven-year-olds are not small ten-year-old and to be mindful of the kinds of experiences that they need to develop foundational skills. Strong low variance routines, the use of visuals, and explicit teaching of classroom behaviours are all important elements of instruction in Year 1 and 2. The more targeted you are in teaching (and reteaching these skills as needed), the more calm and ordered your classroom will be.

Snapshot of Practice 2 – Knowing Your Students is the Key to Differentiation

Karen Michell – Foundation Teacher

Trying to teach whole class can be challenging. The key to differentiating effectively is knowing where my students are up to. Once I know that, then I know what I need to do to move them to the next stage of development. I used to aim my lessons at the middle of the group, but with more experience I now know how to use the gradual release model better and provide support both to those needing extra help and those needing an extension. My strugglers join in with the main lesson, but then have time with my paraprofessional colleague every day to focus on phoneme/grapheme correspondence and word work. This is very systematic so that they have as many exposures as possible and can review exactly what they need to. When it comes to applying the phonics in grapheme and word-level work, I alternate the questions between groups. So, I have a word for my 'low' group, a word for the main group, and then a word for the high-flyers. I also adjust the task. My strugglers will just have graphemes or CVC words, but my high-flyers will have a word matrix to complete including multisyllable words.

Karen's Advice for Other Teachers

- Do a pretest to know what students know and what they can do. Make sure you work from your data.
- Find a set routine that works for you and stick with it, adjusting as needed to meet student needs.
- Don't be afraid to try new things but keep it simple.
- Sit students in their 'groups' on the floor so that you can support them.

Snapshot of Practice 3 – Providing Effective Feedback

Nadine MacAninch – Year 2 Teacher

Feedback needs to be very specific. It lets the students know that they are supported. I let them know: what they have done well, what they can improve on independently, and what we are going to work on together next. The growth has been especially pleasing for my most vulnerable students and their confidence has really grown. I give feedback in a couple of different ways. Each day I have a 'carpet crew' who know they will be working with me in a small group for about 15 minutes. We repeat the lesson we've just done and I listen to them read, giving feedback. This small group allows me to respond to the huge variation of needs in my class. I also give feedback digitally. I have the students place their work on the online platform we use to communicate with parents and I record feedback videos for six of them each day. I let them know who will be getting feedback so they know what will happen. This is not just great for students but is an ongoing record for parents. At first it felt like a lot of work, but the impact of it was so high that it was worth it. Finally, I seek out certain students during partner reading time. I let them know about the goals that I have written in my book and give them feedback on those goals as I listen. In this way, I'm able to be specific and personal in the feedback for every child across the week. They understand that it's not about failure, but about learning.

Snapshot of Practice 4 – Supporting Diverse Learners in a Multi-Age Setting

Karen Lane – Multi-age Teacher

In a multi-age setting, you can strengthen learning by pairing younger and older students. This helps the older students consolidate learning and supports the younger ones. I use layered questioning with some students repeating the modelled input, but others being asked for a more complex answer. It's necessary to shape lessons to meet students where they are up to in both interest and content so that engagement remains high, particularly when working at the 'top of the rope'. I have an overview of instruction but am always prepared to adjust as needed, keeping things simple and then broadening or deepening in response to student needs and interests. In writing, I'll give the younger students a 'straight' sentence to transcribe but give the older students a sentence to edit or expand on. Sometimes the science or history content is a bit advanced for the younger students, but they are generally o.k. because they have the support of a buddy and lots of modelling. It really is a judgement call about where to 'pitch' the learning.

Karen's Advice for Other Teachers of Multi-Age Classes

- Accept that you can't do as much as you may want to, depending on your context.
- Work with your teaching assistants to upskill them to teach a phonics or reading lesson to a small group.
- In practising the earlier content, help older students understand the role of overlearning.
- Try and have tasks that are self-sustaining – everyone knows what to do.
- It's important to explicitly support students to learn to self-regulate and manage themselves, otherwise you have chaos.
- Do the best you can with the resources you have and don't give up on things too quickly.
- Reteach the 'how' of routines as much as you can.
- Increase engagement with strategic opportunities for student choice.

Troubleshooting

Q – What if my students get bored with low variance routines?

A – It's true that young children are attracted to novelty and bright shiny things, but this doesn't mean that we have to change things up all the time. We can provide novelty by means as simple as asking students to help you decide what coloured whiteboard marker you will use or orienting the group differently on the mat. A portable whiteboard makes this much easier. By and large, children don't get bored when they have a clear feeling of success and achievement. Keep fostering that sense of 'can do' and children will come to value the low variance routines.

Q – I have a set of visuals but I have a student with their own visuals from the speech therapist. What do I do?

A – The visuals from the speech therapist are the student's communication. Wherever possible, work with the same visuals that your student/s with additional needs have. This will help them to settle and engage in the classroom and these will be quickly adopted by the other students too.

Q – I tried to implement routines but they didn't work.

A – There are three key words when it comes to establishing any routines: insistent, persistent, and consistent. Insist that all children join in (taking students with additional needs into account). Be persistent over time. It might take a few weeks for routines to be firmly embedded in your classroom. Consistency is critical to helping your students know 'what happens here'. If you insist on the expectations one day but not the next, they won't know what you want from them. It can be tiring to be these three things, but it will pay off in the end.

Reflecting on Practice

- What low variance routines do I have established in my classroom?
- How can I support students to build automaticity with these routines?
- How will I manage feedback in my classroom?
- How will I structure opportunities for myself as a teacher to lead full-participation joint construction?
- Reflecting on my students who have difficulty managing classroom expectations for behaviour, what experiences can I provide to support these students learn the things they need to? What adjustments do I need to provide to enable this? (Visuals, timetables, feedback, goal setting)

References

Dehaene, S. (2021). *How we learn: Why brains learn better than any machine…for now*. Penguin Books.

Lovell, O. (2020). *Sweller's cognitive load theory in action*. John Catt Educational.

Mariani, L. (1997). Teacher support and teacher challenge in promoting learner autonomy. *Perspectives, a Journal of TESOL-Italy, 22*, 5–19.

Sweller, J. (2021). Analysis Paper 24 (AP24): Why Inquiry-Based Approaches Harm Student Learning. The Centre for Independent Studies Limited. Retrieved September 7, 2021, from https://www.cis.org.au/app/uploads/2021/08/ap24.pdf

8 Organising the Literacy Block

A well-organised literacy block is like a permaculture garden. Every aspect has more than one job to do and everything is interconnected. Nothing exists in isolation. This is not always an easy thing to achieve amongst busy school timetables and seemingly conflicting programs and tools, but if you keep things simple, it is not only possible, but also can be an expectation in your classroom. In a structured literacy block, there is little room for children to be working without guidance. The goal is that children receive fully guided instruction for the whole two hours of the block to provide the most direct path to learning. Even when students are completing individual work, there is an adult available to guide, support, and provide feedback. Whether you can achieve this depends a great deal on the size of your school, the approach your school takes to timetabling classroom paraprofessional staff, and the level of shared instruction that your school is willing to engage in. Regardless of what resources you have available to you, there are always compromises in teaching. Remember, when you say yes to one thing, you have to say no to something else. The trick to creating a streamlined literacy block is having a crystal clear picture of what is *most* important in helping your students reach reading and writing proficiency. This chapter provides you with an outline of what a literacy block might look like, some routines and structures you can set up to keep everything running smoothly, and explains how daily shared writing enables you to reinforce each aspect of what is taught throughout the block.

The Big Picture of the Literacy Block

Every skill and piece of knowledge we want our students to learn must be taught, reviewed/practised, and developed through the support of context. Each step of the literacy block needs to contribute to one of those undertakings. Figure 8.1 views the early primary literacy block through the lens of the top and bottom of Scarborough's Reading Rope, we can see that each part serves multiple purposes.

Key Components of a Literacy Block

There are six key areas of a comprehensive, structured literacy block.

94 Structured Literacy Practices

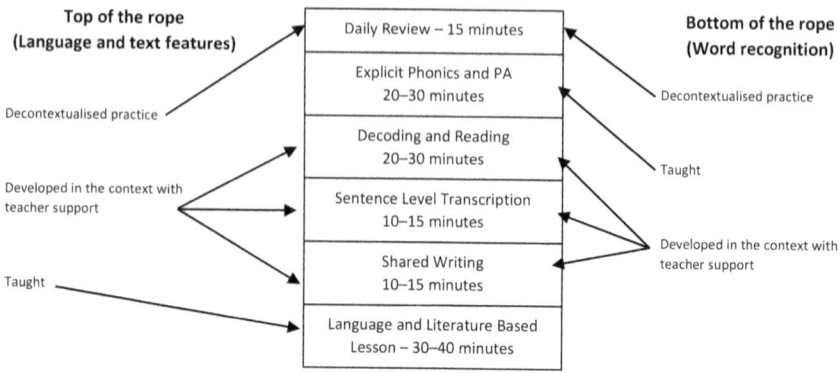

Figure 8.1 Intersection of Scarborough's Reading Rope with the Literacy Block

Daily Review – Approximately 10–15 Minutes

Your daily review is a short, fast-paced chance to consolidate phoneme/grapheme correspondences, blending, segmenting, vocabulary, and other concepts you might have been teaching. It's great if you can start the day with the review, but on days where the timetable doesn't allow for it, you can pop it in wherever you can fit it in.

Explicit Teaching of Phoneme/Grapheme Correspondences and Word-Level Skills – 25 Minutes

See Chapter 11 for further details.

A daily, low variance routine is a core part of a structured literacy approach. In the early years, this will involve phonics and word-level reading and spelling. Students should both read and spell in each lesson. Using a sustainable routine that is the same each day, insisting on full participation, and building in feedback, consolidation, and skill building can ensure rapid growth for students. While teaching this low variance routine, it is important to notice when students are 'wobbly' on content and then reteach it the very next day. When it comes to phonics, content must be pitched at the optimum level for each student to experience active engagement. Not too easy, not too hard. You can maximise efficiencies in this section of the block by connecting phonics and handwriting and teaching phonemic skills in the context of reading and spelling words during decoding and encoding tasks.

Sentence-Level Transcription – 15 Minutes

See Chapter 12 for more details.

In the early years, we need to provide explicit and supported instruction in how to put pencil to paper and produce a sentence. Use sentences that contain known phoneme/grapheme correspondences and irregular high frequency words so that students can focus on building stamina for writing more than one or two words. Handwriting skills must also be built to automaticity. Complete this section as a joint construction focusing on embedding word-level skills through sentence-level production. Children do not think up their own sentences for this. You already have the sentence chosen from a decodable text or to match the sequence of phonics you are teaching.

Decoding and Reading (20 Minutes)

See Chapter 12 for more details.

It is in this section of the block that students engage in partner practice. This is where oral reading of texts occurs, but only once students are able to read CVC words with some fluency. Providing books before students have reached this point is of little value. Match the texts to students' reading development and have each student work with a partner who is reading the same complexity of text that they are. This ensures that each person has the benefit of feedback if they make an error. Some students may be reading words, some fully decodable texts, and others mostly decodable texts. This part of the block does not replace your whole class lessons with rich text. It is a chance to practise reading aloud, lifting the words from the page, and developing reading rate as well as other aspects of fluency. Irregular high frequency words are taught in this part of the lesson to support students to read their texts.

Shared Writing (15–20 Minutes)

See Chapter 9 for further details.

If the transcription routine is about getting sentences down on the page, shared writing is a chance to engage in the joint construction of sentences containing rich vocabulary and syntax concepts you have been teaching. Provide a stimulus, model the type of language you want students to use, have students talk with a partner, and select students to share their responses. From there, co-construct the sentence on the board, having students help to spell the words. If students have the necessary transcription skills, they might then write the sentence, but if they don't, it's fine to keep this as a purely oral exercise. The focus is on oral sentence production and language development. If you are short on time (or simply want to extend literacy across the curriculum), you can use this structure in science, maths, history, and geography or any other curriculum area. After all, language and writing belong across the whole day.

Language and Literature-Based Lesson (30–40 Minutes)

See Chapter 9 for more explanation.

This is the part of the literacy block where you utilise rich text and focus on language, teaching the concepts from the top of Scarborough's reading rope and writing. This is where you explicitly teach vocabulary, genre, examine characters, text structure, and then have students write. In the early years, you would also teach morphology and syntax here.

Tub Time

Tub time is not part of the literacy block, as such, but is a routine that may help you keep your literacy block and the rest of your day on track. You can use it at any point in the day that suits your needs. I have always favoured using Tub Time in the middle of school day when children were getting restless. However, if you find that you need to do small group work, it supports that work by creating a quiet, calm environment where every child is engaged. Tub time is an adaptation of the Montessori Tray time that I observed in an early childhood setting when my own children were small. I watched in amazement as three-year-old children calmly retrieved a tray, took it back to a table, worked with it, and then returned the tray. As a teacher, I have used this routine for a variety of purposes with a variety of ages. I also think of 'Tub Time' as an individual invitation to play in the Foundation year.

In Foundation, the routine involves setting up a number of tubs, baskets, trays, or boxes (usually one for each child plus two or three more) and then allowing them to have full agency over which they choose to engage with. Figure 8.2 shows a possible set up for Tub Time resources. The tubs contain

Figure 8.2 Tub Time Set up. Photo Courtesy of Mikalya Luxton. *Used with Permission*

non-academic tasks (puzzles, Lego, fine motor activities, books, and puppets) that children will be able to engage with on their own. The purpose of this routine is to:

- Provide some downtime and a brain break.
- Teach self-regulation skills – how can you work collaboratively if you can't manage yourself?
- Support the development of choice making and provide an opportunity for agency in the day.
- Provide a sensory/hands-on activity.
- Introduce the expected behaviours for small group work and general classroom engagement.
- Enable you to work with a small group without interruption in a quiet, calm environment.

'Miss Jocelyn's' Rules for Tub Time

1 You may only choose from the available activities
2 Keep your eyes on your own activity
3 Work on your own in your own space
4 You may change your activity as many times as you like; however, you must return your activity neatly, quietly, and quickly
5 Tub time is silent time

Suggestions for Making Tub Time Work

- Do not fall into the trap of spending money to find activities or set them up. Every school has storerooms and cupboards full of things that can be used to engage children. Even down to some (old-fashioned!) things such as a magazine, scissors, paper, and glue stick in a tub can be very well received.
- Double up on the most popular activities such as Lego and whiteboards and markers.
- Demonstrate how to use each tub for students to greatly reduce the risk of misuse of the activities.
- Reinforce the 'rules' and have children recite them. Ask a student to model quietly collecting their activity, moving to a desk or location in the room, and then putting their activity away.
- Don't compromise on the boundary around what is available. Tub time is for tubs, not for having free choice of all of the toys in the classroom.
- Be insistent on silence. It helps children learn what a calm, orderly environment feels and sounds like.
- Start with a small amount of time (five minutes) and then build up. When the children's focus starts to wane, bring the session to a close. Their stamina will develop quickly but insist on your expectations.

- Don't 'leave them to it' until you can see that the students can manage themselves. This may mean being available to keep them on track for a week or two before attempting to take a small group during this time.
- Only change out the activities that are not being used or enjoyed. Allocate half an hour each week to change activities. No more. This is supposed to be a low maintenance, simple addition to the classroom.
- Don't get too caught up in insisting that children use the activities exactly as you intended. If you included a peg matching activity and a student simply places the pegs all around a card, there is no need to correct them. As long as they are following the rules, it's fine for them to use the activities as they choose to. Remember, it's about agency!

Growing Independence in Individual Work in Year 1 and 2

As students grow in their skills, particularly in Year 1 and 2, you are going to want your Tub Time activities to include more academic tasks. Before simply swapping out all the non-academic tasks for academic ones, consider the fact that not all children will be ready to move to independent academic tasks in the same way at the same time. Review Figure 8.3 and reflect on which 'number' you could allocate to the students in your class. The higher the number, the higher the capacity the student has for independent, academic work. A student who needs to sit on their own and can only manage themselves independently with a high-interest non-academic task is not going to respond well to sitting at a table with others working on an

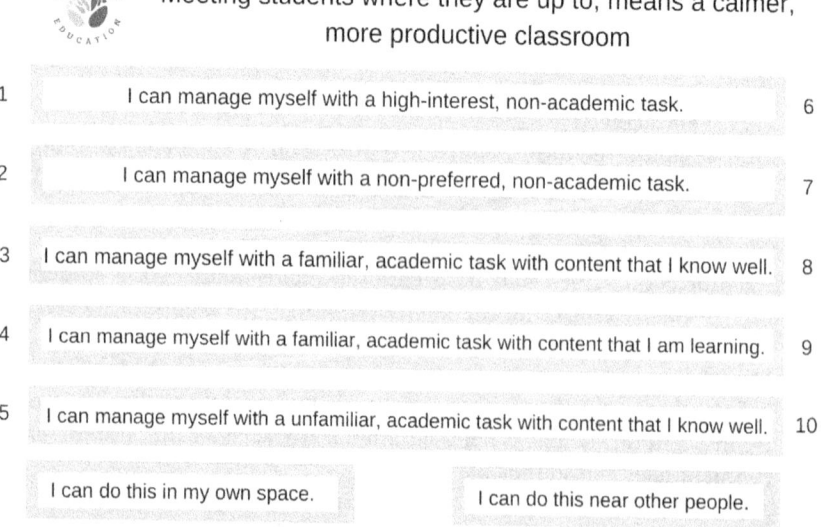

Figure 8.3 Framework to Develop Skills for Independent Tasks

unfamiliar academic task. Very often, a student's challenging behaviour in the classrooms comes about because we have asked them to do something that is outside their scope of development, either personally, academically, or socially. When we meet students where they are up to, we have a calmer, more productive classroom overall.

In order to transition students to independent, academic tasks, choose four tasks that are repeated over and over but have different levels of complexity and a different content focus. For example, you might teach the children to manage four tasks.

N.B. Text refers to graphemes, words, sentences, or paragraphs depending on the students' development.

1. Matching – match text and pictures.
2. Read and draw – read the text and draw a picture.
3. Read, hide, write, check – read text, hide it away, write what you read, and check to see if you're correct. At the paragraph level, this could be extended to summarising for students who are ready.
4. View and write – view a picture and then write text without a model.

All four of these tasks can be used at grapheme, word, sentence, and paragraph levels. The beauty of this approach is that you can meet students where they are up to in both code knowledge and complexity of text AND only have to teach them four routines that grow as their development grows. It also enables you to repurpose resources. The pictures used for matching text and pictures can also be used for 'view and write'. The text used for matching text and pictures can then be used for 'read, hide, write, check'.

Suggestions for Making Independent Tasks Work

- Keep some non-academic tasks in the mix. Children who become cognitively overloaded may need greater access to brain breaks than others. Enabling any child who needs a brain break to have one is a simple way to support your students.
- Reinforce the same rules as for tub time.
- While choice is still a feature of this set-up, you may code the activities so that children can independently choose an activity. So, you could have a coloured circle to represent different sections of the code and a letter 'g, w, s, p' to indicate the level of complexity of the task. Alternatively, you can have a tub for each group in your class that contains a number of activities for students to choose from.
- Don't insist that children sit in their groups if they aren't ready for that. It's ok for some children to be in their own space.

Daily Shared Writing

When it comes to a routine that packs a punch, daily shared writing, outlined in Figure 8.4, is one of the best. It is a versatile, easy to differentiate opportunity to help students develop confidence and understanding of the components of literacy you are teaching in the context of real sentences. Best of all, it begins from an oral starting point, which means that all children can participate fully. The benefits of the daily shared writing routine are as follows:

- Your students are exposed to the thought processes of a proficient writer.
- It reinforces the oral sentence structures you are teaching (whether they be simple, compound, or complex).
- Vocabulary is reinforced.
- It is an additional opportunity for phonemic awareness practice.
- It provides an opportunity for student talk.
- You can revise previously learned, knowledge-based content.
- It transfers across the curriculum. You can use it in any subject area.

The magic in this routine comes from the full participation of every student. Every student talks with a partner. Every student helps to sound out words in the joint construction and every student can engage with the content of

Figure 8.4 Daily Shared Writing Routine

the sentence. It is powerful to include content from other subject areas in this routine, but ensure that students have enough background knowledge and vocabulary of the topic to be able to discuss it with confidence. This routine may end with students writing the target sentence, but it may not. The focus is on developing strong oral sentences and reinforcing previously learned concepts. If students have the transcription skills to write, that's great. If they don't, keep the task oral.

Considerations for Foundation

Foundation is a unique and critical year in that children are making major developmental leaps both socially and academically. The Foundation year is one where the curriculum requirements allow us plenty of time to help students develop core skills. Unless a student has additional needs, there are few reasons for them to arrive at the end of the Foundation year without the ability to read and write simple sentences. But simply having time doesn't make this an easy task. Your Foundation students might be ready for explicit, intensive teaching when they come to your classroom, or they may not. They might need support to negotiate with classmates, pack away their own things, or even take themselves to the bathroom or they might come to your class with the basics of literacy firmly established. The important thing is to not make assumptions about what your classroom will be like and not to make assumptions about a child's capability based on their family background or the neighbourhood they live in. Get to know your students. Find out where they are up to and meet them there. This doesn't mean that you don't start teaching fundamental literacy skills and knowledge at the start of the year. It *does* mean that you will get better results if you are responsive to your students' attention spans and self-regulation capacities. Remember, five-year-olds are not small ten-year-olds, nor are they big three-year-olds. Play-based opportunities are a valuable inclusion in our Foundation classrooms,, but let us be very clear. Embedding 'literacy' into play-based experiences is not instruction. That's what the literacy block is for. Some children will 'pick up' reading and writing through independent or guided opportunities for 'noticing' in the context of play. Most, however, will not. It is up to us to provide explicit, evidence-informed instruction.

'Just give them time' is something that many parents of struggling readers have heard over and over as they expressed concerns about their child's lack of literacy development. This idea may make sense if we view literacy as developing in the same natural way as speech. The problem is that we know that it does not. As we have seen, reading and writing are not biologically primary and are not developmental in the same way as walking and talking. Therefore, waiting to see is really waiting to fail. It is crucial that we identify struggling students as soon as they show signs of difficulty and help them. Chapter 15 outlines considerations and tools for assessment that will help you be there right when students need you to be.

Considerations for Year 1–2

The structure of the literacy block does not need to change much between Foundation and Year 1 and 2. The fundamental components remain the same, but the content changes in line with student development. For instance, in Foundation you will likely focus on building phoneme/grapheme correspondence and reading and spelling with the basic code. This shifts to the complex code in Year 1 and 2. The routines to teach these skills (that we will explore in the following chapters) remain largely the same. In this way, the learning can continue with minimal disruption from the year before.

Snapshot of Practice 5 – Using Tub Time in the Foundation/Year 1 Classroom

Xanthi Rice – Foundation/Year 1 Teacher

I prefer tub time to group rotations because the students can select their own activities according to their stage of development. Rather than having a whole shelf with 20 tubs, each literacy group has a tub with multiple activities. There are core activities that are always there and others that I change over. Students choose the activity they wish to do from their group tub and then do this on their own at their desks. I use Tub Time as a way to enable me to work with a small group reading decodable texts and providing revision opportunities. Since implementing Tub Time, my classroom has become more settled, and I have far fewer interruptions when I am working with a small group. I think that this is because the students are more engaged when they choose the activity themselves and they are sitting on their own. When a new task is introduced, either myself or my classroom assistant models how to use it for the children so that they know what to do. I only use Tub Time for a short time. Explicit teaching is now the norm in my classroom. However, Tub Time does allow both myself and my assistant to work with a small group each day and give targeted support and teaching.

Xanthi's Advice for Other Teachers

- You don't need a lot of tubs to start with. Just have enough activities for each student.
- You don't need to spend a lot of money to set your activities up. There are lots of downloadable activities online and you probably have some in your classroom already.
- Use a low variance routine to use the tubs and teach the routine with non-academic tasks such as playdough or Lego.
- Don't try and make the tub time session too long. Once children get restless, they aren't likely to be learning much and will likely be a distraction to each other.
- It's ok for the tasks to be playdough or something fun from time to time. Sometimes children just need a brain break.
- Tub Time doesn't have to happen every day.

Snapshot of Practice 6 – Making the Literacy Block Structured in Year 1

Dan Colquhoun – Year 1 Teacher

After 10 years, I returned to teaching Year 1 and knew that I wanted to change things. I had learned so much about structured literacy and was keen to put it all into practice. I started by shifting the focus of the lesson from small group instruction to whole group. It just seemed such a waste of time to me to have students trying to learn on their own. I wanted my students to all be doing something purposeful all the time. There are now three broad parts to my 2-hour literacy block:

- Phonics and Word Level
- Writing and Language
- Small group reading (Not a rotation. I don't see every group every day)

When I came back to Year 1, I knew that I wanted the literacy approach to be one where every child succeeded. I had learned that when we teach the structure of language, children don't have to memorise words because they can read and write any words they want to. I don't have reading parts of the block and writing parts of the block. Everything is integrated.

Dan's Advice for Other Teachers

- Make your classroom predictable with routines that the students know.
- Help children be independent in managing resources.
- Even kids who struggle have skills. Often, they have the knowledge, but just aren't automatic yet.
- Don't be afraid to give children challenging texts to read once they know the phonics and irregular high frequency words in them, but make sure an adult supports them so that they don't start looking at pictures or skipping words.
- It's great to have tools and lesson plans, but you need to know why you are doing what you are doing.
- Extend high flying students by going deeper with the same content that the rest of the class is learning.
- Aim to have children reading as much as possible to another person each and every day.
- Assess skills and knowledge of reading (phonics, phonemic awareness, spelling, etc.) at the start of the year and then monitor learning throughout the year.
- Teach the 'top of the rope' (concepts at the top of Scarborough's Reading Rope) as explicitly as you teach decoding and phonics.

Troubleshooting

Q – How do you fit it all in?
A –

1. Focus on what's important. If it isn't the most direct path to learning to read and write, change it.
2. Include solid, repeatable instructional routines that lead to automaticity. The more time students spend trying to answer the question 'what's happening now?' the longer everything will take. Set timers, watch the clock, and set a brisk pace for lessons. Be mindful though that there is a point at which the pace is so fast that learning can become compromised, so be realistic.
3. There are times when you just don't have time to do the daily shared writing in the literacy block, so include it in another subject area like science or HASS. This will also help strengthen learning in those areas.
4. Don't get off track. It's really easy to go off on 'teacher tangents' and wander down the fascinating road of morphology or etymology. Pick your times when this is appropriate and be strict with yourself in your focused time. What seems like an enrichment opportunity for you might just be distracting your students from the learning at hand and be the cause of time management challenges.
5. Be persistent, insistent, and consistent with your expectations about student engagement. It's not ok for you to spend 15–20 minutes in every literacy block waiting for students to be quiet or move to desks or put things away. Be clear and firm about what you expect and provide praise when this is done well.

Q – How much do you differentiate?
A – From my perspective, the only part of the literacy block that you absolutely need to manage content in a differentiated way with is phonics and word-level decoding. It's much easier to support the other areas with students at the same development level; however, it is possible to manage content in a way that all students can access.

Reflection Questions

- How does my current literacy block reflect the core components of structured literacy teaching?
- What is my plan to differentiate content so that each student receives the instruction they need with an appropriate level of challenge while supporting their cognitive load?

- How can I work with my colleagues to support all of our students to access appropriate content for their development?
- How am I supporting my students to complete independent work where necessary?
- What routines will I teach and use for each section of the literacy block?
- How will I resource the work in each section of the block?

9 Oral Language and Vocabulary

Creating an Oral Language-Rich Classroom

Our classrooms should be language-rich environments. First, our own enthusiasm for and use of rich language provides an important model for the children. We are naturally primed for language and to 'pick it up' from the world around us. For English speaking students, Tier 1 language develops quite naturally; however, Tier 2 vocabulary needs to be explicitly taught and its development supported. (see Chapter 1 for further explanation of tiers of vocabulary) We teachers can do this by using rich language structures as we teach every day in conjunction with explicit vocabulary lessons.

Jim Cummins developed the language framework of basic interpersonal skills (BICS) and cognitively academic language proficiency (CALP) to explain the language demands of school (Cummins, 1981). While this theory was intended to relate to students with English as an additional language or dialect (EALD), there are important implications for us as primary teachers. Namely, how we understand the challenges that our students might experience engaging with different types of texts throughout their school lives. Cummins talked about 'context embedded' and 'context reduced' opportunities for using language. Context embedded language use can be thought of as being 'more concrete'. That is, there are things to look at and more clues given during the communication. This might take the form of an in-person conversation or a simple, hands on task in the classroom. Context reduced communication, however, relies on a person's capacity to process more formal/academic language. There are fewer 'clues' to rely on when engaging in the task. Having an awareness of the difference between BICS and CALP means that we can plan for meaningful development in both areas as it is appropriate for our students. Table 9.1 gives the different types of tasks and where they sit in the BICS and CALP framework. Most students will develop skills and knowledge to participate in context embedded tasks, but it is through intentional, explicit instruction in context *reduced* tasks that we can participate fully in the academic tasks required to be successful in school. It is in the cognitively demanding, context reduced quadrant that many students struggle and a strong focus on vocabulary, language structures, text structures, and conceptual understandings is required so that our students will be able to interact with the material that they encounter.

DOI: 10.4324/9781003244189-9

Table 9.1 BICS Versus CALP, Developed by Jim Cummins (1981)

Context embedded	Context reduced
BICS – face to face, everyday conversation, drama activity, retelling a familiar event, listening to a familiar or simple story	BICS – telephone conversation, written instructions for a basic task
CALP – hands-on maths task, teacher-led science experiment	CALP – most subject areas at school where content is written about and read, writing information reports, reading texts with complex sentence structures, concepts, or language

One of the simplest routines we can introduce to help children extend their language use is to engage them in purposeful partner talk. Partner talk is a scaffolded opportunity for students to discuss the target content or language you wish them to learn. The steps, as described by Hollingsworth and Ybarra (2012), are given in Table 9.2.

Table 9.2 Partner Talk Lesson Plan

Steps	Teaching actions
1. Provide a stimulus for students to discuss. This could be a picture, sentence, video, or story	Referring to a labelled diagram, 'This week we have been learning about insects. We have named the body parts (head, thorax, abdomen) and learned that insects all have 6 legs and 2 antennas. They might have wings but might not. Examples of insects are bees, flies, and beetles'.
2. Present a question for students to answer. Provide a sentence starter for the discussion to come to encourage students to speak in full sentences	'Class, I'd like you to describe the different body parts of an insect to your partner. You can start your partner talk with, "An insect has…" Say that after me. An insect has (students repeat) An insect has (students repeat)'.
3. Ask students to talk with their partners (set up turn taking supports as needed)	'Put your hand up if you are partner number 1. Partner number 1, talk with your partner and tell them about the body parts of an insect'. After one minute, 'Class, it is now time for partner number 2 to describe an insect'.
4. Monitor student talk and support those students who you know will need extra help in this routine	Circulate throughout the group, listening to responses and supporting students as needed
5. Call on 'non volunteers' to share responses before moving on with the lesson	'I heard many great explanations of the body parts of an insect. Well done everyone. Johnny, can you please share with the group what you said to Jill?' Repeat with two more students
	'Today we are going to draw our own insects and label them'.

In oral language partner work, it can be useful to partner a more developed language user with a less developed language user. This allows the less developed language user to have a peer model. Assign the more developed student to speak first so that they can provide an example. Even if the weaker language user simply copies what their partner said, this scaffold is a marvellous one to help them develop their language skills.

Using Picture Books to Teach Vocabulary

Picture books provide a rich and valuable source of modelling for language structures and vocabulary. When selecting a picture book to use as the basis of this work, consider the following:

- Ensure that the book contains the language structures you are planning to teach. If you wish to focus your unit of work on adjectives, make sure that the book contains adjectives. If you are teaching compound sentences, make sure that the book contains compound sentences.
- Plan to have the level of complexity of the text placed just above the level of language development of your 'fast lane' learners. All children require stretch to develop their skills.
- Think about genre and match the text to your writing focus. While the major focus in writing is on sentence and paragraph development in the early years, we still need to help children understand the macro- and microstructures of the genre we are teaching such as text structure and specific syntax considerations.
- Include an emotional hook. Stories are central to human society and providing an emotional hook for students to connect with can make the difference between experiencing and engaging with a text.
- Ensure that the book contains sufficient Tier 2 vocabulary to be a useful model.

When planning to teach vocabulary lessons from a picture book, different teachers may make different choices about the words they choose to focus on. When we teach phonics, there are a finite number of graphemes to teach and over the three years of the early years of school, we can have a reasonable expectation of teaching them all. When it comes to language, however, there are simply too many words to approach it in the same way. Select the Tier 2 words that you think have the greatest value for your students at the time. In their 2013 text, Bringing Words to Life, Beck et al. outline how to choose and teach Tier 2 vocabulary. They recommend the following as a guide to choosing Tier 2 words for instruction:

1. Words are important when they have high utility. That is, they appear frequently across contexts that students will encounter in their learning.
2. Students know what they mean. Be clear about when you are teaching vocabulary and when you are teaching concepts. For example, students will know what it means to 'look at something', but they may not be familiar with the words gazed or peered.

3   Use words that have 'instructional potential'. In short, words that have more than one meaning that will be useful to students. For example, 'select' can mean to choose or can mean something that is special.

The line between the tiers of words is not always hard and fast, but by using the criteria provided above, you will choose words that are most useful for your students.

When it comes to introducing vocabulary, Beck et al. (2013) provide more useful guidance. Table 9.3 outlines an introductory vocabulary lesson.

Table 9.3 Vocabulary Introduction Lesson Plan (Beck et al., 2013)

Steps	Teacher action
1 Read a story	Read the story 'The Three Little Pigs'
2 Contextualise the word for the students	'We have just read the story of the Three Little Pigs. In the story, the wolf wasn't just a little bit hungry, he was ravenous'.
3 Have children say the word	'Say that word, "Ravenous"'. (The children repeat the word ravenous)
4 Provide a student-friendly explanation	'Ravenous means that you are really, really hungry'.
5 Present examples in different contexts	'You might be ravenous after you swim in the pool. You might be ravenous when you come home from school'.
6 Engage children in interacting with the word. Questioning is valuable here	'Have a think. If you were ravenous, would you rather eat half a sandwich or a whole loaf of bread?' (show a picture to reinforce). 'Talk with your partner about what you'd rather eat if you were ravenous. Say this after me, If I was ravenous I'd want to eat...'
7 Have the children say the word again	'Say that word again. Ravenous'. (Children repeat the word.)

It is also important to provide follow-up teaching to keep words circulating and provide many exposure and opportunities to use new vocabulary. You can do this by:

- Creating a vocabulary wall where you place the new words learned. Have students draw pictures of the word in different contexts and share their oral sentences with each other.
- Setting up a points system for when students use particular words in the classroom or in their writing. Make it a collective points system rather than an individual one and when the whole class tally reaches a certain point, the whole class has extra playtime or some other simple acknowledgement.
- Writing new vocabulary on cards and placing them in a box. Each day, draw out a word and review it, having students think of new sentences to use the words in.

Teaching About Sentences

'Sentences are the building blocks of all writing' (Hochman & Wexler, 2017, p. 10). There is a growing awareness by teachers of the importance of sentence-level instruction and children's reading and writing have benefited as a result. However, all literacy begins with oral language and having an intentional plan for teaching oral sentences as a bridge to writing is critical in supporting all students, particularly those who may struggle with language.

There are three types of sentences to consider when planning for instruction.

Simple sentences – Contain a subject (a noun that tells us what or who the sentence is talking about) and a verb (a word that describes what the subject is doing, having, or being (Paramour & Paramour, 2020)). A simple sentence can stand on its own as a complete thought. For example, 'Tim jumped'. Simple sentences can also contain an object (a phrase that shows what the verb is acting on (Paramour, 2020)). For example, 'Tim jumped the puddles'.

Compound sentences – Two simple sentences joined by a coordinating conjunction (for, and, nor, but, or, yet, and so). Each part of the sentence is equally important in understanding what is happening in the sentence (Paramour & Paramour, 2020). For example, 'Tim jumped the puddles but his trousers were wet when he reached home'.

Complex sentences – Contain two parts that are not of equal value in understanding the sentence. They usually contain a main clause and a subordinate clause as well as subordinating conjunction such as *after, because, as, although,* and *since*. For example, 'Even though Tim jumped the puddles, his trousers were wet when he reached home'. The most important part of the sentence is that Tim has wet trousers.

Two recommended texts for further exploring grammar and sentence structure are as follows:

Stone, L. (2015). *Language for life: Where linguistics meets teaching.* Taylor and Francis Ltd.

Paramour, Z. & Parmaour, T. (2020). *The grammar book: Understanding and teaching primary grammar.* Bloomsbury Education.

Curriculum Expectations for Sentence Instruction

At the time of writing, the Australian Curriculum Version 8.4 (ACARA, 2015) expectations of sentence structures are as follows:

Foundation – Use of simple sentences

Year 1 – Awareness of the parts of simple sentences (who, what, what is happening, where it is happening)

Year 2 – Understanding of and use of compound sentences

These expectations might make sense in terms of a scope and sequence across the whole primary school, but they don't necessarily set our students up for success to develop strong writing and reading comprehension skills. To meet reading requirements for the end of Year 2 (reading 90 words per minute of a reasonably complex text), students need to be familiar with a variety of sentence structures and read them fluently. As such, I consider the Australian Curriculum guidelines *at least* points and really the minimum expectation I might have for a student who is a struggling reader and writer.

Another way to view the progression of knowledge and skill development is as given in Table 9.4.

Table 9.4 Timeline of Teaching Sentence Structure Across the Early Years 'At Least' Points

	Oral production	Achieved reading fluency	Automaticity in writing with appropriate structures (at least points)
First Semester Foundation	Simple sentences		
End of Second Semester Foundation		Simple sentences containing basic code graphemes and irregular and known high frequency words. Be able to track the subject of several sentences	(Be able to write simple sentences with some support)
First Semester Year 1	Compound sentences		Simple sentences containing basic code graphemes and known irregular high frequency words
End of Second Semester Year 1		Compound sentences – maintain comprehension with sentences using 'and', 'but', 'so', and 'because'	
First Semester Year 2	Complex sentences	Understand simple and compound sentences with extended noun phrases. 'The quick, black dog with the long tail chased the squirrel in the park and tried to catch it'.	Compound sentences – using and, but, so, because
End of Second Semester Year 2		Complex sentences.	Able to produce complex sentences with a small range of subordinate conjunctions

112 *Structured Literacy Practices*

Of course, you will have students who sit both within and outside of these expectations and it is important that you identify where your students are up to and meet them there.

Fragments and Sentences

Many teachers are now familiar with the task of teaching children the differences between fragments and complete sentences. We teach this concept to help students understand what a complete idea is and to be able to monitor their own writing. Once students are familiar with the concept of fragment and sentence, you can then use this metalanguage when speaking with children about their writing. When teaching this concept to young children, it is very useful to provide picture examples as in Figure 9.1 and to introduce the concepts of 'namer' (who) and 'action' (do) (Bussman Gillis & Chapel Eberhardt, 2017).

Figure 9.1 Subject and Verb Pictures to Support Oral Sentence Instruction

You can introduce this to students using the following script:

1 Today we are going to learn about sentences. It is important for us to share all of the details that a listener or reader needs so that they understand what we are saying. A sentence is only a sentence when we say who or what we are talking about **and** what they are doing. We need a 'who' and a 'do'.

2 Let's look at these pictures. Place a picture from the left and a picture from the right together in the centre of the board. Say the sentence, for example, 'The girl is walking'.

TEACHER: Who is the sentence about?
STUDENTS: The girl
TEACHER: That's Right. The girl is the 'who'.
TEACHER: What is happening? What is she doing?
STUDENTS: Walking.
TEACHER: That's Right. 'Walking' is the 'do'.
TEACHER: Now say the sentence after me. The girl (point to the girl) is walking (point to the picture of walking).
STUDENTS: The girl is walking.

Repeat the steps twice more using different pictures.
   To follow up and consolidate this lesson, display several examples of either sentences or fragments and ask students to tell you if it is a complete sentence or not using 'thumbs up or thumbs down'.

TEACHER: Do we have a 'who' and a 'do'?

You can extend this task by adding words to the pictures and then, when students have the appropriate decoding ability, remove the pictures altogether. In addition, you can extend this lesson by adding prepositions to the sentences. As students' familiarity with the concepts grows, you can use words like 'fragment and sentence' and 'subject and verb'.

Teach About Compound Sentences

Once students have a firm grasp on simple sentences, you can begin to introduce the concept of compound sentences: two simple sentences joined by a coordinating conjunction. In the early years, we can focus on the conjunctions *and*, *but*, and *or* as these are the most common (Van Cleave, 2014). Teaching about compound sentences is not just about writing. Understanding conjunctions provides important contributions to comprehension. Consider the following:

> The boy played on the swings **and** the girl climbed on the monkey bars.
> Did the girl play on the swing **or** climb on the monkey bars?
> The boy played on the swings **but** the girl climbed on the monkey bars.

Using 'and' indicates concurrent action.
   Using 'or' indicates a choice or alternate possibility.
   Using 'but' indicates contrasting or potentially conflicting information.
   To teach students about compound sentences, you can use the structure given in Table 9.5.

Table 9.5 Teaching Compound Sentences Lesson Plan

Steps	Teacher actions
Introduce the concept of compound sentences	'We know how to write great sentences. Now we are going to learn how to put them together to make compound sentences. A compound sentence is two simple sentences joined by a conjunction (joining word)'.
Display a picture and invite students to talk with their partners about what they can see	'In this picture we can see two cats who are playing. They have wool, balls, and cat toys. Talk with your partner and describe what you can see happening in the picture'.
Call on non-volunteers to compile a list of simple sentences. Write them on the board	There are two cats One cat is brown One cat is white The cats are playing with the toys The brown cat is rolling a ball The white cat is playing with the wool
Demonstrate joining two of the sentences with a conjunction	If I want to write more than one thing about the picture, I can use the word 'and' to join two of these sentences. I might write, 'There are two cats and they are playing with toys'. 'The brown cat is rolling the ball and the white cat is playing with wool'.

If students can decode the simple sentences, provide sentence strips with the sentences without capital letters and punctuation. Provide cards with the word 'and'. Have students join two sentences with the word and. If students are not able to decode, complete the task orally before inviting partners to share their compound sentences with each other

How much metalanguage you introduce your students to and your expectations of their ability to use this language is a decision for your school community. Children are often much more capable of learning the Tier 3 vocabulary associated with language than we expect them to be; however, don't get bogged down in this. Focus on concept development and using the skills. You can then encourage metalanguage development over time.

Foundations for Morphology

Morphology is an important part of learning about language. Children come to our classrooms with quite advanced spoken morphological awareness (Seidenberg, 2017). That is, they use prefixes, suffixes, and bases in their everyday speech. They are just not aware that they are doing it. While phonics is a major focus for reading in the early years, there are many good reasons to include morphology in your teaching.

- Morphology is necessary for children to engage with more complex language and texts. If we want students to be able to move beyond simple texts and single syllable words, they need to be able to read words

containing prefixes, suffixes, and Greek and Latin roots and understand the impact they have on meaning.
- Morphological knowledge helps students be more confident and informed spellers. Spelling and meaning remain constant in words, whereas pronunciation can vary considerably. Take the example of past tense 'ed', which can be pronounced in three different ways (/ed//t/or/d/) but is always spelled with an 'e' and a 'd' and always indicates past tense.

One of the reasons that many teachers feel unsure about teaching morphology is that they don't have a solid grasp of the knowledge of how our language works themselves. Many of us were primary school students in the 1980s and beyond and so have missed out on learning about morphology and syntax. Chapter 2 provides information about morphological foundations and a table showing which morphemes to teach in which grades.

Considerations for Foundation

At the time of writing, the Australian Curriculum does not discuss the specific morphology knowledge expected for Foundation; however, there are some key morphemes that we can introduce to our students in the first year of school.

Plural and present tense 's' – once students can blend four phonemes, we can introduce plural and present tense 's'. This is as simple as adding an 's' to base words in phonics lessons. Be mindful, however, of maintaining the sound /s/ at first so that we do not complicate matters for our students who might struggle. For example, adding 's' to the word pig gives us 'pigs'. The letter 's' in this word represents the /z/ phoneme. The phoneme /s/ is maintained when we add the letter 's' to words ending in unvoiced speech sounds (/t/, /p/, /k/, /f/). Once students have gained some proficiency with the irregular high frequency words 'is' and 'has', this does not usually pose a difficulty. Many students will have no problem at all with adjusting the pronunciation of the letter 's' between /s/ and /z/ because they already have that in their spoken language (their brain just puts it together), but to provide equitable access to all students and to facilitate spelling development, it is helpful to be mindful of the different word structures.

Words that maintain the /s/ sound at the end of the word	Words that change the /s/ to a /z/ at the end of the word
tops	runs
cats	pigs
sits	suns
cliffs	dogs
ducks	sings
trips	ribs

Present progressive tense 'ing' can also be introduced without difficulty once students have learned the 'ng' grapheme. This can be introduced orally at any point, of course, but if you are planning for your students to write the words, leave it until digraphs have been learned. It is important to remember that 'ing' is made up of two phonemes and two graphemes /i/ /ng/. Reinforce this code mapping rather than teaching the 'ing' as a unit. When choosing to introduce this morpheme, be mindful of the spelling rule that comes with adding a vowel suffix (a suffix that starts with a vowel letter) to a CVC word. Adding a vowel suffix to a CVC word requires you to double the final consonant in the base word. This doesn't mean that you can't introduce these words, but that you will need to scaffold any spelling for the students.

Base word (single short vowel, single consonant)	Base word + ing
hop	hopping
run	running
swim	swimming
set	setting
drag	dragging

Teaching these kinds of spelling rules in Foundation is not out of the question, but depending on your school context, not all students will necessarily be ready for this learning. Students need to have an understanding of the following:

- Vowels and consonants
- 'Short' and 'long' vowels
- The concept of suffixes

Be sure to explicitly teach the concepts around the code and morphology so that children develop an understanding of why they are doing what they are doing, not just a memory for how words 'should' look.

The other morpheme you can teach in foundation year is 'un'. This is perfectly regular once students know the graphemes 'u' and 'n' and can blend with five phonemes. When students have this morpheme in their repertoire, they can decode words such as undid, undo, uncut, unfit, unpeg, unpack, and unlock.

Finally, you may introduce the past tense 'ed' in your foundation program for students who are ready. The tricky thing about past tense 'ed' is that it comes with three different pronunciations: /d/ as in healed, /t/ as in helped, and /e/ /d/ as in handed. It is likely that you have some students who can manage this complexity, but not all will be ready for it. Address past tense 'ed' as it appears in decodable texts or in students' own writing and then revisit it again in Year 1.

Considerations for Year 1 and 2

Once students have the fundamentals of the basic code and basic inflectional morphemes (s, ing, ed), you can begin to extend their skills. The Australian curriculum requires the following:

> Year 1 – Students can build word families from common morphemes. For example, adding morphemes to the base word pack can give you the following list:
>
> > packs
> > packed
> > repack
> > unpack
> > packing
> > unpacking
> > repacking
> > packer

Students also need to be able to identify the base of a given word. If you said 'unpack' and asked what the base word is, students need to be able to give you the answer 'pack'.

> Year 2 – Year 2 moves students beyond familiar words into the territory of unfamiliar words. The curriculum requires students to be able to read and write unfamiliar words using their knowledge of morphemes.

Essentially, Year 1 teaches 'about' and Year 2 puts it into action. You will extend the number of morphemes you teach in Year 2 (refer to Chapter 2 for a list) as well as help students transfer this knowledge to their spelling.

Snapshot of Practice 7 – Using Shared Reading to Build Comprehension

Charlene Stewart – Year 1 Teacher

Our team developed a template that we all used for our shared reading and comprehension. We identify key vocabulary and background knowledge that needs to be developed and the grammar and sentence structures we want to teach. We worked with a speech therapist to understand and choose three levels of comprehension questions to ask and, utilising 'Questioning the Author' (Beck et al. – 2020), break it into three sections to explore. Students really enjoy the shared reading routine. Our students are from disadvantaged backgrounds and the oral language aspects are really important. Some of the challenges in this have been building teacher knowledge of grammar and sentence structure. These conceptual understandings are critical. It is important to know that this work was not about comprehension strategies and that children need time and repetition to fully engage with a text.

Charlene's Advice for Other Teachers

- Make sure that you are building your own knowledge of grammar, sentence structure, and conceptual understanding of how our language works.
- Try and find a scope and sequence or guide as to what to teach and when. It makes the decisions so much easier!
- Shared reading is about building oral language and a deeper connection with the book.
- Children need time and repetition to really be able to engage with the text.
- Choose a focus and don't try and do too much at once.
- Be ready to teach about text knowledge.
- Pick your comprehension question for your students to meet them where they are up to, but extend and support them.
- Use think, pair, share for everything you do. Children need to talk more!
- If students aren't connecting with what you are teaching, take a couple of steps back and meet them where they are up to.
- Work with colleagues to lighten the planning load.

Snapshot of Practice 8 – Creating a Language-Rich Environment in Year 2

Jo Dick – Year 2 Teacher

In the past 6 years, there has been a real increase in the number of Year 2 children who don't know basic vocabulary like what a baby horse or cow is called. This means that I have to adjust teaching to compensate for children's lower level of language and meet them where they are up to. Each class you teach is different and you need to be flexible. It's not about assuming you can teach the same things year after year. I like to plan for language teaching using a focus text to support the learning, but it's also about the incidental opportunities and making a language-rich classroom. Language learning isn't just for the literacy block. It's for all curriculum areas. I love seeing kids becoming word detectives, noticing words they don't know the meaning of, or/and bringing the words to the group. Increasing the oral language work in the classroom enables everyone to participate and they are excited to join in. It also helps them transfer what they know to the page. When they know what they want to say, writing becomes easier because they can focus more on spelling and putting the words down on paper.

Jo's Advice for Other Teachers

- Provide lots of opportunities for students to speak. Partner work is great for this and having students present things to the class across the school day.
- Class discussion about issues or particular books is also important. Children need to learn the 'behaviours' of discussion and to listen as well as speak.
- Have students share their work with a partner and talk about what they are about to do at their desks. Then ask them to share again when the work is done. This helps keep everyone on track.
- Use a word topic wall across the curriculum so that vocabulary is a part of the whole day.

Reflection Questions

- How am I providing intentional opportunities for students to talk with each other?
- In the Foundation year, what kind of play-based stimulus will I use to encourage the development of both academic and interpersonal language?
- Which morphemes will I teach orally and which will I teach in writing?
- How will I ensure that learned vocabulary is revisited and revised?
- What plans do I have to teach vocabulary and morphology both in and out of the context of rich picture books?

References

Australian Curriculum, Assessment and Reporting Authority (ACARA) 2010 to present. (2015). This material was downloaded (www.australiancurriculum.edu.au) (accessed 19 March, 2022) and was modified. The material is licensed under CC BY 4.0 (https://creativecommons.org/licenses/by/4.0).

Beck, I., McKeown, M., & Kucan, L. (2013). *Bringing words to life* (2nd ed.). Guildford Publications.

Bussman Gillis, M., & Chapel Eberhardt, N. (2017). *Syntax. Knowledge to practice*. Literacy How Professional Learning Series.

Cummins, J. (1981). Empirical and theoretical underpinnings of bilingual education. *The Journal of Education, 163*(1), 16–29. http://www.jstor.org/stable/42772934

Hochman, J., & Wexler, N. (2017). *The writing revolution: A guide to advancing thinking through writing in all subjects and grades.* John Wiley & Sons Inc.

Hollingsworth, J., & Ybarra, S. (2012). *Explicit direct instruction for English learners.* Corwin Press Inc.

Paramour, Z., & Paramour, T. (2020). *The grammar book: Understanding and teaching primary grammar.* Bloomsbury Education.

Seidenberg, M. (2017). *Language at the speed of sight: How we read, why so many can't, and what can be done about it.* Basic Books.

Stone, L. (2015). *Language for life: where linguistics meets teaching.* Routledge.

Van Cleave, W. (2014). *Writing matters: Developing sentence skills in students of all ages* (2nd ed.). Edition. Teacher's Manual

10 Phonological and Phonemic Awareness

This chapter will share specific strategies and guidance about how to provide instruction in phonological and phonemic in the general education classroom across the first three years of school as well as considerations for assessment and supporting students at risk of reading difficulty.

Finding Teachable Moments for Phonological Sensitivity

Phonological sensitivity relates to the words and units in words larger than phonemes (onset and rime, rhyming, and syllables). In the mainstream classroom, it is not usually necessary to devote large amounts of instructional time to the development of these skills. Of course, if students display difficulty in acquiring them, then we should provide whatever targeted instruction they need to do so. Here are some suggestions for ways that you can build this work into your daily routine.

Jump It Out

Jump it out (Table 10.1):

a helps children be aware of words as units
b provides children with a movement break after they have been sitting for a period of time
c provides incidental exposure to complete sentences (not fragments)
d allows you to reinforce facts or knowledge children have been learning (however, this is not its primary purpose) (Table 10.1).

Table 10.1 'Jump it Out' Lesson Steps

Steps	Teacher actions
1 – Select a sentence. This sentence might be an instruction or reinforcement of the material you have covered in the preceding lesson. (To begin with, you can avoid confusion with syllables by selecting one syllable words. Later on, you can include multisyllable words as well)	If you have been learning about insects, you might choose the sentence, 'Ants have 6 legs'
2 – Say the sentence for the students and ask the students to repeat it	Class, we are going to jump this sentence. 'Ants have 6 legs'. Have the students repeat the sentence after you orally
3 – Have the students repeat the sentence jumping once for each word spoken	Ok, now let's jump it out! 'Ants have 6 legs'.
Optional – choose a second sentence for children to jump to and repeat steps one to three. You can do 'arms up' as an alternative to jumping. Follow the same steps by having children raise one arm for each word spoken	

Syllable Blending While Giving Instructions

There is no better way to ensure that instructions are followed than to have students repeat them back to you. In this activity, segment the last word of instruction and have students blend the syllables together to say the word. This kind of activity is particularly useful for students with phonological delay, developmental language disorder, or English as an additional language or dialect because it is simple and context embedded. See Table 10.2 for details.

Table 10.2 Syllable Blending in Instructions Lesson Steps

Steps	Teacher actions
1 – Decide on the instruction you wish to give. Use the most direct speech possible, avoiding multistep instructions. *Multistep instructions are fine in general, but they don't work well for this task*	You might decide on the instruction – 'sit on the carpet'. *Note that it is the kind of instruction that when a student repeats it, they can internalise it to be applicable to them. If you said, 'I'd like you to sit on the carpet', it might not make sense when they repeat it*
2 – Say the sentence for the students, segmenting the last word into syllables	'Sit on the car-pet'. 'Chop' the syllables car-pet with your closed hands
3 – Have the students repeat the sentence exactly as you have modelled it before saying the blended word	Students say, 'Sit on the car-pet. Carpet'.
This routine might take some teaching, but once students know what to expect, it will be a snappy, effective routine for both syllable blending and instruction giving	

Syllable Segmenting During Transitions

Use this routine, outlined in table 10.3, when you wish students to move to do something where they might have to wait for their turn (washing hands, getting bags, blowing noses, collecting a book to read). It prevents a stampede of children in the classroom and allows you a one-on-one opportunity to support and assess syllable segmentation (Table 10.3).

Table 10.3 Syllable Segmenting During Transitions Lesson Steps

Steps	Teacher actions
1 – Choose a student and sing the syllable song to the tune of 'open shut them'	*Can you chop it* *Can you chop it* *Can you chop your name _____?*
2 – The student then 'chops' their name into the appropriate number of syllables. If they are unable to perform this skill, model it for them and have them repeat it. This is also an opportunity to assess this skill. Simply keep a checklist and tick off when students can perform the skill	

Rhyming During Transitions

For many children, the ability to produce rhyming words will not develop until they have a solid grasp of the alphabetic code and can blend and segment with ease. This task, as outlined in Table 10.4, introduces the skill of recognising rhyming words which can be done from preschool onwards. The full version of this rhyme originally appeared in the book Alligator Pie by Dennis Lee in 1974 (Table 10.4).

N.B. Ensure that you work out all possible rhyming words for your students' names when you choose a letter to avoid any embarrassing, inappropriate words being produced!

Table 10.4 Rhyming During Transitions Lesson Steps

Steps	Teacher actions
1 – Choose a student and sing the rhyming song substituting the first phoneme of their name with a /w/	*A wibbly wobbly woo* *An elephant sat on you* *A wibbly wobby /w/-rhyme of the child's name (Wark)* *An elephant sat on …*
2 – Students identify the child whose name has been rhymed with	*(students all say) Mark!*
3 – The selected students then proceed to complete the task (wash hands, collect their bag, etc.)	

You can substitute any animal and beginning letter, for example

A tibbly tobbly too	A hibbly hobbly who	A gibbly gobbly goo
A tiger sat on you	A hippo sat on you	A goose sat on you
A tibbly tobbly Tark	A hibbly hobbly Hark	A gibbly gobbly Gark
A tiger sat on…(Mark)	A hippo sat on…(Mark)	A goose sat on…(Mark)

A Word on Nursery Rhymes

Nursery rhymes have been an important part of the early years classroom for a very long time and there is a good reason for this. In years gone by, children would sing the nursery rhymes and learn them by heart. In modern classrooms, we are more likely to show a video clip of the nursery rhyme complete with fun cartoon images. Wherever possible, turn off the screen during nursery rhyme singing. This keeps the focus on listening and the production of the words rather than on consuming the visual content. For some children, the visual is such a distraction that they are unlikely to be paying any attention at all to the nursery rhyme when a cartoon is present.

Phonemic Awareness

Phonemic awareness is the awareness of and ability to manipulate phonemes (sounds) in words.

The skills involved are:

- Identifying the initial phoneme
- Identifying the final phoneme
- Identifying the medial vowel in a consonant-vowel-consonant word
- Blending phonemes
- Segmenting phonemes
- Adding phonemes
- Deleting phonemes
- Substituting phonemes

It should not be taken for granted that phonemic awareness will develop naturally and for many children, it does not develop without explicit support (Moats, 2020). Oral phonemic work is fine; however, there will be more 'bang for your buck' if you include graphemes or concrete materials in your lessons.

Being able to isolate and identify phonemes is the fundamental skill of the game, 'eye spy'. It is the first step on the path to phonemic awareness and can be introduced in preschool and early Foundation for all students. Table 10.5 outlines a lesson sequence for this.

Table 10.5 Early Phoneme Identification Lesson Steps

Suggestions for teaching this concept	Teacher actions
Identifying the initial phoneme (continuous sound) Show a picture of the target object Say the word, emphasising the initial phoneme. Have students repeat the word after you. (Also emphasising the initial phoneme) Ask students to identify the initial phoneme *N.B. Choose words that start with continuous sounds so that you can draw out the first phoneme (f, l, m, n, r, s, v, w)*	*Display a picture of the sun* We are finding out 'What sound sun starts with'. 'Say the word sssssun'. Students say, 'Sssssssun' 'What word does sun start with?' Students say /s/
Identifying the initial phoneme *(containing a stop sound at the beginning of the word such as t, p, b, d, g)* Display three magnets or blocks Display a picture of the object Say the target word, having students repeat the word after you. As you say the word, point to the magnets or blocks, one tap for each sound Ask what the first sound is *You may need to repeat the initial phoneme two or three times to make this clear* *p – p – pig, but discontinue as soon as possible to set children up for success in reading and spelling*	*Display three magnets or blocks* *Display a picture of a pig* 'We are finding out What sound pig starts with'. Say /p/ /i/ /g/ pointing to one magnet or block with each phoneme you say. Have the students repeat you 'Say pig'. Students say pig 'What sound does pig start with?'
Repeat the above steps for identifying the final and medial phoneme in consonant-vowel-consonant words	

You do not need to wait for students to have developed the above skills before beginning the work of teaching blending and segmenting; however, ensure that you monitor student skill development and respond accordingly to prevent gaps in student understanding.

Chapter 11 focuses on blending and segmenting in the context of phonics lessons, so this chapter will focus on incidental opportunities for blending and segmenting and supporting students who may be struggling to develop these critical skills.

Incidental Opportunities for Blending and Segmenting

You can provide incidental opportunities for blending and segmenting in the following ways:

- While giving instructions. 'Children, I would like you to sit on the "m-a-t"'.
- 'Please get the pencil that is r-e-d'.
- In your morning routine, display two pictures (a mop and a map). Ask, 'Which word am I saying? m – a – p'. Students repeat m – a – p and then point to the picture that matches the word you have said.
- As exit tickets before going out to recess or lunch. Show a picture of a dog and ask the student to count the phonemes on their fingers as they segment 'd – o – g' before heading out for the break
- Use children's names as the target word. 'Whose name am I saying? j – a – n. That's right! Jan, can you please collect the lunch basket?'
- During shared writing opportunities, ask students to help you sound out words. If your shared sentence is 'The dog can jump', have the students sound out the words before you write them on the board.

All of the above suggestions are context embedded oral opportunities to practise blending and segmenting. They are part of creating a language-rich classroom with multiple opportunities to practise skills; however, they do not replace the explicit teaching with graphemes explored in Chapter 11.

Phonological Sensitivity and Phonemic Awareness in Year 1 and 2

There is nothing to prevent you from using the techniques described in the Year 1 or 2 classroom; however, if a child arrives in Year 1 or 2 without these skills, they require immediate intervention, not just opportunities for exposure. If a child experiences difficulty in developing these skills, it is preferable for intervention to have commenced in the Foundation year, as soon as the difficulty was noticed. However, this does not always happen. Children come to us from other schools or are missed in the data collection during the Foundation year in our own school. Regardless, Year 1 and 2 teachers must step in and support their students to develop these skills to prevent them from falling further behind.

Phonological and Phonemic Awareness 127

The following routines provide different levels of support for students experiencing difficulty in acquiring blending and segmenting through the mainstream lesson alone. Not all students will need the step-by-step approach outlined in the following lesson sequence; however, students at Tier 2 and 3 may require a very responsive, intentional approach.

Beginning Blending (I Do) – Model and Deconstruct

This is the 'I do' part of the teaching. You are modelling the process of blending for the student. Use blocks before students have learned graphemes, or graphemes once they have automatic phoneme/grapheme correspondence. This lesson is outlined in Table 10.6.

Table 10.6 Beginning Blending (I Do) Lesson Steps

Steps	Teacher actions
Step 1 – Say the phonemes of a word	/b/ /a/ /t/
Step 2 – Place a block or magnetic letter, one as you say each phoneme	/b/ ☐ b /b/ /a/ ☐ ☐ b a /b/ /a/ /t/ ☐ ☐ ☐ b a t
Step 3 – You blend, the student copies	/b/ /a/ /t/, 'bat' (the student repeats you)
Step 4 – Display a picture of a bat	

128 Structured Literacy Practices

Beginning Blending (We Do) – Joint Construction

Table 10.7 outlines the joint construction part of the teaching. You are modelling the process of blending for the students and they are 'helping' you. Use blocks before students have learned graphemes, or graphemes once they have automatic phoneme/grapheme correspondence. Provide wait time during the activity to give the student the chance to answer, but when it is clear that they do not have the correct response, provide it for them.

When selecting pictures for this task, start with words that are completely different from each other and then increase the stretch by using minimal pairs (words that have just one phoneme difference).

Table 10.7 Beginning Blending (We Do) Lesson Steps

Step 1 – Display two pictures	
Step 2 – Say the phonemes for one of the pictures	/c/ /a/ /t/
Step 3 – Model with concrete materials moving one block/magnetic letter for each phoneme	c ▢ c - a ▢ ▢ c - a - t ▢ ▢ ▢
Step 3 – Student repeats with their own materials. In a small group, ensure that each student has their own set of materials	c ▢ c - a ▢ ▢ c - a - t ▢ ▢ ▢
Step 4 – The student attempts to blend the word	'cat'

If the student provides an incorrect response, model sounding out the word and blending it. Then have them copy you

Phonological and Phonemic Awareness 129

Beginning Blending (You Do) – Supported Practice

The lesson outlined in Table 10.8 requires the student/s to blend on their own. Use blocks before students have learned graphemes, or graphemes once they have automatic phoneme/grapheme correspondence. Provide wait time during the activity to give the student the chance to answer, but when it is clear that they do not have the correct response, provide it for them.

Table 10.8 Beginning Blending (You Do) Lesson Steps

Steps	Teacher actions
Step 1 – Model with concrete materials/ magnetic letters and say the phonemes	t □ t - a □ □ t - a - p □ □ □
Step 2 – Ask students to repeat the phonemes and blend the word	'Say the sounds after me. /t/ /a/ /p/. What is this word?'
Step 3 – Provide feedback	'Very good. Well done!' or 'My turn. /t/ /a/ /p/, tap. Your turn'. Students repeat you 'Great listening. Good job'.
If needed, students may tap the graphemes or block as they say the sounds	

Move backwards and forwards through these levels of support as needed. Once you have taught the skills and students have demonstrated that they can work with the lowest level of support possible, start there each day and move backwards through the levels if students experience difficulty.

Once children have reached the point where they can tell you what a word is after you say the individual phonemes, you can say that they have achieved *oral blending*.

Once children have reached the point where they can tell you what a word is after you show them a written word and they can say the phonemes and then blend them, you can say that they can *blend with graphemes*.

130 *Structured Literacy Practices*

Beginning Segmenting (I Do) – Model and Deconstruct

Table 10.9 Beginning Segmenting (I Do) Lesson Sequence

Step 1 – Display a picture and say the word.	'tap'
Step 2 – Model segmenting the word and mapping with concrete materials or magnetic letters before blending the word	t ☐ t - a ☐ ☐ t - a - p ☐ ☐ ☐ 'tap'
Step 3 – Have the student copy you	Student repeats what you have just done, saying /t/ /a/ /p/, 'tap'

Beginning Segmenting (We Do) – Joint Construction

Table 10.10 Beginning Segmenting (We Do) Lesson Steps

Step 1 – Display a picture and say the word	'map'
Step 2 – Segment orally (no concrete materials or graphemes)	/m/ /a/ /p/
Step 3 – Have student repeat you and place the concrete materials or graphemes on the table	/m/ /a/ /p/ m ☐ m - a ☐ ☐ m - a - p ☐ ☐ ☐
Step 4 – Show the word to the student so that they can self-check and fix any errors	

Beginning Segmenting (You Do) – Supported Practice

Table 10.11 Beginning Segmenting (You Do) Lesson Steps

Step 1 – Say the word	'bat'
Step 2 – Ask the student to segment the word and say how many sounds there are	'Sound out bat' 'How many sounds are there?'
Step 3 – Provide concrete materials or graphemes for student to 'spell' the word	Student says, /b/ /a/ /t/ b ☐ b - a ☐ ☐ b - a - t ☐ ☐ ☐
Step 4 – Show the word to students so that they can self-check and fix any errors	

More Phonemic Awareness Skills

Beyond blending and segmenting, students will develop the skills of phoneme addition, deletion, and substitution. As with all phonemic skills, once students have learned them, there is no need to continue instruction. Phonemic skills are a means to the end of effective reading spelling, not a means in and of themselves.

Considerations for Promoting Automaticity in Phonemic Skills

The more familiar we become with how our spelling systems work, the stronger our phonemic skills become. We can promote knowledge development in the following ways:

- Intentionally include base words and morphemes in phonics lessons. For example, students read the word 'plant' and then they read the word 'plants'. Explain that you made the new word by adding 's'.
- Ask students to identify the base of words. For example, if you are spelling the word 'hopping' in shared writing, ask students what the base word is (hop).
- Use syllables to break down longer words for spelling.

If you wish to explicitly work on addition, deletion, and substitution, consider the following:

- Include these opportunities in phonics lessons rather than finding a separate time. Performing these skills with graphemes will result in stronger learning.
- Be careful that you are actually engaging the students in a phonemic task rather than simply a blending one.

Blending task	Manipulation task
'Make the word "pat" with magnetic letters. Now swap the /a/ for an /o/ (students switch the letters out). What word do you have?'	'Make the word "pat" with magnetic letters. What would we have to change to turn this word into "pot"?' You are then looking for students to switch out the 'a' and the 'o' without having to pull the whole word apart and put it back together again

Assessment

Assessment is important in its role in identifying students who are experiencing difficulty. It is critical that we do this and intervene as soon as possible when we notice that a student is struggling, particularly as phonological and phonemic skills are a critical indicator of future reading challenges. As well as screening for a potential difficulty, assessment plays an important role in helping us make decisions about instruction. The National Reading Panel (NICHD, 2000) found that approaches that focused on a narrower range of skills were more effective than those that attempted to teach a large range of skills at once. Knowing where students are up to in their development allows you to meet them there and provide the instruction that they need. To this end, it is not necessary to have a norm-referenced assessment for classroom use. An informal assessment or screener will provide the information you need. At the end of the day, the question that our phonological and phonemic awareness assessment needs to answer is, 'Can the student perform the following skills?' Once you know that, you'll know where to focus your teaching efforts. Many high-quality systematic synthetic phonics programs include a phonological and phonemic awareness assessment. You can also find phonological awareness assessments online from a range of sources, including your education system's own internal resources.

Snapshot of Practice 9 – Teaching Phonological and Phonemic Awareness in the Foundation Year

Brynell Francis – Foundation Teacher

I used to take it for granted that once the students learned some phonics, they would all be able to just read words. I now know that I have to be really intentional in this.

In phonological and phonemic awareness, students can come to the Foundation classroom with such different levels of development. So I make sure that I complete an assessment at the start of the year to give me my baseline data and again at the end of the year to be able to measure impact. In between, I observe and complete informal assessment in lessons. From there I am able to plan which skills to focus on. When I first started teaching phonological and phonemic awareness, I relied on a structured program from a book. Now that I know what I need to teach I do things differently. In our classroom, phonological sensitivity is done throughout the day and embedded into the everyday activities of the room.

The impact of this has been huge and the growth we have seen has been amazing. The other thing we saw was that by embedding blending and segmenting into phonics lessons, the students' phonics learning became much more meaningful. They knew that they were going to actually use this new knowledge they were learning."

Brynell's Advice for Other Teachers

- Go slowly. You don't have to have it all down pat straightaway.
- Try and build phonological sensitivity into your routines instead of spending 10–15 minutes on it every day. Those minutes add up!
- Focus on developing one or two skills at a time, not all of them at once.

Troubleshooting

Q — My Students can select the correct pictures from two options when I say the sounds, but can't do it without the pictures.

A — Make this task slightly more challenging by using a minimal pair (words that only have one sound different such as pat and pan) to push the student to discriminate between the words. When you do remove the pictures from the task, use words that have continuous sounds (e.g. m, n, l, f, v, r, s). When we speak, we 'smoosh' the sounds together. When we are developing phonemic awareness, we are working to separate the phonemes from the word. Using continuous sounds can make this easier.

Q — My student can blend orally, but not with graphemes.

A — If a student is having trouble blending, check that they can recognise the graphemes you are asking them to read with instantly. If they can't, use different graphemes or spend more time focusing on phoneme/grapheme correspondence. If they can, use words with continuous sounds and introduce pictures (one written word and two pictures) as a support, but step back from this as skills grow.

Q — My student's blending is robotic and stilted.

A — Use words that contain continuous sounds and encourage 'continuous blending'. So rather than sounding out /m/ /a/ /p/ as three separate sounds with breaks in between each one, make the blending continuous m, ma, map. Ask the student to say the phoneme of the words in their head before saying the word aloud ('read with your eyes, then with your mouth').

Q — My student can blend one syllable words but not multisyllable words.

A — Students need to be able to blend single syllable words with ease before they will be able to tackle multisyllable words. Go back and check this before proceeding. Start with compound words such as 'sunshine' and 'runway'. Write each syllable on a separate card (or fold a card along the syllable break) and have the students read them one at a time before putting them together. Explicitly teach students about morphology (base words, prefixes, and suffixes) and help them identify the base of words as well as add morphemes to base words. This awareness of structure helps them see the 'parts' of multisyllable words instead of one long jumble of letters.

Reflection Questions

- How am I monitoring the skill development of my students?
- What criteria am I using to decide which students need intervention support?
- How often do I embed blending and segmenting with graphemes?
- How am I working with my paraprofessional colleagues to ensure that they understand phonological and phonemic awareness and how to support its development?
- What is the ratio of oral work to work with graphemes I currently have?
- Do I discontinue work in early skills once students have demonstrated that they can perform them?

References

Lee, D. (1974). *Alligator pie*. Harper Collins Publishing.
Moats, L. C. (2020). *Speech to print* (3rd ed.). Paul Brooks Publishing.
(NICHD) Eunice Kennedy Shriver National Institute of Child Health and Human Development, NIH, DHHS. (2000). *Report of the National Reading Panel: teaching children to read: Reports of the subgroups (00-4754)*. U.S. Government Printing Office.

11 Phonics

Whether you are teaching the Foundation year or Year 1 and 2, you are likely to have a range of 'levels' of development in your class. The aim is to narrow this development gap as much as possible to allow you to maximise instructional time. This chapter does not explain how to run group rotations, and indeed it is preferable that this is not a regular feature of your lessons. Fully guided instruction in phonics yields the best results and I encourage you to work towards eliminating situations where children are 'learning on their own' or 'doing hands-on tasks as exposure'. While I do work with schools that have achieved this goal, the reality is that for many teachers, the timetabling and other changes needed to make this happen are out of their hands. So do the best you can with what you have to work with, knowing that every step you take towards a structured approach to reading instruction is a gift to your students. This chapter outlines what and how to teach phonics in a mainstream teaching environment across the first three years of school, including how to adjust practice to support the full range of learning needs in your class.

Deciding on the Pace and Intensity of Learning

Systematic synthetic phonics approaches utilise a set sequence of content to structure learning. This means that you and your students have a clear understanding of where you are in this sequence and what the next steps will be. As well as allowing you to organise content, the sequence enables you to make decisions about the pace and intensity of teaching that may be needed by different groups of students.

The aim of any phonics instruction is to keep the largest number of students possible together in the 'main' group of learners. It is much easier to teach a group of students who are all within a similar range because you can target content and pace of instruction to meet the students' needs. How close you get to this ideal will depend on your school context, the type of instruction that has occurred in the past, and the opportunities you provide within your lessons for review and consolidation. If you do not have enough consolidation in your instruction, students may well fall behind one by one until you end up with five or more groups within your class. This is a recipe for overwhelm for both you and your students. The situation might also exist where, when you review your new class data, you find a wide range in every classroom. If this is the case, you might consider an alternative arrangement to every teacher teaching phonics and decoding to their own students, until such times as your range narrows. There is no magical, one-size-fits-all solution when it comes to supporting the range of learners in your class. The needs of students is the driver of your approach in this and knowing each student's data story is vital to prevent wasting precious instructional time and cognitive overload.

Why can't We Just Teach the Whole Class and 'Catch up' Those Students Who Need It?

It would be wonderful if it was this easy! The answer really depends on the learning profile of the students who need the catch-up. Students might fall into the category of students who:

- Do not have any working memory or retrieval challenges and have simply not had the opportunity to learn the phoneme/grapheme correspondences they should have up until this point.
- Do not having diagnosable challenges, but benefit greatly from an opportunity for additional practice. With this support, they can remain with the 'main' group in your class.
- Who have compromised working memory and retrieval challenges where the student becomes cognitively overloaded very quickly when there is too much content being presented at once. Students require many more exposures than their peers to commit new learning to long-term memory. The more we ask these students to learn at once, the more muddled they become.

For students who do not have learning challenges but have a case of 'never been taught', we can expect that with some additional review of the parts of the sequence they don't know yet, they'll catch up with the class, depending on how far 'behind' they currently are. Similarly, students who can keep up with the main group with some extra repetitions or review of the phoneme/grapheme correspondences can be expected to access the core content that the rest of the class is working on. However, for students experiencing difficulty with working memory or retrieval, trying to catch them up by having them learn with the main group and then adding additional catch-up content may simply be too much for them. This also depends on how much catching up there is to do. For students experiencing difficulty, it is preferable to provide 'right there' teaching that meets them at the point in the code they are up to. Appropriate instruction will provide the intensity of teaching and the number of repetitions they need to learn to mastery before moving on. This concept of learning phoneme/grapheme correspondences to mastery is important for both mainstream learners and those who require additional support.

Fast Lane Learners

Within any class, there will be students who I call the 'fast lane learners'. While slower lane learners need more repetitions and greater intensity of teaching, fast lane learners do not need as much intensity or as many repetitions to learn to read. For these students, one or two exposures to a grapheme may be sufficient to get them on their way. Asking these students to learn alongside the main group can be a recipe for boredom and disengagement. This doesn't mean that these fast lane learners do not benefit from the same structured, sequential phonics teaching as their peers, but that they don't need as much of it.

For all learners, we need to recognise that instruction should proceed at the pace and with the intensity that responds to the students, not the pre-determined pace of a program or a teaching approach that provides a one-size-fits-all series of lessons. Some teachers I have worked with have found that their class is all working at the same point. This comes about as a product of solid, skilled teaching and a little bit of luck. However, the majority of teachers find that there is a range (sometimes across three or four years of achievement) in their classroom and they need to adjust teaching to meet these students' needs.

Conduct a Phonics Lesson

Systematic synthetic phonics lessons include the following components:

- Learning a new grapheme
- Reviewing previously learned graphemes
- Writing graphemes
- Reading words
- Spelling words

Different programs or tools may do this slightly differently or in a different order, but the fundamentals are consistent. The lesson outline below is a suggestion for what you might do in your phonics lesson.

The Basic Code

Magnetic Letters or Handwriting?

There are many activities that involve the use of magnetic letters and they definitely have a temporary place in our lessons. Use magnetic letters when students do not have fluent and correct handwriting (Table 11.1).

Table 11.1 Steps to a Basic Code Phonics Lesson

Step	Teacher actions
1 Introduce the phoneme/grapheme correspondence you are teaching	'Today we are learning how to write the sound /f/'. Show pictures of objects that begin with /f/ to reinforce the target phoneme by saying the words and having the students say them after you Show students the position of their mouths and explain how their breath works in producing this phoneme 'When we say /f/, our top teeth are on our bottom lip and we push air out of our mouths. Everybody say this sound with me /f/'.
2 Show the grapheme (using the language 'one of the ways' makes it clear that there is greater complexity to come without overwhelming students' working memories)	Show the students a card with the letter 'f' 'The letter 'eff' is one of the ways we can write /f/. What do we say when we see this letter?' Students say /f/. Repeat this several times to reinforce
3 Practise handwriting (moving students to desks and then back to the mat during the lesson gives them a movement break and sitting at a desk for writing tasks ensures correct posture and facilitates pencil grip) Ask students to say the phoneme you are teaching as they write. This provides multiple repetitions of the phoneme/grapheme correspondence You might choose to have small group work with a classroom assistant or parent helper for this task if they are unable to perform it on their own	'Now we are going to practise writing this letter.' Using whichever handwriting mnemonic/rhyme you have available at your school, model writing the target letter on the board. Have the students write the letter in the air or on the floor Students move to desks and, at your signal, practise writing the letter f. 'Keep writing the letter "f" until I say to stop. As you write, I want to hear you saying /f/ each time you write'. Monitor students as they write, providing support and redirection as needed
4 Review of previously learned graphemes	Bring the students back to the mat and show a range of cards that have the graphemes students have previously learned. Place the new grapheme into the deck as an additional review opportunity. Note which graphemes students are 'wobbly' on and put them aside to reteach the next day

(*Continued*)

Table 11.1 Steps to a Basic Code Phonics Lesson (Continued)

Step	Teacher actions
N.B. If students are blending and segmenting, move to the following steps. If they aren't, refer to the blending and segmenting routines in Chapter 10 for options	
5 Read words Providing an instructional lag for the basic code means that students (who are likely consolidating both phoneme/grapheme correspondences and phonemic skills) have a higher degree of success when reading the words	Select three or four words that contain graphemes the students have previously learned (but not the current day's new grapheme). Hold the card up and ask students to sound the words out before telling you the whole word. Explain the meaning of any words as necessary Ensure that the group answers together
6 Grapheme recall Grapheme recall supports long-term retention of phoneme/grapheme correspondences and primes students for success in word-level spelling. This step also provides some 'wait time' between reading and spelling words so that students are more engaged in segmenting and transcribing in the following task instead of 'copying from memory'	Have students move back to their desks quickly and silently Have a look at the words you are going to ask students to spell and say the graphemes out of order one by one having them write the grapheme in their books
7 Spell words A high degree of success is important in this step. If a student corrects an error (fixes it), allow them to then tick the word. The tick is for engagement and focus, not 100% correct answers all the time	Using the same three or four words as in Step 5, say the target word. Have the students repeat this word. Repeat. Ask students to 'sound out the first word', mapping in the way that your school uses (counting on fingers, writing lines, tapping on arms, etc.). Ask students to write the word Making sure that the board is visible to all students, ask them to sound out the word for you as you write the word on the board 'Tick it or fix it'

As soon as students have correct and confident handwriting, remove the magnetic letters from lessons. The sooner that practice opportunities mirror the actual act of writing the better. Additionally, there is a helpful multisensory aspect of forming letters that students will not have if they are selecting magnets instead of writing themselves.

If students still need the support of magnetic letters when they reach the stage of learning digraphs, avoid providing magnets where the letters of the digraph are joined. Having to select the individual letters of the digraph mirrors the task of recalling the parts of the digraph in writing. Sometimes, our scaffolds are well intentioned but only serve to make our students dependent on the support. Of course, if you have a student with additional needs who requires this adjustment, then provide it.

Moving on From the Basic Code

It is tempting to rush into the complex code as soon as children know the most common, consonant digraphs, but providing a little more time for consolidation means that students will have strong foundations to carry them into the next stage of learning.

Before moving children on to the complex code, consider the following questions:

- Can they blend words?
- How developed is their phonemic processing? Can they read and spell CVC, CCVC, CVCC, CCVCC, and CCCVCC words?
- Can they map words with graphemes?
- Can they correctly form graphemes?
- Do they have automaticity in the above knowledge and processes? Is reading and spelling smooth and effective or stilted and slow?
- Are they able to read text consisting of several sentences?
- Can they write a simple sentence on their own?

If the answer to any of the above questions is 'no', it is worth spending time consolidating knowledge and skills before moving on. Continual growth is built on strong foundations. Different children will develop automaticity with differing levels of ease and review, so it's important that you know your students well and have a clear understanding of their learning profiles and needs.

Teaching the Complex Code

There are a few different ways to approach the complex code content. I am sharing one possibility (that makes sense to me), but if your school's program presents things differently, don't worry. As long as we are covering the necessary content in the early years, carefully consider student cognitive load and are maintaining a cumulative, systematic approach, students will be fine.

When planning for phonics teaching, I start with (what I call) the early complex code. That is, one representation of the remaining phonemes of English not covered in the basic code. When we consider the frequency with which graphemes occur, focus on graphemes that appear most often in single syllable words. This might look like:

Early complex code: ay, ee, igh, ow, oo (hoop), oy, or, ar, oo (look), er, ou, are (dare)

Alternate spellings: ow (snow), oi, ir, a_e, i_e, o_e, u_e, ea, ai, ie, aw, ur, ear (near), ew, and other alternative spellings of vowel and consonant phonemes. See Chapter 2 for an outline of when to teach what.

If you are teaching Year 1 or 2, it is well worth spending a couple of weeks reviewing previously learned phoneme/grapheme correspondences before moving on. This presents gaps that can cause difficulty.

When it's time to move on to the complex code, rest assured that you don't need to have a new method of teaching. With a few tweaks, the phonics lesson from the basic code can serve you very well. Items in bold in Table 11.2 are those that are different from the previous routine for the basic code.

Introducing Multisyllable Words

Multisyllable words come in a range of forms

1. Words that end in inflexional suffixes (s, es, ed, ing).
    To teach these words, show the word in its base form before showing the word with the suffix on the end.
2. Compound words (stingray, sunset, driveway). These words are made up of two free bases (morphemes that can appear on their own).
    To teach these words, display each syllable (base) on its own for students to read and then combine them.
3. Multisyllable words such as carpet, garlic, and guitar.
    To teach these words, you can either use the same method as for compound words or display the word with a syllable break clearly marked. Students decode the word before viewing it without the syllable break and decoding it again.
    For example, car / pet
      carpet

Review and Consolidation

One of the keys to ongoing growth and helping students to keep up with the pace of learning in your classroom is to include multiple opportunities for review and consolidation. This can take many forms and be done across the school day. Keep review adult led when content is new and include partner practice when it's time to consolidate understandings.

Table 11.2 Complex Code Phonics Lesson Steps

Step	Teacher actions
1 Introduce the phoneme/grapheme correspondence you are teaching	'Today we are learning a new way to write /ay/'. **Say words (and write them on the board if you choose to) that contain that grapheme** rain train aim ail
2 Show the grapheme (using the language 'one of the ways' makes it clear that there is greater complexity to come without overwhelming students' working memories). **If you have taught one representation of the phoneme previously, point this out so that students understand where the new grapheme fits in**	**Explain the grapheme, including spelling patterns.** For example, 'This representation of /ay/ is a digraph. Two letters are used to represent one sound/phoneme. This /ay/ is never used at the end of an English word because English words cannot end in the letter "i". Say that with me. "English words don't end in i"'. Have students say that sentence with you to reinforce
3 Practise writing (moving students to desks and then back to the mat during the lesson gives them a movement break and sitting at a desk for writing tasks ensures correct posture and facilitates pencil grip) Ask students to say the phoneme you are focusing on as they write. This provides multiple repetitions of the phoneme/grapheme correspondence You might choose to have some students work with a classroom assistant or parent helper for this task if they are unable to perform it on their own	'Now we are going to practise writing this **grapheme**'. Model writing the target grapheme on the board saying the phoneme as you do so. Have the students write the grapheme in the air or on the floor Students move to desks and, at your signal, practise writing the grapheme. 'Keep writing the grapheme /ay/ "a-i" until I say to stop. As you write, I want to hear you saying /ay/ each time you write'. Monitor students as they write, providing support and redirection as needed
4 Review of previously learned graphemes	Bring the students back to the mat and show a range of cards that have the graphemes students have previously learned. Place the new grapheme into the deck as an additional review opportunity. Note which graphemes they are 'wobbly' on and put them aside to reteach the next day

(Continued)

Table 11.2 Complex Code Phonics Lesson Steps *(Continued)*

Step	Teacher actions
5 Read words Instructional lag is unnecessary once students are learning the complex code; however, you may wish to use it for students with additional needs **Depending on students' development, you might like to include both single syllable and multisyllable words in this step**	**Select three or four words that contain the new grapheme.** Hold the card up and ask students to sound the words out before telling you the whole word. Explain the meaning of any words as necessary Ensure that the group answers as one
6 Grapheme recall Grapheme recall supports long-term retention of phoneme/grapheme correspondences and primes students for success in word-level spelling. This step also provides some wait time between reading and spelling words so that students are more engaged in segmenting and transcribing in the following step instead of 'copying from memory'	Have students move back to their desks quickly and silently Have a look at the words you are going to ask students to spell and say the graphemes out of order one by one having them write the grapheme in their books. Include any graphemes you wish to assess
7 Spell words A high degree of success is important in this step. If a student corrects an error (fixes it), allow them to then tick the word. The tick is for engagement and focus, not 100% correct answers all the time **Depending on students' development, you might like to include both single syllable and multisyllable words in this step**	Using the same three or four words as in step 5, say the target word. Have the students repeat this word. Repeat. Ask students to 'sound out the first word', mapping in the way that your school uses (counting on fingers, writing lines, tapping on arms, etc.). Ask students to write the word Making sure that the board is visible to all students, ask them to sound out the word for you as you write the word on the board. 'Tick it or fix it'

Teacher Led Review

- Daily review sessions in morning routines. These review sessions are rapid-fire and specifically targeted at content students are learning. Include graphemes students have learned most recently (yesterday), some from a little while ago (last two weeks) and some from a long time ago (last term). This type of review can be done whole class but differentiated for different groups. 'Higher' groups get to practice previous material and 'lower' groups get exposure to the content that is to come. This 'exposure without expectation' is a great thing, but doesn't replace explicit teaching. Some children will 'pick up' learning in this way, but many won't. That's ok. You will target teaching exactly at what these children need when the time comes.
- Review within your phonics lesson – if time allows, you might include reading and spelling of words containing graphemes that students have previously learned.
- Exit and entry 'tickets' as students leave and enter the classroom.
- Incidental opportunities for practice – keep a deck of grapheme cards with you at all times and call children to you when time permits for a 20-second practice.
- During shared writing activities, provide students with whiteboards and markers. When you come to a word containing a grapheme students know, ask the students to spell it themselves before you confirm the spelling on the board.
- To ensure that students have a firm understanding of the complexities of the alphabetic code, include items in your review to revisit alternate spellings in both reading and writing words.

Supported Practice

- Include grapheme and word-level partner practice in your day. For example, before students read their decodable texts, review words or graphemes that students might find tricky. The Reading Success in Action Series contains partner practice booklets for this purpose.
- Have a 'student leader' for the day who will show grapheme cards to the class on entering the classroom or during transitions between activities.
- Homework – send home grapheme and words 'cards' printed on A4 paper for students to practice at home. Only send these home when students are familiar with them.

Consolidating Alternate Spellings

It is not unusual for students to progress well when learning one grapheme/ one phoneme correspondences, but then become muddled when alternate spellings are introduced. For these children, it isn't just about not knowing which spelling option to use in which words, but 'forgetting' graphemes that they have previously learned.. An activity that has worked well for my students is to, after initially learning the alternate spellings, work with a sentence containing all learned alternate spellings.

For example, the bird turned on its perch.

1 Write the sentence as a joint construction.
2 Cover the sentence and ask the students to write it on their own.
3 Reveal the sentence and have students mark it, making any necessary changes.
4 Repeat step 2, twice more.
5 Covering all written sentences, ask the students to 'imagine' the sentence and write down all of the ways to write the target phoneme.
6 Show a deck of cards containing the target graphemes and other previously learned graphemes. Ask the students to say the phoneme for each grapheme you show.

Repeat this task as many times as necessary and include items such as 'write down all the ways you know to write the phoneme /er/' and 'Write two words that have this grapheme making two different sounds "ow"' (students might write snow and how).

A second activity that is very helpful is word sorts. This can be done in a number of ways including:

1 Read a number of words containing different spellings of the same phoneme (fern, purl, bird, etc.) and ask students to write them in the correct 'column' on their boards (see below). In this example, students need to have had several exposures to these words as there is no guideline or 'rule' to govern when to use which spelling option.

Er	ur	ir
Fern	purl	bird

The use of other alternate spellings is more rule governed, such as with 'ai' and 'ay', as it is not 'legal' to use 'ai' at the end of a word in English.

2 Present a number of words with alternate pronunciations of the same grapheme. For example, 'ow' which can be used for /oa/ as in snow or /ou/ as in crowd. Ask students to decode these words, sorting them according to the pronunciation of the phoneme in the word.

It may be difficult for some students to remember all the alternate spellings of phonemes or when to use them, but embedding these concepts into your everyday lessons and maintaining a cumulative sound wall or alphabetic code chart will be very helpful in making the complexities of the code clear.

Sound Walls and Code Charts

There has been an increase in the popularity of 'sound walls' in classrooms recently. For many teachers, this poses a significant shift in practice away from word walls containing high frequency words for students to copy or alphabet walls that have words listed according to starting letter regardless of what phoneme they begin with (think apple, ape, aeroplane, any). Sound walls perform the same function as alphabetic code charts in that they make the code visible.

However, just putting the code on the wall and hoping that children will 'absorb' its content is unlikely to add any value to your reading instruction. Sound walls and code charts are useful only when we integrate them into our teaching and our classroom interactions. Suggestions for effective use of a sound wall include:

- Have the wall or charts at student eye level, near where you teach your reading lessons. This enables you to refer to it during instruction.
- If you use a sound wall, have a plan for how you will fit everything into the space, but don't put it all up at once. One of the lovely features of a sound wall is that it can be co-constructed with students as you introduce new graphemes.
- Take advantage of 'teachable moments' to introduce less common graphemes to the wall. Some representations (e.g. ey in they, grey, prey, and hey) only appear in a few words. Rather than devoting instructional time to that grapheme, add it to the sound wall when you encounter it in your regular lessons. You may then choose to include these 'special group' words in your daily review.
- If you are using an alphabetic code chart, use post it notes to add these 'special group' graphemes to the chart as they appear.

Resourcing Phonics Lessons

It is easy to spend large amounts of money on resources to teach phonics, but it really isn't necessary. A ream of thick A4 card and some pictures printed from the internet are all you need to be ready to teach. The following is a basic list of items you'll need to teach phonics systematically:

- A set of 'sound cards'. For a large group, use an A4 card, and for a smaller one, half, or quarter A4. Write the graphemes you are teaching on the card in thick marker. This also allows you to use the font you are teaching for handwriting.
- If teaching the basic code, a set of pictures beginning with the target sound. You can find these for free on the internet.
- Word cards. Cut your thick A4 card into quarters and write the words on them as you need them. Most systematic, synthetic programs/tools come with cumulative word lists.

- A way to store and organise your sound and word cards into sets. Craft or photo storage boxes that contain smaller containers are ideal. These can be found in department and craft stores for a reasonable price. They fit a quarter A4 card nicely and mean that you will always know where your resources are.
- Half A4 or full A4 books for students to practise writing graphemes, spell words, and write sentences during the literacy block.

If your card is thick enough, there is no need to laminate any of the cards you use as they will not be handled by students.

> **Snapshot of Practice 10 – The Difference between Teaching Phonics in Foundation and Year 1 and 2**
>
> *Diane Herman – Early Years Teacher*
>
> There are key differences between teaching phonics in Foundation and Year 1-2. With Foundation, we are having to start from scratch in most areas. I want to make sure that I am not leaving any gaps that will cause difficulty later on, so our pace is slower. It is critical to ensure that the Foundation Year is strong because otherwise the foundations will crack when the students are in Year 3 and 4. In Year 1-2, the routines are very similar to those used in Foundation; however, we can increase the pace of lessons. We still insist that students sound out with new graphemes and morphemes. This maintains the focus on how words are built. In Year 2, phonics instruction shifts to alternate spellings including understanding when to use particular graphemes and making decisions about spelling. There's actually a lot of learning to do after the initial phonics teaching and this also extends to morphology and etymology.
>
> *Diane's Advice for Other Teachers*
>
> - Group rotations don't maximise learning time. Students need to be learning all the time, so focus on teacher led instruction.
> - Insist on correct phoneme pronunciation. Make sure there is no schwa when the students say the sounds.
> - Make sure that all skills are automatic and strong.
> - Take the time to work with parents so that they understand your approach.
> - When you get your new class in Year 1 and 2, make sure you review all previously learned phoneme/grapheme correspondences because sometimes there are gaps.

Troubleshooting

Q – When writing the graphemes in phonics lessons, some students finish before others.

A – Avoid this 'fast finishers' situation by using a timer instead of writing the grapheme a particular number of times. All students begin at the same time and end at the same time. This discourages students from rushing in order to be the first finished.

Q – Phonics lessons running over time.
A – Fast-paced, effective lessons are the goal. At times though, slow student responses or off-track behaviour means that lessons run overtime. You can keep everyone together by

   a displaying a timer and challenging students to 'beat the clock' by staying on task,
   b ensuring that you are familiar and fluent with the lesson structure and move seamlessly between activities in the lesson,
   c having all of your materials ready and at hand to avoid wasted time, and
   d being explicit about the quick, sharp responses you are expecting from students in your lessons.

Q – Students are having trouble remembering graphemes, even after several exposures.
A – Some students will come to this learning more quickly than others and we need to adjust teaching to suit. For students who require more exposure than their peers, try providing additional opportunities for practice and reducing the number of correspondences you are asking them to learn. Include reading and spelling of words in lessons and include handwriting rather than tracing in lessons for a multisensory aspect. Use picture mnemonics that have the handwriting formation embedded in the image and verbal prompt but be careful not to overextend the use of the mnemonic. The mnemonic provides a scaffold, but students should be moved on from them as soon as possible.

Reflection Questions

- What sequence of graphemes will I teach?
- How will I select the language to use in lessons that reflects the complexity of the code? For example, 'One of the ways to write the sound /_/' instead of 'H says/h/'.
- Where will I source the cumulative word list for my lessons?
- How will my lessons be resourced?
- What plan do I have to include reading and spelling words in each phonics lesson?
- What is my plan for introducing multisyllable words? How will I know that my students are ready for this step?

12 Using Decodable Texts

In the early years, reading comprehension is much more heavily influenced by decoding ability than it is by language comprehension. This is because students already possess the oral language skills necessary to understand the texts they are being asked to read (Moats, 2020; Seidenberg, 2017). As such, the primary focus for the use of decodable texts is lifting words from the page. This doesn't mean that we don't attend to comprehension at all, but that it is not the major focus of our lessons.

Moving on From Traditional Guided Reading

It is not only the types of texts we give children, but the way in which they are used that is changing. Traditional guided reading involved 'levelling' children based on benchmark assessment (see Chapter 15 for more information) and then grouping them in the classroom according to these levels. Lessons focused on teaching children to use a range of strategies for decoding (looking at pictures, thinking about what makes sense, finding little words inside big words) and a range of strategies for comprehension. Both the decoding strategies promoted in balanced literacy guided reading programs and the heavy reliance on comprehension strategies are being replaced with structured literacy practices. Table 12.1 outlines the alternatives to these main goals of guided reading.

Table 12.1 Alternatives to Guided Reading Practices

Guided reading practice	*Suggested alternative*
Use of levelled texts in small group reading lessons. Texts assigned after benchmark assessment	Decodable texts are used in partner practice and assigned according to phonics knowledge
Teaching children to lift words from the page using a range of strategies including:	The primary strategy for decoding is through the structure of the word exploring:

(Continued)

DOI: 10.4324/9781003244189-12

Table 12.1 Alternatives to Guided Reading Practices *(Continued)*

Guided reading practice	Suggested alternative
• Look at the picture • Chunk the word • Flip the vowel • Get my lips ready • Skip the word and come back to it, thinking about what makes sense • Stretch the word out • Ask for help (so someone can just tell you what it is) • Looking at the sounds in the word (if this is suggested, it is as a last resort)	• The phoneme/grapheme correspondences in the word • The morphological structures in the word (prefixes and suffixes) Looking at pictures is a part of making meaning rather than lifting the words from the page. Asking 'does that make sense' is about comprehension monitoring to identify where decoding errors may have been made, rather than guessing a word based on the meaning of the sentence
Comprehension was taught through extensive use of strategies such as: Making connections Inferring Creating mental images Asking questions Determining importance Monitoring understanding Summarising Synthesising	While some comprehension strategies have a more solid research base than others, the role of strategies in comprehension is not as prominent as previously believed Instead, the role of actively building background knowledge and vocabulary is recognised and explicit, and intentional teaching of knowledge plays a much larger part in comprehension instruction. Additionally, attending to syntax and being able to track meaning across sentences using pronouns is a more productive use of time than comprehension strategies

Now that the 'what' of shifting away from guided reading has been established, let us explore the 'how'. Traditional guided reading involved breaking the class up into small groups with the classroom teacher working with one small group at a time while the other students worked on 'stations' or 'centres' until it was their turn to work with the teacher. There are several challenges with this style of teaching.

1 The work done with students as they read their levelled readers was based on misunderstandings of how we read. For children who possessed the 'protective factors' of processing that just put it all together, this approach posed little or no challenge to learning to read. They were able to recognise patterns and develop orthographic mapping and long-term memories of words without much explicit instruction. However, for many students, this approach led to low levels of reading, frustration, and a reduction in engagement in learning.
2 Students were required to work independently for a significant amount of time. The assumption that working on 'engaging' activities would strengthen learning is now being challenged. Stanislas Dehaene's description of four Pillars of Learning states that students need their

attention directed, error feedback provided, active engagement facilitated (actually thinking about the learning), and consolidation of learning for learning to be strong. Independent work on 'fun' tasks that often do not require students to think about reading or spelling at all does not meet the criteria for learning set out in the four pillars (Dehaene, 2021).

3 Breaking into small groups immediately cuts down on the amount of time available for active, engaged, and explicit instruction. In a 60-minute lesson, students may only be actively engaged with learning (presuming that the work done with the teacher is evidence informed) for 10 minutes. This results in students only being engaged in learning from the teacher for 50 minutes per week instead of the potential 300 minutes. That's a potential loss of instructional time of 166 hours each and every school year.

A Lesson With Decodable Texts

Lessons with decodable texts might be conducted in a number of ways including using the suggestion below.

1 Pre-reading activities
2 Partner reading
3 Post-reading activities and discussion
4 Sentence-level transcription

Pre-reading Activities

When working at the class level (or with a larger group), there is a limit to how much support can be provided to individual students. To ensure a high probability of success in reading the chosen decodable text, pre-reading activities can be used to set students up for success. These activities might include:

- Reviewing graphemes, irregular high frequency words, or regular words contained in the text that students might be less familiar with.
- If all students are reading the same text, this can be done with the teacher leading from the front. If students are reading different texts, they can complete this with partners. Decodable texts often have review graphemes and words in the front of the text to be used as pre-reading.
- Reminding students about how to work with their partners and providing support. Instead of partners simply telling each other what a word is when they stumble, encourage them to say 'sound it out' or 'read all through the word' when their partner makes an error.
- Pre-teaching vocabulary that students may be unfamiliar with.
- Teaching any irregular high frequency words that students are not yet familiar with.

Partner Reading

There are two situations that teachers may find themselves in:

1. Working with a large group of students all at the same level of development in phoneme/grapheme correspondence and phonemic skills.
2. Working with their whole class who are at different points in their reading development.

Regardless of which of these situations arises, pair children who are at the same point in their reading development for partner reading. This ensures that both students are able to receive support and error feedback. Pairing a more developed reader with a less developed reader (who are working on learning different parts of the code) means that the less developed reader will be the only one receiving error feedback as they read. If you would like to have buddy reading to support less developed readers, do this in another part of the day, for example, after lunch.

If you are sharing your students across classes for reading lessons, selecting a decodable text and using it in lessons is a simpler undertaking than if you are conducting partner reading with a class of students at different points in development. However, both options are viable and can result in a great outcome for students. The key to making this work is:

- Having detailed knowledge of each student's reading profile.
- Arranging decodable text resources so that they are easy to locate and store. It is well worth spending time making sure that your central text resources are well organised and in line with your school's chosen sequence of teaching phoneme/grapheme correspondences and irregular high frequency words.

Students should read their decodable texts three times.

> Reading 1 – For accuracy
> Reading 2 – For fluency
> Reading 3 – For meaning

Having a visual to support the focus of these three readings will help students understand the success criteria for the lesson. Students will also benefit from hearing you read the text aloud to reinforce expression and phrasing, but only do so *after* the students have read the text. You are aiming for maximum engagement in decoding.

Post-reading Activities and Discussion

While our decodable text reading time isn't for in-depth exploration of comprehension (we can use rich text in a whole class lesson for that), we do want children engaged in thinking about what they have read. This can be achieved in a variety of ways. You will likely find that different approaches are more suitable for different grades and that the suitability of the tasks will vary depending on whether your students are all reading the same text or whether they are reading different texts.

Discussion

Many decodable texts contain text-related questions in the back of the book. If these are present, they can be used to promote reflection of the text and enable you to monitor how much of the text students have remembered. If your texts do not contain these questions, or if you find that your students cannot read the questions in their texts themselves, you might like to ask some generic text-dependent questions such as:

- Who were the characters in the text?
- What was the problem the characters had?
- How was the problem resolved?
- What do you think might have happened next?
- What might have happened before the story?

This discussion can be conducted as 'partner talk' before feeding back to the main group for you to expand on ideas and answers.

Independent Follow-up Tasks

As much as I encourage teachers to work whole class, the reality exists that this is not always possible. You may work in a small school where you are the only teacher for two or three grades or your school leadership may not grant permission to share students between classes. Whatever the reason, it's entirely possible that you may find yourself in a situation where you need to manage the learning needs of children at vastly different stages of reading development. Inevitably, this means that you will need to group children within your class and that some kind of small group lesson is required. This doesn't mean that you have to do rotations or have your students work in unproductive groups. There are several worthwhile activities to do with decodables as a follow-up.

No or Minimal Preparation Activities

1. Have students keep a 'reading journal' where they record who the character was, draw a picture of a scene, and write a sentence about the scene (not copied from the book).
2. Work with a partner on a 'mini spelling test'. One partner chooses a word from the text for the other partner to write. They then mark the word and swap roles.
3. Have students search for a particular grapheme or phoneme in the book, making a list of all of the words that contain that grapheme before

reading them to a partner. This is particularly useful for students who are learning alternate spellings for the complex code.

4 For Year 2 and above, provide a base word from the text and have students create word families before writing sentences that relate to the text. For example, play becomes plays, playing, playful, and playfully.

Resourcing

One of the biggest challenges that teachers have in using decodable texts is resourcing. A considerable number of books are required to have enough for instruction as well as home reading in every class. This issue is often compounded by the fact that schools will likely have spent a significant amount of money on levelled texts and resources and either don't have funds set aside for decodables or feel pressure to use the levelled texts so that they don't go to 'waste'. Here are some key points to think about in resourcing decodable texts:

- Decodables are a necessary tool while children are learning all aspects of the code, not only the first year of school or the basic code. Continuing to use decodables as core instruction through to Year 2 and while learning the full complex code means that all students, including those at risk, will receive the kind of instruction that will prevent the need for intervention in the upper primary years.
- It is more cost-effective to provide decodable texts and appropriate instruction for all students who need it in the early years than provide years of 'intervention' all through the primary years. Of course, some children will continue to require additional support, but this should be a very small number of children across the school.
- There is no rule that says that decoding practice can only occur when using a book. Stories or passages printed on A4 pieces of paper with a single picture to aid comprehension are just as effective as a book. The books are nice, but not essential.
- You do not have to send your precious, limited decodables home for home reading. As per the point above, passages on paper do nicely for home reading. Similarly, an online library of books can be very helpful. A growing number of online platforms exist where teachers can assign texts to students for home reading on a phone, tablet, or computer. At the time of writing, examples of this are Decodable Readers Australia, Read Write Inc, and Get Reading Right. It is important to ensure that the decodables included in the online library align with your scope and sequence or that you have aligned them appropriately.
- It isn't necessary for each classroom to hold a full set of texts. You can have a central resource of all of the school's decodables that are signed in and out as needed.
- When it comes to 'after lunch' or home reading, you can have a number of 'book boxes' (the same number of boxes as you have classrooms). These boxes can contain decodable titles from across a range of reading

development levels marked in a way that children recognise. Children can then choose their own book from this box for in-class or home reading. At the end of the week, the box is rotated to the next classroom. In this way, every class receives a 'new' box of books each week. By the time the box comes back to your classroom again, the students will have moved to a different 'level' of decodable and so will not be re-reading the same books.

What To Do With All the Levelled Texts?

Schools have invested significant resources into their levelled texts. Sometimes this occurs at the same time that the school is beginning its structured literacy journey. While levelled texts aren't great for core instruction in a structured literacy approach, they can still be used in a number of valuable ways.

- **Guided speaking** – If you have sets of early levelled texts and they have engaging pictures, you can use them for guided speaking. More than ever before, teachers are reporting that our young children are coming to school with low levels of oral literacy proficiency. Using the books as a stimulus for oral language tasks is a great idea. You can either display one or more pictures on a screen for a whole class activity or use them in small group, oral language activities such as asking and answering questions or describing pictures. If the books have the text along the bottom of the page, just cut off the lower portion of the book and leave the pictures.
- **Cross curricula texts** – Many levelled reader series have non-fiction texts with wonderful photos and graphics. Sort your levelled texts into topics such as 'plants', 'space', 'environment', 'the ocean', or whatever else arises rather than levels. These book sets can then be accessed during cross curricula learning such as science, humanities, or arts as a stimulus for knowledge building or to be part of vocabulary or oral sentence structure work.
- **Interest-based reading** – Once you have the books sorted into topic sets, students who are ready to move on from decodables (they know the alphabetic code and can approach unfamiliar words without guessing) can read from the books regardless of 'level' for interest-based reading at school and home.
- **'Read to me' texts** – Younger students may like to take higher levelled texts home for parents to read to them as a story. If you choose this option, ensure that you communicate with families effectively so that parents understand how to use the text with their child.
- **Writing exemplars** – Some levelled texts make great, short exemplar texts for writing across a range of text types. Read them to the children and then use them to unpack the text structure and features with your class.

Sentence-Level Transcription From Decodables

We know that reading and writing are closely connected. When we teach both decoding and encoding, (reading and spelling) as reciprocal processes, we strengthen our students' learning considerably. A powerful way to enhance sentence-level proficiency is to use sentences from decodable texts for sentence-level transcription. We often assume that just because students can write words, they can write sentences. This isn't always the case. Sentence-level writing can be a complex task for our young learners. Additionally, including sentence-level writing with a high degree of scaffolding means that your students will gain confidence in using their newly acquired phonics and morphology knowledge in the context of sentences, not just words. Sentence-level transcription draws on the joint construction and supported practice sections of the explicit teaching model as outlined in Table 12.2.

Table 12.2 Sentence Level Transcription Lesson Steps

Steps	Teacher actions
Step 1 – Display a picture from the decodable texts	'Class, today we are going to write a sentence from our book'.
Step 2 – Model the language – think out loud about the picture, modelling the language you want to reinforce	'In the story, Sam was unhappy. Un means "not" or "the opposite". So if Sam was unhappy, he was not happy. Sam was unhappy because he fell in the pond'.
Step 3 – Devise a new sentence and use 'I say, you say'	'Sam fell into the pond. Say that after me. Sam fell into the pond'.
	Point to the students and have them repeat your sentence
	'Sam fell into the pond'. Point to the students and have them repeat your sentence
Step 4 – Joint Construction – with students, jointly construct the sentence on the board. Discuss punctuation, spelling, morphology, meaning, irregular high frequency words, etc. as appropriate	'What was our first word?'
	Students say 'Sam'
	'Sound out Sam with me'
	Students sound out the word sam /s/ /a/ /m/
	Teacher writes Sam on the board
	Repeat with the remaining words
Step 5 – Read the sentence	'Let's read'
	You point to the words as the students read them
Step 6 – Students write the sentence. Hide or rub the sentence off the board and ask students to write it down in their books. You do not want them copying from the board as this is a passive process. Covering rather than rubbing off means that students can 'sneak a peak' if needed. This makes it a low stakes activity and one in which every student receives support	

This sentence-level routine is versatile and can also be used to:

- Provide a 'run up' for students before a more complex writing task.
- Include writing across the curriculum such as in science, humanities, and health.
- Embed contextualised practice of concepts learned in other areas of English.
- Practise using new vocabulary or revise previously learned vocabulary.

The value of a supported sentence writing task cannot be overstated. Use the same routine regardless of age, simply increasing the sentence complexity and vocabulary of the sentence. This routine helps all students feel safe and supported as they develop their writing automaticity and using it regularly will mean that all students can be successful in sentence-level writing.

Snapshot of Practice 11 – Using Decodable Texts in the Year 1 and 2 Classroom

Alison Fahey – Year 1 and 2 Teacher

Decodable texts have been a revelation to me. I was concerned that they wouldn't be challenging, but even my very capable readers thoroughly enjoy reading them. When the decodable text is complex enough, it helps students develop fluency and comprehension. Now that they can sound out the words, they want to read at home. In the classroom, the students read decodables with partners. It took a little while for them to be familiar with the learning behaviours such as sitting close enough to their partner and following along as their partner points to the words, but with some practice the partner reading became well established.

I also connect our sentence-level transcription work to the decodables children are reading. We jointly construct a sentence on the board based on a decodable text the students are reading. Students who need a simpler approach only complete this simple sentence, but other students add a conjunction and then write the second half of the sentence on their own. This provides an extension for the students who are ready for more. It's so great to see children who wouldn't normally want to write sharing their ideas in our class Author Chair.

Alison's Advice for Other Teachers

- Match the decodables to your phonics focus.
- Group your more complex levelled texts by interest and let your students read them when they are up to it.
- Include your new vocabulary in your sentence-level work that comes from your decodable text where it matches your phonics teaching.
- Whisper phones are great to help children monitor their own reading.

Troubleshooting

Q – Some students find the sentence transcription too easy and are looking for more challenges.

A – To extend students who are ready for it, ask them to add a conjunction (and, because, so) and then write the second part of the sentence themselves. They can then share their extended sentence with a partner or the class.

Q – Some students cannot write the whole sentence that the rest of the class can write.

A – When this situation arises, it is important that your struggling students participate as much as they can in the joint construction. At the very least, they will receive additional practice in blending and segmenting and will have the chance to see different ways to spell words and review irregular high frequency words. If you have a student who cannot write the full sentence, only ask them to write at the level of transcription they currently possess. If they can only write single graphemes, have them do that. If they can only write single words, have them do that. If they can only write a three-word fragment, have them do that. It is important to meet students where they are up and the transcription routine is an easy way to do that.

Q – I want to send decodables for home reading but my school insists that I send levelled texts home.

A – The simplest thing to do is to send the book but make it clear to the parent that you do not expect the child to read it themselves. (Send some grapheme cards, word cards, and decodable texts/passages home too.) Communicate with parents what you *do* want the student to do with the levelled book. This might include:

- Discussing the pictures and making connections with their own experiences.
- Going on a 'sound' or irregular high frequency word hunt. Have students look through the book and find the 'sounds' or irregular words you are currently teaching.
- Having the parent read the book to the student.

Reflection

- How closely aligned are our decodable texts to our phonics scope and sequence?
- How do we differentiate this?
- Are we teaching both reading and writing of sentences at the same time?

- How are we making good use of our levelled texts so that we don't waste these resources?
- How are we setting our students up for success in partner reading routines? Are we providing enough instruction in these routines so that partner practice is effective?

References

Dehaene, S. (2021). *How we learn: Why brains learn better than any machine…for now.* Penguin Books.

Moats, L. C. (2020). Speech to print (3rd ed.). Paul Brooks Publishing.

Seidenberg, M. (2017). *Language at the speed of sight: How we read, why so many can't, and what can be done about it.* Basic Books.

13 Irregular High Frequency Words

A quick search online for 'reading instruction resources' will lead you to a plethora of downloadables and books dedicated to teaching 'sight words'. The practice of presenting the most frequently occurring words as whole words and expecting children to remember them as units has a strong and unfortunate history. Teachers may well have had varied experiences of this practice with some children taking to it without difficulty, progressing through the first, second, and then third 100 words, while others struggled to get past the first 20. The ability to read these 'sight words' greatly predicted the ability of the students to progress through the levels of the school's levelled reading scheme and was seen as a prerequisite to fluent reading. Children were presented with flash cards, games, and word diagrams containing boxes that they were required to 'match' to the printed words in a list (Figure 13.1).

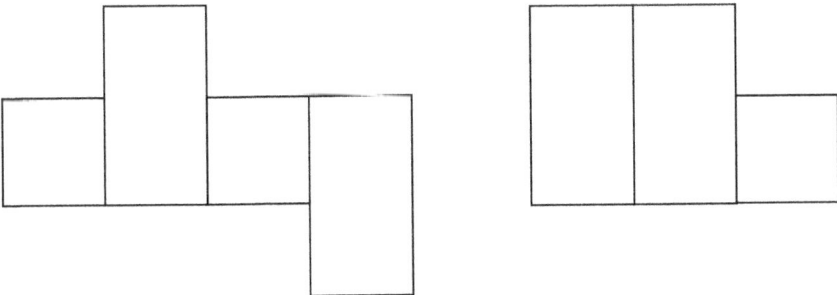

Figure 13.1 Sight Word Boxes

Practice has significantly shifted in this area in recent years. The driver of this change is the growing understanding that we don't process words as global shapes, but through the letter/sound correspondences and patterns that we have embedded in our long-term memory via repeated exposures. Even proficient readers process these correspondences. They just do it simultaneously rather than one at a time (Dehaene, 2009). Our understanding of how automatic reading develops has also evolved. Understanding that it is through knowledge of the alphabetic principle and multiple opportunities to blend words that we embed words and orthographic patterns into our long-term memory for automatic recall further supports this shift in practice.

What Irregular High Frequency Words Are

The first thing to note is that less than 4% of words in English are truly irregular when we account for phonics, morphology, and etymology (Moats, 2020). For the purposes of this section, the word 'irregular' refers to the fact that students have not yet learned the phoneme/grapheme correspondences contained in the words.

Rather than talk about 'sight words', I will refer to irregular high frequency words (IHFW) for the remainder of the chapter for reasons that will soon become clear. There are noticeable differences between the words included in the 'sight word' approach and the current recommendations for this area.

Table 13.1 Sight Words Versus IHFW

Sight word list (32 words)			IHFW list (21 words)	
a	all	on	a	he
be	as	one	be	her
I	are	said	I	his
and	At	so	of	one
in	but	they	is	said
is	for	we	the	so
it	had	with	to	they
of	have	you	was	we
that	he		all	you
the	her		as	
to	his		are	
was	not		have	

A close look at the two lists in Table 13.1 shows that both lists have words in common, but the IHFW list contains fewer words than the 'sight word' list. The difference is that the IHFW list does not contain any words that a student could sound out using their basic code knowledge. Words such as 'at', 'on', 'it', 'not', and 'but' all contain the basic alphabetic code that students learning through a systematic synthetic phonics approach learn first. The words that remain on the IHFW list, therefore, are those that contain phoneme/grapheme correspondences the students have not yet been taught. Once students learn the correspondences, the word is no longer 'irregular' and they are able to use their phonics knowledge to decode it as with any other word.

There are two main reasons to include IHFW in your teaching program.

1. They facilitate reading decodable texts. It's quite difficult to construct meaningful sentences without verbs; 'is', 'was', 'has', 'have', 'be', 'are', and 'were' are all forms of the verb 'to be'. 'He', 'her', 'they', 'their', 'me', 'you', 'I', 'we', and 'she' are all pronouns that make it possible to write more complex sentences and passages.
2. When we teach IHFW through the alphabetic principle, we help our students understand the complexity of the English alphabetic code. Students will learn very early on that the phoneme /z/ can be represented by both the letter 'z' (zip) and the letter 's' (is, has, was). They will learn that the sound /o/ can be represented by the letter 'a' (was, want) as well as the letter 'o' (hot).

In short, irregular high frequency words are words that you are expecting children to read that contain phoneme/grapheme correspondences you have not yet taught in your explicit phonics lessons.

Which Words and How?

Rather than having a list that students work through from top to bottom, it is more effective to align your IHFW teaching to the decodable texts you expect students to read. This means that students will be able to apply the new words in the context of both sentence reading and writing instead of learning a set of random words out of context. When deciding which words to teach, refer to the recommendations of the main decodable texts series you are using in your classroom. The authors of these series have carefully written their texts and chosen words to support student learning. When utilising several different series of decodable texts, it can be challenging to arrange content in a way that responds to the different sequences in the texts. To do so requires the teacher to examine each text for the included IHFW and place the texts in order so that students will have already learned the words before they encounter them.

You might also note which IHFW students are using in their writing and include those as well. However, be careful not to overload your students' working memory with too many words.

The first way to make learning IHFW easier to learn is to begin with the words that have the smallest number of irregularities.

For example, if the students have learned the basic phoneme/grapheme correspondences for 'i' and 's', there is one regular part 'i' and one irregular part (circled) in the word 'is'. i⒮

Whereas if the students have learned the basic phoneme/grapheme correspondences for 'w', 'a', and 's', there will be two irregular parts in the word 'was'. w⒜⒮

However, if students have learned the word 'is' and had ample opportunity to encounter it in both reading and writing, 'was' may only contain one irregular part. w(a)s

Similarly, let's consider the word 'the'. 'The' contains the voiced phoneme /th/ and schwa (little grunt noise that is our most common vowel). If students have learned that 'th' represents the voiced /th/, then there is only one irregular part. However, if they are not up to this learning yet, both the 'th' and the 'e' will be irregular.

We can see that there are no hard and fast rules for when phoneme/grapheme correspondences are actually irregular. It all depends on what previous learning has occurred.

The second way to make learning IHFW easier to learn is to point out the orthographic connections between words and connect new learning to established knowledge. This means that when teaching a new IHFW, it is a good idea to ask yourself which words the students already know that contain the same spelling pattern. For example, if the students have learned the word 'to', when you teach 'do', you can bring this to their attention. When they are learning the word 'she', if they have already learned 'he', you can show both words and make the connections explicit. A list of 31 common IHFW arranged into their patterns is given in Table 13.2.

Table 13.2 IHFW Arranged According to Letter Sound/Spelling Patterns

's' as the phoneme /z/	'o' as the phoneme /oa/	'ere' as the phoneme /air/
is was has as his	go so no	where there
'e' as the long /ee/	'th' as the voiced /th/	'o' as the phoneme /oo/
he she be we me	the they	to do who
've' as the phoneme /v/	'y' as the phoneme /igh/	'a' as the phoneme /o/
have give live	my by	was what want
Modal verbs		
should, could, would		
Words with common spelling patterns that will eventually be introduced in your phonics program		
all are for her or		
Words with lesson common spelling patterns		
of one said you two here were your their		

Just because words contain a less common spelling pattern, it doesn't mean that there aren't very good explanations for why the words are spelled the way they are. John Ayto's (2011) book 'Dictionary of Word Origins' is a terrific source of information about the history of words such as 'said', 'here', and 'you'. Teachers can also visit www.etymonline.com for details of the origin and history of words.

Teaching Routine

Children are ready to begin learning IHFW when they have a grasp of the basic code and are confidently blending and segmenting. Trying to teach IHFW to children before they know any phoneme/grapheme correspondences makes every single word irregular and cognitively overloading. Trying to teach them before blending and segmenting have developed means that students are left memorising strings of letters instead of thinking about how the words are constructed.

Teaching IHFW may or may not include a discussion of the origin of the word or an in-depth explanation of the phonological connections between words. Each word comes with its own history and story. Each group of students comes with differing levels of background knowledge, cognitive load, and capacity to examine words depending on their age and stage of reading development. As a teacher, use your judgement when it comes to how much or how little word exploration you include in your teaching. The teaching sequence given in Table 13.3 is a starting point and you can take it in the direction that makes sense to you.

Table 13.3 Teaching Irregular High Frequency Words Lesson Steps

Step	Teacher action
1 Say the word you are teaching. You say, I say	'Today we are going to read and spell the word "said". "Said" is a very old word that used to be pronounced "saith". We don't say that anymore, but some of the spelling has stayed the same as it was a very long time ago'.
	Point to yourself and say 'said'
	Point to the students and have them say 'said'
	Repeat this several times
2 Map the word you are teaching with lines or boxes indicating which sounds children already know	As you draw the lines, say the phonemes for the word /s/ /e/ /d/
	Then tick underneath the lines indicating which sounds the children have already learned. 'You have already learned how to write the sounds /s/ and /d/'.

Figure 13.2 Map the Word

(Continued)

Table 13.3 Teaching Irregular High Frequency Words Lesson Steps *(Continued)*

Step	Teacher action
3 Have the children sound out the word with you as you write in the graphemes they already know	'Let's sound out the word "said" together'. Students sound out the word 'said' – /s/ /e/ /d/. Write in the 's' and the 'd'

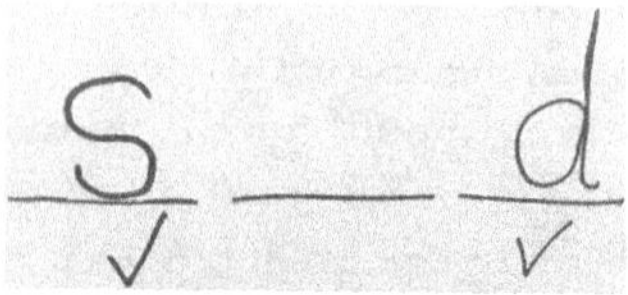

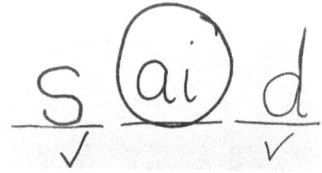

Figure 13.3 Write in the Regular Part

4 Circle the position of the unfamiliar grapheme and model how to write it. Explain the 'tricky' part of the spelling	'We know the /s/ and the /d/, but the /e/ in the middle of this word is a bit tricky (circle). Let me show you'. Write in the unfamiliar grapheme. 'We write the sound /e/ in this word using the letters "a" and "i"'.

Figure 13.4 Write in the Irregular Part

5 Write the word underneath sounding out as you write	

Figure 13.5 Rewrite the Word
'Watch as I write the word again /s/ /e/ /d/'

(Continued)

Table 13.3 Teaching Irregular High Frequency Words Lesson Steps *(Continued)*

Step	Teacher action
6 Have the students map the word on their boards or in their books with lines and then write the word underneath as demonstrated	'It is your turn to write "said" now'.
	'Start by mapping the word with lines. Let's sound it out. /s/ /e/ /d/. Show me your boards'. Have students chin their boards so you can ensure that they have the correct number of phonemes
	'Ok, now write the letters onto your lines, remembering the tricky part'.
	'Show me your boards'.
	You might leave the word on the board the first couple of times you practice, but ensure that you remove this scaffold in time so that students are drawing on their memories for the spelling of the 'tricky part' and not just copying

Practising Irregular High Frequency Words

Instruction in IHFW does not end with the above introduction. It is necessary to provide opportunities for practice both in and out of context to help students embed the spelling of IHFW into long-term memory.

As discussed in Chapter 8, independent activities that do not provide the opportunity for error correction are not a great option for young children. Consolidation only occurs when students pay attention, experience error correction feedback, and are engaged in thinking. To maximise consolidation, it is best to provide adult led review sessions where knowledge and skill are rehearsed and reviewed.

Some of the ways to provide this rehearsal and review are discussed next.

Decontextualised Practice

- Daily review sessions led by the teacher where you engage children in both reading and spelling (not copying) of the IHFW they are currently learning.
- Bring small groups to a table for guided, explicit practice with an adult as time allows.
- Partner work where students take turns to read a list of words and then give each other a 'spelling test', with feedback.
- Computerised practice of IHFWs. If choosing this option, ensure that the software isn't introducing words the children haven't learned yet reinforces the phonological aspects of the words (sounds).
- Short games with a helper such as bingo or partner games such as '4 in a row'.

Contextualised Practice

- Reading texts (decodable sentences, passages, or books).
- Using those texts to go on word hunts and then writing down a list of words that students then share with a friend, taking turns to read.
- Including words for review in daily transcription and shared writing lessons.

If you find that you have differentiated groups in your class, it's perfectly fine to have everyone in the same review session and present content for all groups. Just remember that exposure alone is unlikely to result in new learning. Even if less developed students see the 'higher' groups' words time and again, this is not a replacement for the explicit teaching outlined in this chapter.

When it comes to home learning and parent expectations, it is important to help them understand that the methodology around this has changed. Parents who have had older children go through school bringing home 'sight word lists' may well expect that to be a core part of instruction from day one. Make a short video to show parents how to tackle these words. It would be a shame to have your hard work in the classroom undone by home practice that encourages memorising from sight.

Snapshot of Practice 12 – Teaching and Consolidating High Frequency Words

Larissa Marchant – Foundation Teacher and Deputy Principal

I have changed the way I teach irregular high frequency words over the years. I used to do a 'sight word' program with whole words but have changed that now to a structured, explicit approach where we use the alphabetic code to explain words and decode. Instead of just having a list of words that children learn 'by sight', I choose the words to teach that align with our phonics program and the decodable texts we are reading. Many of the words that we used to think of as 'sight words' can just be sounded out (such as 'it', 'and', 'on', 'that'), so we look at where they fit into the phonics sequence and just teach children to sound them out. Over time, the students become more automatic. When it comes to irregular words, we:

- Identify the regular and irregular parts of the word
- Make links to other words with the same pattern
- Practice the words as many times as the students need.

I have tried many different things over the years to reinforce irregular high frequency words. I've tried games and activities in play-based learning but found that not all children will engage sufficiently with this to transfer the words to their long-term memory for reading and spelling. Explicit instruction is important to ensure that every student learns well. The most effective thing I have found is to have the students come to a small group table where I lead them in practice. They both read and spell the words they are practising, and I can make sure that I target specific words to specific children, giving them personal feedback along the way. The other thing that I have found worked well is differentiated dictation booklets to match the needs of the students. Students having to retrieve the words to use in structured sentence work helped them be able to transfer their knowledge in their own writing.

Larissa's Advice for Other Teachers

- Avoid tracing and copying activities. This is passive and doesn't require children to actually think about the words.
- While you might include the words in your play-based learning opportunities, this doesn't replace explicit teaching with structured practice at the word and sentence levels. Play based learning is great, but explicit teaching makes sure that everyone is learning.
- It's ok to try a new way to teach. Just be ready to change things if what you are doing isn't resulting in great learning for students. If something doesn't work, it doesn't mean you are a bad teacher. Trial and error is part of the experience.

Troubleshooting

Q – Students just can't remember the words.

A – Try slowing down the number of words that are introduced at once and providing extra consolidation time. Ensure that students have a firm grasp on phoneme/grapheme correspondence and blending and segmenting. If this is 'wobbly', go back to this instruction and pick up IHFW instruction when knowledge and skill are firmer. Increase the number of repetitions and reduce instances of copying. It is better to support students to recall the spellings from their long-term memory rather than have them copy from the board.

Q – Students try to sound out the IHFW as if they are fully decodable.

A – It can be helpful to review IHFW before students read their text. You might also have them go on a 'word hunt' before reading to front-load the fact that these words are tackled in a slightly different way from other words. If students are reading from a printed passage or text, have them circle or underline the IHFW before reading. It's much better for them to find the words themselves than to present them with a pre-marked passage simply because when students find the words, they are actively engaging with the text. When it is pre-marked, they aren't doing that.

Reflection

- How am I aligning IHFW instruction to the decodable texts my students are learning?
- Do my students have the necessary, prerequisite skills and knowledge to effectively learn IHFWs?
- Does our school have consistent methods across classrooms of teaching IHFW?
- How have I communicated our updated methods of teaching with parents?
- How have I supported all classroom-based staff to feel confident teaching IHFW through a phonological and morphological route instead of through learning as whole units?
- How am I conducting formative assessment to ensure that students are developing a solid grounding in this area?

References

Ayto, J. (2011). *Dictionary of word origins*. Skyhorse Publishing.

Dehaene, S. (2009). *Reading in the brain: The new science of how we read*. New York: Penguin Books.

Moats, L. C. (2020) *Speech to print* (3rd ed.). Paul Brooks Publishing.

14 Text Level Reading

While there has been an enormous (and pleasing) push for students in the early years to be reading decodable texts, we must not forget that the inclusion of a range of texts is an important feature of instruction. As soon as students are equipped with the skills and knowledge to do so, we should have them reading decodable and mostly decodable texts. Of course, we should be reading rich texts *to* students from day one right across the curriculum and making these texts available when they are able to tackle them for themselves, even if that requires scaffolding. After all, engagement with texts is a wonderful way to develop oral comprehension in preparation for the day when students will be reading these rich texts by themselves.

The key to moving into wider and more independent reading is engaging students in practices that prepare students for 'self-teaching'. David Share's self-teaching hypothesis (Share, 1999) provides an important understanding of the skills and knowledge required to move into reading more complex texts (read more about this in Chapter 5). Some of your students will develop this ability seemingly effortlessly, others will be accelerated by intentional teaching, and a third group will require explicit instruction in tackling unknown words. Your knowledge of your students' learning profiles and knowing how to respond to their individual needs will help you meet each student where they are up to. As with everything, attending to this area of instruction is not a one-size-fits-all proposition.

Moving on From Decodable Texts

There are three types of texts to include in our instruction. The first is decodable text, the second is what I call 'mostly decodable' text, and finally there are rich, uncontrolled texts. Most students will read all three types of texts at different points in their reading development journey. The timing of when children will engage with each type of text will vary from child to child and how we use these texts at different points across the early years will also vary.

Let's begin by examining exactly what each type of text is.

DOI: 10.4324/9781003244189-18

Fully Decodable Texts – Fully decodable texts are texts that are controlled for complexity at the phonics, vocabulary, and syntax level. They provide an opportunity for students to practise reading with the graphemes and irregular high frequency words they have learned. They also assist students to build their reading stamina. Chapter 12 explores this more and describes how to use them in your classroom.

Mostly Decodable Texts – This term is my invention and I find it a useful one to distinguish between a text that will contain zero surprises and one that has a certain number of unfamiliar words and/or graphemes. In terms of the ratio between known and unknown, my conservative estimate is 90% known to 10% unknown. This number just makes sense to me as a way to support student cognitive load and not interfere with fluency and comprehension. You may have a different view on this and I invite you to manage it as makes sense to you. Very often, the existing levelled texts in our schools are great as mostly decodable texts. More complex 'decodable' texts can also fall into this category. Other sources of these texts can be online platforms focused on knowledge building.

A text may be fully decodable for one child and mostly decodable for another. It really depends on the background knowledge of the student. This can be the case for any text, so it's important to recognise that the texts themselves are just texts. The defining factor about decodability is determined by the knowledge and skill of the student.

Uncontrolled Texts – Uncontrolled texts are just that. These rich texts have been written with language and story/information in mind, not phonics. Examples of these texts are chapter books and informational texts. It is important that we read uncontrolled texts *to* students all the way through the early years and facilitate student engagement with them in a range of contexts. If a student wants to borrow uncontrolled texts from the school library to look at the pictures or read them with an adult, that should be encouraged. Limiting a child's access to rich text because they cannot yet decode them sends the unhelpful message to the student that they are not clever enough for those texts. We need to foster students' relationships with books, adjusting expectations of how much they decode themselves in accordance with their skills.

Uncontrolled texts play an important part in the development of language and text knowledge. Using these texts as the model for the vocabulary, language functions and features, we want students to develop a critical part of literacy instruction, both for reading and for writing.

It is important to recognise that there is no discrete point at which students move from engaging with one text to another. There is likely overlap in the use of these texts and, ideally, teachers include all three in instruction. Of course, that means we need to adjust the scaffolding and support provided to match the students' level of knowledge and skill.

To illustrate what this looks like in practice, let us consider the needs of three different students and how a teacher may respond to meet their needs (Table 14.1).

Table 14.1 Responding to Student Needs in Text Use across the Curriculum

Student profile	Teaching response
Student A is learning the phoneme/grapheme correspondences of the basic code. They can blend words independently and are developing increased independence in reading sentences	Fully Decodable Texts – used as core instruction in the classroom as well as for home reading
	Mostly Decodable Texts – Student A's teacher uses mostly decodable texts as shared texts across the curriculum to ensure that the students are developing their knowledge of curriculum concepts, vocabulary, and language. Student A is not expected to decode these texts for themselves, but rather follow along as the teacher reads. They then engage in partner talk and classroom work based on the content of these texts
	Uncontrolled Texts – Student A has full access to a range of fiction and non-fiction texts from the school and classroom library for home reading with parents at home and quiet reading time in the classroom. Student A's teacher reads to students several times a day from these texts, including in science, health, and history/geography classes
Student B has mastered the basic code and is learning multiple representations of the extended/complex code. They can read IHFW by sight and are confident to read paragraphs containing the phonics that they are familiar with. When they approach an unknown word, Student B can use their phonics knowledge to partially decode the word and they are growing in confidence to be able to complete the 'self-teaching' required to work out the pronunciation of the word on their own	Fully Decodable Texts – used as core instruction in the classroom. These texts align with the phoneme/grapheme correspondences the class is learning and contain a range of sentence structures and Tier 2 vocabulary
	Mostly Decodable Texts – because Student B has shown that they are ready for 'self-teaching', their teacher knows that they are able to manage these texts without difficulty. To support their use across the curriculum, Student B's teacher pre-teaches any 'tricky' words that contain unfamiliar graphemes or vocabulary before having students read the text with a partner. Student B takes 'mostly decodable' texts home for home reading
	Uncontrolled Texts – Student B has full access to a range of fiction and non-fiction texts from the school and classroom library for home reading with parents and classroom quiet reading time. At home, Student B shares the reading with their parents. Sometimes they read aloud for short periods of time and other times their parent reads to them. Student B's teacher reads to students several times a day from these texts, including in English, science, health, and history/geography classes

(Continued)

174 Structured Literacy Practices

Table 14.1 Responding to Student Needs in Text Use across the Curriculum *(Continued)*

Student profile	Teaching response
Like Student B, Student C has mastered the basic code and is learning the same multiple representations of the extended/complex code as Student B. However, this has come about through intensive and regular Tier 2 support both in and out of the classroom. Student C sometimes still requires support to distinguish between IHFW and 'regular' words and tends to guess when they come across an unfamiliar word	Fully Decodable Texts – used as core instruction in the classroom *as well as for home reading*. These texts align with the phoneme/grapheme correspondences the class is learning and contain a range of sentence structures and Tier 2 vocabulary. Student C has the opportunity to read these texts multiple times including in the regular classroom lesson and also with their teacher after lunch or with a classroom assistant at another time in the day
	Mostly Decodable Texts – because Student C isn't quite ready for mostly decodable texts, their teacher ensures that there is sufficient scaffolding when they are read in class. To support their use across the curriculum, Student C's teacher pre-teaches any 'tricky' words that contain unfamiliar graphemes or vocabulary. They then make sure that Student C has a strong reading partner to read these texts with or supports them in small group reading with an adult during the lessons where they are used
	Student C's teacher knows that they will likely need additional support to learn the important 'self-teaching' needed to read more complex texts on their own. As such, the teacher explicitly models what to do when an unfamiliar word appears in a text, including how to think about the structure of the word and its meaning within the sentence
	Uncontrolled Texts – Student C has full access to a range of fiction and non-fiction texts from the school and classroom library for home reading with parents and classroom quiet reading time. Student C's teacher reads to students several times a day from these texts, including in English, science, health, and history/geography classes

Including Mostly Decodable Texts Across the Curriculum

'Every lesson is a language lesson' was the mantra of the English as an additional language or dialect (EAL/D) advisors when I worked in remote schools. They were right. I would also add that every lesson can be a reading (and writing) lesson. When we remember that 'reading' is not just about decoding but also about vocabulary, sentence structure, parts of speech, text structure and pragmatics, any time we read texts to and with students across the curriculum, we are building their understanding and skill in language and reading. This means that whether we are helping students understand the vocabulary and structure of a written maths question, unpacking an information text in science, or helping students find connections between a picture book and the concepts they are learning in history, we are immersing them in the world of language and reading. All too often, reading and writing are confined to the English Lesson. This is a great shame and means that we are missing important opportunities for teaching and learning. The use of mostly decodable texts across the curriculum can help students engage widely with texts across the curriculum.

Lesson Structure with a Mostly Decodable Text

Preparing to Teach

It is important to be aware of the current phonics knowledge your students possess before engaging with this lesson structure. Preparation is also key. Do not try and 'wing it' when students are at a critical stage of learning. To prepare well for using a mostly decodable text, it is necessary to:

- Examine the text and identify which words may pose some difficulty for students either because they contain graphemes/morphemes students will be unfamiliar with or are words that the students may not know the meaning of.
- Decide whether you need to adjust some of the wording to reduce 'irregularity' or whether the ratio of 'regular' to 'irregular/unknown' words is within the range that will not tax student cognitive load to the point that they cannot access meaning. This will vary from classroom to classroom, so make your decision based on your knowledge of your students. Remember, you are looking for the 'sweet' spot. Not too easy, not too hard.
- Identify which students will be able to read the text with a partner and which students will need the support of an adult either to decode themselves or have the text read to them.

Let's consider the example below. A year 1 class has been learning about narrative structure and descriptive language through the text 'Joe and the Stars' (Cummings & Brecon, 2021). The teacher has decided to build background knowledge about stars through the use of a 'mostly decodable' text from the ReadWorks website.

The students in this Year 1 class have learned one representation of 42 of the phonemes of English (the basic code plus ar, or, air, er, ou, oy, ay, ee, igh, oa, oo, a_e, e_e, i_e, o_e, u_e) as well as a range of irregular high frequency words. They are blending and segmenting with automaticity.

The teacher would like the students to read the text from ReadWorks with a partner. Having examined the text, the teacher has identified that there are several words that many students may find tricky as they contain graphemes that have not been taught explicitly yet. There are no issues with vocabulary in this text.

Having examined the text and planned for the scaffolding and support in the lesson, the teacher is ready to teach the lesson as given in Table 14.2.

You might also wish to adjust a text based on the vocabulary it contains. While we do not want to 'dumb down' texts, we do want to consider cognitive load and accessibility when planning for lessons. As with the phonics content, the level of adjustment required will vary from classroom to classroom. Keep in mind that children's reading comprehension and ability to engage with more complex texts depends on the scaffolded interaction with 'stretch texts'. When texts are too easy, there is simply no learning and growth.

Table 14.2 A Lesson with Mostly Decodable Texts

Steps	Teach actions
1 Pre-reading activities. Unpack 'tricky' or unfamiliar words for students pointing out the phoneme/grapheme connections, morphology, and meaning (10 minutes)	'Class, we have been reading the book, "Joe and Stars". In this book, Joe loves to look at the stars at night. Today we are going to learn about what stars are and why we can only see them at night.'
	'You know how to read most of the words in the text we are going to read, but there are some that might be a bit tricky. Let's look at them together before we read.'
	Group words that have similar features and structures and explain the graphemes/morphemes/structure of the word
	e.g. "The words *both*", *only*, and *closer* all have the letter 'o' representation the long /oa/ sound. Let's sound those words out (write the words on the board as the students segment them orally)
	both – /b/ /oa/ /th/
	only – /oa/ /n/ /l/ /ee/
	closer – /k/ /l/ /oa/ /s/ /er/
	Repeat this with the other words
	m**a**ny
	b**ur**ning
	evening
	oth**er**
	Point out to students that there are two different representations of the phoneme /er/ in this text. 'There are two different graphemes for the phoneme /er/ in our reading today. There is 'e-r' that we have already learned and there is 'u-r' that we haven't learned yet'.
	You may choose to have the students highlight or underline the unfamiliar graphemes to prompt them as they read

(Continued)

Table 14.2 A Lesson with Mostly Decodable Texts *(Continued)*

Steps	Teach actions
2 Partner reading. Keep those students not yet ready for this level of decoding with you and read *to/with* them. Partner remainder of the class with more and less developed students (5 minutes)	'Class, it is now time to read your text about stars with your partner. Remember, when you come to a word you aren't sure of, sound it out. If you are stuck and can't remember what the sounds are, ask your partner. If you are both stuck, ask a friend. Remember that good readers don't guess words. If your partner makes a mistake on a word, encourage them to sound it out and then help them if they need it'. Have students read the text with a partner, swapping readers each paragraph, while you (or your paraprofessional colleague) read with students who might need additional support. Vary this support to meet the needs of the students
3 Teacher reads the piece aloud for fluency and consolidation of concepts (5 minutes)	'Class. It is my turn to read this text to you now. Please put your finger under the first word and follow along as I read'. Read the text aloud modelled with fluency and prosody (phrasing and expression)
4 Students re-read the text (5 minutes)	It is now your turn to read again. If you read first last time, it's your turn to read second. As you read, I'd like you to think about these questions that I have written on the board. Read each question one at a time and have students repeat the question aloud for their partners • What are stars? • Why can't we see stars in the daytime?
5 Post-reading – think/pair discussion (5 minutes)	'We have now read this text three times. I'd like you to talk with your partners about the questions you were thinking about while you read. What are stars and why can't we see stars in the daytime? Remember to give your answers to your partner in full sentences'. After the partner talk is finished, call on non-volunteers to share their answers with the group
6 Checking for understanding (5 minutes)	Have students write two or three sentences in their books or on their boards so that you can see that they have understood the reading

Practices That Promote Fluency

Fluency is not an activity we do, but the result of practices that support students to develop automatic, accurate, and expressive reading. We don't *do* fluency. We promote it through:

- Ensuring strong word-level reading through our phonics lessons and the inclusion of both blending and segmenting daily.

- Promoting language learning through explicit vocabulary instruction and the creation of a language-rich environment. After all, students will read words more fluently if they already have them in their spoken vocabulary. This is also critical for students to be able to take advantage of 'self-teaching'.
- Providing appropriate, explicit morphology instruction from the Foundation year. This teaching can be simply embedded inside phonics lessons to start with and then deepened a little more in Year 1 and Year 2.
- Ensuring that you are aware of your students' reading needs and goals so that you can make them aware of what they need to do to improve their reading. Specific and effective feedback is required to help them know when they are on the right track and when they need to adjust.
- Modelling appropriate prosody through oral reading daily and making students aware of the role of punctuation.

To identify if your students are making appropriate progress in this area, it is important to consider factors across all three components of fluency: accuracy, automaticity, and prosody.

Accuracy – Teachers are very used to examining the accuracy rate of students' text-level reading. It is a cornerstone of benchmark reading assessment. However, the way that we examine student errors has now changed and when we are seeking to provide instruction that promotes fluency, it is necessary to carefully consider not just how many errors a student makes, but what the cause of the errors is. These may be due to:

- Not recognising learned graphemes in the context of text-level reading.
- Not having sufficient flexibility with the complexity of the alphabetic code to 'self-teach' when encountering an unfamiliar word. For example, you may have taught that 'ow' can represent both /ou/ and /oa/ in your phonics lessons, but the student might not be tapping into this knowledge when presented with an unfamiliar word in the text they are reading.
- Not having sufficient practice in reading multisyllable words to be able to think about both phonics and morphology when reading these words in a text. They may be able to read the word 'open' on their own, but lack the strategies to read 'reopening' in a text.
- Having been previously taught ineffective word attack strategies such as looking at the pictures and looking at the first letter of the word to 'have a guess'. If these habits are ingrained, it can take time to redirect and build new habits.

Once you have identified the reason for the inaccuracy in students' reading, you can adjust instruction to meet their needs.

Automaticity – As we saw in Chapter 1, automatic, effortless reading comes from the development of orthographic mapping. Strong instruction that helps students understand how our language works coupled with repeated decoding and encoding of words (reading and spelling) forms the

Table 14.3 National Assessment of Educational Progress Fluency Scale (Pinnell, 1995)

		National assessment of educational progress fluency scale
Fluent	Level 4	Reads primarily in larger, meaningful phrase groups. Although some regressions, repetitions, and deviations from the text may be present, these do not appear to detract from the overall structure of the story. Preservation of the author's syntax is consistent. Some or most of the story is read with expressive interpretation
Fluent	Level 3	Read primarily in three- or four-word phrase groups. Some small groupings may be present. However, the majority of the phrasing seems appropriate and preserves the syntax of the author. Little or no expressive interpretation is present
Non-fluent	Level 2	Reads primarily with two-word phrases with some three- or four-word groupings. Some word-by-word reading may be present. Word groupings may seem awkward and unrelated to the larger context of a sentence or passage
Non-fluent	Level 1	Reads primarily word by word. Occasional two-word or three-word phrases may occur, but these are infrequent and/or do not preserve meaningful syntax

foundation for this work. It is important to note that the alphabetic principle is just one part of this picture. Morphology also has a place for its impact on the reading of multisyllable words.

Prosody – The ability to read with expression and accurate phrasing is the final piece of the picture when it comes to fluency. To ascertain where your students sit in their prosody development, you might refer to the 1992 National Assessment of Educational Progress (NAEP).

This fluency scale describes qualitative indicators of fluency development seen in Table 14.3 (Pinnell et al., 1995).

Practices That Promote Reading Comprehension

Like fluency, comprehension is not something that we do. It is a by-product of strong reading instruction overall and the development of background knowledge to enable the student to engage with the text.

We promote it by:

- Actively building background knowledge.
- Explicitly teaching vocabulary and creating a language-rich environment.
- Making the links between students' existing knowledge and the content of the text explicit.
- Explicitly teaching about syntax (sentence structure) and parts of speech.
- Ensuring that word-level reading is accurate and automatic so that cognitive energy can be freed up to think about what is being read.

Just as with fluency, the errors students encounter provide the guidance for where to target instruction. Students' difficulties could be related to:

- Unfamiliar vocabulary.
- Not having sufficient decoding skills to read automatically.
- Not being able to maintain awareness of pronouns from sentence to sentence.
- Not actively making connections between the macro- and micro-structures of a text. For example, a student may not yet be able to relate an event of a story to where it fits in with the whole text (a key skill in discussing the beginning, middle, or end of a story).
- Developmental language disorder or some other language-related difficulty. If you have ruled out a decoding basis for students' reading comprehension challenges, make a referral to your school's speech therapy services.

Snapshot of Practice 13 – Comprehension in Foundation

Liz Foley – Early Years Teacher

Decoding had the biggest impact on how well my Foundation students were comprehending what they were reading, but I still programmed for oral comprehension work. A lot of this work has had an oral focus because that's where it all starts. We spent lots of time on reflection and discussion/writing about the content of the texts we were reading, whether that was using decodable or picture books. Part of our lessons has been to put both decodable texts and rich text on the screen. I then model how to engage with the text, exploring the features and language. We have also had a significant focus on building background knowledge with hands-on experiences so that the children understand what they are reading.

Liz's Advice for Other Teachers

- Make sure you build a rich language environment. Don't simplify your classroom talk.
- Model language and text interactions.
- Focus on building strong decoding to facilitate fluent reading.
- Encourage students to ask questions when they don't understand something. This is the beginning of monitoring their comprehension of reading.

Snapshot of Practice 14 – Teaching Morphology to Boost Comprehension

April Brown – Year 2 Teacher

One of the things that has moved the needle on comprehension for our students has been teaching morphology. Because we have taught suffixes explicitly, students know when and how things happen. I use a mix of intentional teaching and incidental inclusion. The intentional teaching is often closely connected with.

vocabulary instruction, and I draw attention to suffixes in stories and writing. It's important to check what students need to know for the texts you are using and teach that. Connect this as much as possible to spelling patterns. I'm not sure that morphology needs to be taught as a stand-alone lesson all the time in the early years. Our students are doing really well having it embedded in other areas of learning.

Snapshot of Practice 15 – Building Background Knowledge

Suzanne Powell – Foundation Teacher

We have had many conversations about comprehension over the years, moving from strategies to vocabulary and oral language development. Knowledge building has also been a huge part of this work. To make sure that children understand the texts, I spend time every day building the field about the concepts and language structures and features of the texts we read. The impact on students has been amazing. I have never had students being able to talk and write so well. The focus on sentences and writing positively impacted their ability to comprehend what we were reading and exploring. You can use decodables for basic comprehension work by asking students to think about 'who is…', 'what was…', and 'when did…'. Once you have done this, have the students go to their desks and draw and label everything they can remember from the decodable sentence/short passage before describing it to a partner.

Suzanne's Advice for Other Teachers

- Children can't comprehend a text that they don't know anything about, so you need to build knowledge.
- Don't try and make a full 'comprehension' lesson out of decodables. While they can be a stepping stone to reading comprehension, the main focus is decoding.
- Don't try and use several texts to teach one concept. Instead, embed and reinforce several concepts with one text.
- Remember that expressive and receptive language skills go hand in hand, so include them both in all lessons.

Troubleshooting

Q – My students seem to be following along with mostly decodable texts ok, but are struggling to discuss what is in the reading.

A – The text may be too complex for where they are up to at the moment. Perhaps switch to a simpler text and then reassess. Your students may also benefit from a little more time spent unpacking and practising with the vocabulary from the text and any 'tricky words'.

Q – Most of my students are ready for mostly decodable texts, but I have some who just aren't. How do I encourage them to participate in reading across the curriculum?

A – If students don't have enough knowledge of the alphabetic code and/or are not blending appropriately, do not put them in the position of asking them to read. Keep on reading *to* them and having them follow along so that they can engage with the language and ideas of the text. At the same time, keep building knowledge and skills so that they are narrowing the gap between their decoding and their comprehension.

Q – Where do I find appropriate 'mostly decodable' texts?

A – Your existing levelled readers (particularly the non-fiction titles) make great mostly decodable texts; however, you will need to examine them carefully to ensure that there are not too many 'irregularities' for your students. Big books, websites, online encyclopaedias, and non-fiction texts written for children can also form part of these resources. Whichever texts you choose, be clear about how you will use them to the greatest effect. There is nothing wrong with reading these *to* children until they can read them for themselves.

Reflection

- How am I embedding the three different types of texts across the curriculum for my students?
- What data/observations am I using to determine when a student is ready to move on to reading mostly decodable texts on their own?
- How often am I including the reading of the uncontrolled text to my students across the curriculum?
- How am I matching the type of text provided for home reading with my students' current level of reading development?
- How is our school ensuring consistency in these matters across classes and the school?

References

Cummings, P., & Brecon, C. (2021). *Joe and the stars*. Scholastic Press.

Pinnell, G. S., & Others. (1995). *Listening to Children Read Aloud: Data from NAEP's Integrated Reading PerforMance Record (IRPR) at Grade 4*. Center for the Assessment of Educational Progress. Retrieved April 7, 2022, from https://files.eric.ed.gov/fulltext/ED378550.pdf

ReadWorks Inc. (2021). 'Why don't we see the stars in the daytime?' https://www.readworks.org

Share, D. (1999). Phonological recoding and orthographic learning: A direct test of the self teaching hypothesis. *Journal of Experimental Child Psychology*, 72, 95–129. Retrieved May 11, 2021, from https://citeseerx.ist.psu.edu/viewdoc/download?doi=10.1.1.540.6045&rep=rep1&type=pdf

15 Skills-Based Assessment

Assessment is a key part of any structured literacy approach. It helps us find out where our students are up to so that we can provide appropriate instruction, tells us where they are sitting in relation to other children their age, and, most importantly, assists us to measure the impact of our teaching. Until recently, the main method of reading assessment in most schools has been benchmark assessments aligned with a levelled reading program. These assessments identified what instructional and independent 'reading level' students were currently reading at. They were based on the assumption that children would use a range of 'cues' to decode words, with the benchmark assessment identifying student errors to understand where difficulties were occurring. The levels of the texts used were not controlled for phonics knowledge, but rather vocabulary and text complexity. Unfortunately, the 'cues' previously taught and assessed are ineffective for developing strong reading skills for many students and assessing with benchmark assessment doesn't give us the complete picture of a student's reading development.

Many teachers and schools are now seeking alternatives to benchmark assessment and moving to a skills based approach to reading assessment. This chapter will outline several factors in choosing assessment, understanding the purpose and methodology in assessing, and considering 'achievement checkpoints' across the first three years of school.

Assessing Decoding

We know that reading comprehension in the early years of school is heavily influenced by a child's ability to decode (Moats, 2020). As such, decoding is a major focus of reading assessment in the early years. When we consider the assessment we conduct to explore decoding, it's important to understand the knowledge and skill that we will be assessing. This includes:

- Phoneme/grapheme correspondence
- Oral blending
- Blending with graphemes

- Blending with pseudo words
- Segmenting with graphemes (optional)

Assessing Phoneme/Grapheme Correspondence

To determine whether a student has sound phoneme/grapheme correspondences, we need to be clear about what we are looking for. With what degree of automaticity can the student identify the phoneme that corresponds with the graphemes you are asking them about? Is their response lightning fast or are they spending time 'umming' and looking at the ceiling? Can the student both recognise and recall the correspondences? That is, can they say the correct phoneme/s when you show a grapheme and write the correct grapheme/s when you say a phoneme?

Blending

While we include graphemes in blending exercises as soon as students know a few correspondences, most children will blend orally before they do so with graphemes. That is, if you say /d/ /o/ /g/, the student will be able to tell you that the word is 'dog'. It is a good idea to include a few words for oral blending in your assessment so that you can identify when students have reached this important milestone and provide additional support to those who have not. Once students have learned to blend orally and they know some phoneme/grapheme correspondences, you can begin to assess blending with graphemes. The ability to do this effectively is heavily dependent on having strong phoneme/grapheme correspondences, so ensure that students are strong in the correspondences you are including in the assessment. If a student is wobbly on b/d, it's unlikely that they will be able to consistently read words containing these letters. When assessing blending, monitor whether students are sounding out one phoneme at a time or whether they are blending in their head and then telling you the whole word. This is an important milestone in the development of automatic word-level decoding.

Another important milestone in word-level decoding is when students begin to be able to decode pseudo words (also called nonsense words or alien words). This can be a contentious point for some commentators who claim that structured literacy teachers are teaching children to read nonsense and are not focused on meaning. This is far from the truth. Pseudo words provide certainty that students are indeed blending using phonics knowledge and not just recalling a word that has been orthographically mapped. Students do not become confused by this and as pseudo words are only seen once, there is no danger of these becoming mixed up with 'real words'. The ability to read unknown words, words from other languages, names, Dr Seuss books and to break words into syllables for easier decoding depends on the ability to blend things that may not immediately make sense. Pseudo words for assessment purposes are an important inclusion in any decoding assessment.

To truly say that a student has a depth of knowledge and skill, I like to know that the student can both blend and segment (spell) with the phoneme/grapheme correspondences they have been learning. While the blending assessment is done one on one, the segmenting assessment can be done whole class or whole group. Simply read out a list of words containing the correspondences you have been teaching and include some pseudo words (tell the students that's what they are) for a quick, simple assessment.

Assessing Fluency and Comprehension

As we have seen, fluency is made up of accuracy, automaticity, and prosody. When assessing early years reading, we might consider several levels of fluency.

Accuracy – how accurately are students identifying phoneme/grapheme correspondences, reading individual words, and decoding sentences?

Automaticity – how speedy and effortless is the connection of phonemes and graphemes correspondences, word-level decoding, and text-level reading? What is the student's reading rate at the text level?

Prosody – how smooth is the phrasing of sentences and texts? How well is the student exhibiting appropriate expression when reading sentences and texts?

The most easily quantifiable measure of fluency is reading rate. It is the measure that we can have an unambiguous 'score' for. However, all three elements of fluency are important and having all team members, including classroom assistants, with a clear understanding of expectations will mean greater consistency for students.

Text-Level Assessment

In my experience, there is little to be gained in formally assessing at text level until students can read at approximately 40–50 words per minute. Until students reach this point in development, individual assessment at the grapheme and word level combined with teacher observation during classroom activities is sufficient to monitor student progress. However, once students have learned a significant amount of the complex code and are reading at 40–50 words per minute, it is worth adding text-level monitoring to their assessment. I am not saying that it is wrong to assess at text level one on one before this point, but that I don't think you don't have to.

Questions to Consider When Assessing Fluency in Text-Level Assessment

- At what rate is the student reading? (Are you timing?)
- Are they reading with appropriate expression?
- Are they reading with appropriate prosody (phrasing)?

- Are they attending to punctuation?
- What kinds of words are interrupting fluency? (Multi-syllable? Words with particular suffixes? Loan words from other languages?)
- When errors have been made, what is the cause of the errors? (Omitting words, substituting words, reading only the first part of the word and then guessing the rest)

Part of benchmark reading assessment has involved asking 'comprehension questions' and using these to determine how well a student is 'comprehending' what they are reading. Some benchmark assessments even claim to be able to identify which comprehension skills a student is using in their reading to allow teachers to focus on developing further skills. The challenge with this approach is that assessing comprehension is not as simple a task as many teachers believe. The National Reading Panel (NICHD, 2000) found that viewing comprehension as a purely strategies based activity is misleading. Yes, some skills are valuable in building comprehension (summarising, identifying the main idea); however, comprehension is more influenced by background knowledge, vocabulary, and knowledge of syntax than it is the ability to use a range of 'strategies'. As such, it is difficult to reliably assess comprehension as a transferrable skill. At a basic level, you might ask the student some literal questions or ask them to retell the passage they have just read. Ascertaining a student's ability to infer though is more difficult as inference relies heavily on background knowledge. So, when assessing comprehension, how do we know if a student's inability to answer questions is because they do not know how to infer or because they lack the background knowledge to infer about the passage they have read? In the early years, I think that it is much more useful to focus on assessing decoding in one-to-one assessments and use in-class activities and tasks specifically designed around a particular text you are studying to monitor language and comprehension growth.

Regardless of which approach you take to this, there are some important questions to consider.

- What level of comprehension are you hoping to measure? (literal, inferential)
- Can the student recall the facts or events in the texts?
- Can the student display inferential understanding? (once background knowledge and vocabulary have been established)
- Can the student infer at the local level (using pronouns to track meaning, inferring the meaning of unfamiliar words, filling in unstated information)?
- Can the student infer at the global level (knowing how part of the text relates to the whole and talking about how a character develops through a text)?

Further Considerations for Reading Assessment

Choosing Assessment Tools

The challenge many schools face in moving away from benchmark assessments is what to do instead. There is no one perfect tool that will answer all of your assessment questions, so being clear on what information you need and what your school's needs are before implementing a new tool is critical.

Consider the following:

- Does the tool answer our assessment questions?
- How much time does it take to administer?
- Does it help us understand where students are up to and align with our phonics and reading approach so that our next teaching steps are clear?
- How easy is it for our teachers to administer compared with our previous tools? (teacher cognitive overload is important to consider)
- How will we ensure consistency and reliability across classes with this tool?
- Do we need to have additional qualifications to purchase and use this tool or is it available for in-school use?
- Is this a screener or assessment? What do we really need?
- How easy will it be for our teachers to analyse and interpret data to inform their teaching?
- How often is the tool designed to be administered? Does this fit with our school's desired assessment schedule?

If you have the option of more than one tool, you might consider trialling two or three and have teachers feed back to the group for shared decision-making. This process will take longer than a school leader choosing on the teaching staff's behalf; however, involving teachers in the process will help you have a stronger decision about which tool to use and increase the chances that it will be used comprehensively and effectively in classrooms.

Developing Assessment Capable Learners

Assessment capable learners understand what assessment is, what it is for, and how to get the best out of the process. They are involved in data conversations and understand their own progress and growth. For younger children, this can be as simple as using the same phonics and word-level assessment recording sheet each time you assess a student, but using a different coloured highlighter to mark correct responses. When you sit down with the student, you can say:

> (Before assessing)
>
> Last time we checked in on your reading I used a pink highlighter. I was so proud of how many pink marks I was able to make on your sheet! Today

I am going to use a green highlighter. I want you to know that however many green marks I make today I am proud of all of your hard work.

(After assessing)

Let's have a look at how many green marks I was able to make. Have a look! I made 8 green marks on your check-in sheet. That's 8 new sounds you've learned. Well done! I can see that you know these sounds here (point to them) and that you are learning to read words with these sounds. We are going to work together on helping you sound out nice and quickly with these new sounds you have learned.

A conversation such as the one above helps the student understand that they have been successful. (You set the success criteria of new green marks at the start) and also to know the next steps in their learning. We often hear that we want students to know what their next steps in learning are. They aren't going to know this on their own. In my opinion, a great data conversation involves the student in the process and makes a direct link to the content of your classroom lessons. You might also consider having an individual record of learning sheet for each student. As they learn new correspondences and skills, they can colour in the sheet and be a part of their own data collection. This sheet can then be reviewed at regular intervals to set goals with the student.

Snapshot of Practice 16 – Using a Data Wall in the Foundation Classroom

Eldon Jenkin – Foundation Teacher

I have always liked using data in my teaching and have been working on making it more visible and meaningful for students. I have worked hard to help students understand the role of data and that learning is a long-term undertaking. Part of this was breaking up the learning into small chunks and defining success as growth. My students now understand that:

- Practice is important
- Mistakes prime our brain for learning
- Everyone will make growth in their own way and time. It's not a race!

When introducing a data wall in my classroom, I worried about some students feeling discouraged and embarrassed by it. Most students were hugely motivated by the data wall and were eager for assessment to occur. It also helped them feel in charge of their learning. We do need to be sensitive when supporting students who need additional support. One of the considerations is making sure that every student has something represented that they are successful in. If a student doesn't want their data on the wall, it's important to respect that.

Eldon's Advice for Other Teachers

- Make your data collection and storage simple and sustainable. If it's labour intensive, it's hard to maintain.
- Make sure you explain to parents the idea behind a data wall if you decide to do one and help them understand what success looks like.
- Explicitly teach children how learning and the data wall are connected.

Troubleshooting

Q – My team is having trouble letting go of benchmark assessment.

A – The challenges of reading assessment are sometimes less about knowing how to conduct assessment or manage data and more about finding a new level of certainty after moving away from the familiar. Finding this new level of certainty requires reframing what success means for your students. Once your team can articulate this, you will be an important step closer to effective reading assessment practices.

Q – Some students have difficulty engaging with the assessment.

A – The provision of adjustment for assessment needs to be noted in a student's individual learning plan and then provided as needed. Some students have difficulty sustaining attention during the assessment. Break down the assessment into small chunks and conduct it over a series of days. Other students with anxiety might find direct questioning or reading aloud confronting and challenging. If a student struggles with answering direct verbal questions, provide the questions and allow them to answer them in a written form. If reading aloud is distressing, enable them to record their reading onto an iPad that they can take charge of.

Q – It can be difficult to determine whether students who have significant articulation challenges or are non-verbal for some reason can blend.

A – You can provide adjustments for these students by providing pictures of the words you want them to read. You would do this by showing them the word and providing a range of pictures. The student can then decode the word and point to the corresponding picture.

Q – Our school might have moved on from benchmark reading assessment but our region/district or central office might still require them.

A – Identify your most experienced teaching assistant/s and have them conduct the benchmark assessment. This ensures that the data is provided as required, but doesn't place the pressure on teachers to spend precious time on this task.

References

Moats, L. C. (2020). *Speech to print* (3rd ed.). Paul Brooks Publishing.

(NICHD) Eunice Kennedy Shriver National Institute of Child Health and Human Development, NIH, DHHS. (2000). Report of the National Reading Panel: Teaching children to read: Reports of the subgroups (00-4754). U.S. Government Printing Office.

Appendix 1

A List of Lesson Plans

Table 7.1 – Establishing Learning Behaviours
Figure 8.4 – Daily Shared Writing Routine
Table 9.2 – Partner Talk Lesson Plan
Table 9.3 – Vocabulary Introduction Lesson Plan
Table 10.1 – Jump it out Lesson Steps
Table 10.2 – Beginning Segmenting (You Do) Lesson Steps
Table 10.3 – Syllable Segmenting During Transitions
Table 10.4 – Rhyming During Transitions
Table 10.5 – Early Phoneme Identification Lesson Steps
Table 10.6 – Beginning Blending (I do)
Table 10.7 – Beginning Blending (We do)
Table 10.8 – Beginning Blending (You do)
Table 10.9 – Beginning Segmenting (I do)
Table 10.10 – Beginning Segmenting (We do)
Table 10.11 – Beginning Segmenting (You do)
Table 11.1 – Steps to a Basic Code Phonics Lesson
Table 11.2 – Steps to a Complex Code Phonics Lesson
Table 12.2 – Sentence Level Transcription Lesson Steps
Table 13.3 – Teaching Irregular High Frequency Words Lesson Steps
Table 14.2 – A Lesson with Mostly Decodable Texts

Glossary

Basic Code The phoneme/grapheme correspondences of single consonants, short vowels, and most common consonant digraphs (th, ch, ng, sh).
Complex Code Alternative spellings of the speech sounds of English.
Comprehension The ability to understand what is said and read.
Dialect A form of a language specific to a region.
Explicit Instruction An approach to instruction that involves direct teaching through an 'I do, We do, You do' structure, characterised by the full participation of every student and close monitoring of student progress
Fluency Smooth, accurate, and expressive reading.
Full Participation Lesson A lesson structure where every student is actively engaged in a task or responding to a question. This often involves partner talk, writing on whiteboards and feeding back response to the teacher who formulates a complete response from students' partial responses.
Grapheme Letter or letters that represent phonemes.
I Say, You Say An instructional technique where the teacher provides a model for language and the students repeat what the teacher has said.
Linguistic Relating to language.
Morpheme Smallest unit of meaning in a language. For example, prefixes, suffixes, bases.
Morphology The study of words and their parts including prefixes and suffixes.
Norm referenced A measure of achievement that compares a student with other students of the same age.
Orthography The spelling system of a language.
Partner Practice The practice of two students taking turns to engage with a text, list of words, set of phoneme/grapheme correspondence cards for the purpose of rehearsal.
Parts of Speech The category words are assigned to including nouns, verbs, adjectives, and adverbs depending on their function in a particular sentence.

Phonological Sensitivity Early phonological awareness relating to units larger than the phoneme level including syllables and onset and rime.
Phonemes The individual 'sounds' we say when we speak.
Phonemic Awareness An awareness of the individual phonemes in words and the ability to manipulate them.
Phonics The relationships between phonemes and the letters and letter combinations that represent them.
Orthographic Mapping The cognitive process where the way a word looks, the way it sounds, and what it means are bonded into long-term memory.
Response to Intervention A multi-tier approach to support where students who require additional instruction receive it in a structured, intentional, and responsive manner.
Scaffolding The process of support where structures are provided to assist students in their learning.
Syntax The arrangement of words in sentences.
Systematic Synthetic Phonics Instruction A form of explicit phonics instruction characterised by teaching phoneme/grapheme correspondences and then how to blend them together to read words.
The Big Six A set of core ideas crucial to effective reading instruction including oral language, phonological and phonemic awareness, phonics, vocabulary, fluency, and comprehension.
Vocabulary The number of words that a person understands and can use.

More from Jocelyn

Read the No-Nonsense Educator blog at
www.jocelynseamereducation.com/blog

Join the On the Structured Literacy Bus Facebook group at
https://www.facebook.com/groups/onthereadingbus

Purchase the Reading Success in Action Decoding Instruction series at
https://www.jocelynseamereducation.com/products

View tips and instructional clips at
https://www.youtube.com/c/JocelynSeamerEducation

Index

Note: *Italicised* folios refers figures and **bold** refers tables.

accuracy 17; skills-based assessment 185; student reading with 17; text level reading 178
active engagement 38, 57, 66, 94, 152
advice for teachers 50–51, 90, 91, 102, 103, 118, 119, 133, 148, 158, 169, 180, 181, 189
analytic phonics instruction 14, 16
Archer, A. 37
assessing decoding 183–185; *see also* decoding
assessing fluency 185–186; *see also* fluency
assessing phoneme 184
assessment 132; capable learners 187–189; choosing and conducting 73; consistent 66; of educational progress fluency scale **179**; formal 47, 62; formative 65; informal/one-to-one 62, 72–73, 132; multiple-choice 73; reading 72–73, 183, 186, 187, 189; tools 187; *see also* skills-based assessment
attention 35, 41, 66, 82, 88, 101, 164, 189
automaticity 12, 17; development in students 87–88; in phonemic skills **130–131**, 131,; skills-based assessment 185; text level reading 178
Ayto, J. 164

background knowledge 17–19, 58, 181; building in children 59; novice learners lacking 35; vocabulary and 118
basic code: code knowledge instruction 70; phonics **28**, **139–140**, 141; teaching 147
basic interpersonal skills (BICS) 106, **107**

Beck, I. 16, 108–109, **109**
Beginning Teacher Evaluation Study 37–38
Big Six: comprehension 18–20; fluency 17–18; ideas in reading instruction 9–10; oral language 10–12; phonemic awareness (PA) 12–13; phonics 13–16; phonological awareness 12–13; theoretical basis of *10*, 10–20; vocabulary 16–17
blending 50, *127*, 184–185; with graphemes 129; joint construction 130, **128–129**; model and deconstruct 130; phonemic awareness 12; and segmenting 126; supported practice 129; of syllable 122, **122**
Bowen, C. 49
Brown, A. 180

challenges 91–92; of child's reading development 17; of establishing effective instructional practices 19; learning 137; in oral language 11; reading 48, 132, 189
Clarke, P. J. 20
code charts 146, 147
Code Read Dyslexia Network 49
cognitive load theory 34–36, 41, 75, 81–82, 87, 176
cognitively academic language proficiency (CALP) 106, **107**
Colquhoun, D. 103
complex code 102; phonics lesson steps **143–144**; teaching 141–142
complex sentences 110, **111**
compound sentences: defined 110; teaching 108, 113–114, **114**

comprehension 18–20; assessing fluency and 185; instruction *30*; and language processing 47; oral 11–12, 16–17, 171; reading 29, 58, 118, 176, 179–181; shared reading to build 118; skills 19, 186; strategies 19
consolidated alphabetic phase 9
consolidating alternate spellings 145–146
consolidation **44**, 66, 142–146, 167, **177**
contextualised practice 168
cross curricula texts 156
Cummins, J. 106, **107**
curriculum: decodable texts across 174–175; expectations for sentence instruction 110–111; Foundation year 101; student needs in text use **173–174**

daily review 30, **32**, **44**, 94, 145, 167
daily shared writing *100*, 100–101
decodable texts 75–76, *76*, 150–160; guided reading 150–152, **147–148**; independent follow-up tasks 154–155; lesson structure with 152–154, 175–176, **176–177**; levelled texts 156; resourcing 155–156; sentence-level transcription **157**, 157–158; text level reading 171–172, 174–175, **176–177**; trouble-shooting 159
decoding: assessing 183–185; basis for students 180; and reading 95
decontextualised practice 167
Dehaene, S. 41, 65–66, 81, 151
developmental language disorder (DLD) 48
dialect 14, 24, 26, 60, 122
Dick, J. 118
Dictionary of Word Origins (Ayto) 164
differentiation 89; high impact teaching 86–88; options in literacy block **43–46**; reading difficulty 40–42
discussion 2, 19–20, 119, 153–154

effective feedback 90, 178
Ehri, L. 8–9, 15
Eide, D. 24
English: alphabetic code **25**; as complex language 14, 24; influenced by cultures and languages 24; orthography 24–25
English as an additional language or dialect (EALD) 106, 174
Essentials of assessing, preventing and overcoming Reading difficulties (Kilpatrick) 11
exemplars, writing of 156
explicit instruction 13, 27, 56, 63–64, 168–169, 171

Explicit instruction: Effective and efficient teaching (Archer and Hughes) 37
explicit teaching 12, 56, 60, 83, 94

Fahey, A. 158
fast lane learners 67, 108, 138
feedback 38, 65, 66; corrective 41; effective 90, 178
fiction/non-fiction texts 12, 19, 56, 59, 182
fluency 17–18; assessing 185–186; text level reading 177–178
Foley, L. 180
follow-up lessons 62
formal assessment 47, 62; *see also* assessment
Foundation **28**, 50, 62; considerations for 115–117; in literacy and numeracy 36; literacy block 101; for morphology 114–115; teachers 88–92, 133, 181, 188–189
fragments 112–113
Francis, B 133
full alphabetic phase 9, 15
full participation lesson 57, 82, 84, 94, 100
fully decodable texts 172, **173–174**

Gough, P. B. 7, 8
graphemes 14, 26–27; correspondences 50, 69, 75–76, 88, 94, 165, 184; fluency in 17; and phonemes 14; students 145; teaching 70
guided reading 150–152, **151**; *see also* reading
guided speaking 156

handwriting 35, 94–95, 138, 141, 147, 149
high impact teaching 81–92; considerations for Foundation teachers 88–92; differentiation 86–88; learning behaviours 84; low variance routines 81–84; strategies 36–38; visuals 85–86, *86*; *see also* teaching
Hughes, C. 37
Hyatt, K. J. 49

incidental opportunities 64, 119, 126, 145
independent follow-up tasks 154–155
independent practice 83–84, **84**
independent tasks work *98*, 99
inferencing skills 19
informal/one-to-one assessment 62, 71–72, 132; *see also* assessment
instruction *see* explicit instruction
instructional lag 74, **144**
instructional routine visuals 86, *86*, 104

instructional visuals 85–86
interest-based reading 156
intervention: program 20; response to 49; tier 2 51; tier 3 50–51
intrinsic load 35
irregular high frequency words (IHFW) 161–170; described 162–163; practising 167–169; teaching routine 165; troubleshooting 169; words lesson steps **166–167**
'I say, you say' 57, 157

Jenkin, E. 188–189
Johnston, R. 15
joint construction 82–83, 95, 100, 128, **157**
jump it out 121; lesson steps **122**

Kilpatrick, D. 11
knowledge building 59–60, 156, 172; *see also* background knowledge
Konza, D. 10
Kuhn, M. R. 17

Lane, K. 90
language-based lesson **44–45**, 95–96
language disorder (LD) 11, 48, 50
Language for Life (Stone) 29
language processing 47, 70
learning behaviours 84, **84**, 155
Learning Difficulties Australia 49
lesson plan: partner talk **107**
lessons: with decodable texts 152–154
lesson structure with decodable text 175–176, **176–177**; *see also* decodable texts
levelled texts 33, **147**, 155, 156, 172
linguistic 7, 8, 24, 60
literacy block 29–32, *31*, 93–105, *94*; components of 93–96; daily shared writing *100*, 100–101; differentiation options in **43–46**; foundation 101; growing independence in individual work in year 1 and 2 98–99; independent tasks work 99; lower primary *31*; troubleshooting 104–105; tub time 96–97; for year 1–2 102–103
literacy instruction 9, 29, 41, 58, 75, 172
literature-based lesson 30, **32**, 95–96
long-term memory 9, 34–35, 63, 67, 75, 161–162, 167, 168–169
low variance routines 66, 81–84, 86, 89, 91, 102; building the field 82; independent practice 83–84; joint construction 82–83; model and deconstruct 82; supported practice 83

MacAninch, N. 90
magnetic letters 65, 138, 141
Marchant, L. 168–169
Mariani, L. 81–82
McKeown, M. 19
meta-analysis 12–13
Michell, K. 89–90
minimal preparation activities 154–155
Moats, L. 29
monitoring progress 71–73
morphemes 14, 25, 27, 117, 131, 134, 148
morphology 27; explicit 174; foundations for 114–115; instruction 28, **28**; knowledge 157; oral and written 56; teaching 180–181
morpho-phonemic language 25, 27
mostly decodable texts 76–77, 95, 171, 172, **173–174**, 174–175, **176–177**; *see also* decodable texts
multi-age classes 91
multi-age teacher 90–91
multiple-choice assessment 73; *see also* assessment
multiple meanings of words *58*, 59
multisyllable words 71, 89, 134, 142, **144**, 178–179

National Assessment of Educational Progress (NAEP) 179, **179**
National Inquiry into the Teaching of Literacy 14
National Reading Panel 60–61, 132, 186
non-fiction/fiction texts 12, 19, 56, 59, 182
no preparation activities 154–155
norm referenced 62, 72, 132
nursery rhymes **124**, 124

oral language 10–12, 48; children facing difficulties 48; classroom 106–108; deficits 20; development 12, 16, 17, 55–57, 181; difficulties 48
orthographic mapping 9, 17, 151, 178
orthography 24, 25

pace and intensity of learning 136–137; *see also* learning
partial alphabetic phase 9
partner practice 95, 142, 145
partner reading 90, 153, 158, **177**
partner talk lesson plan **107**
parts of speech 10, 11, 56, 174
perceptual motor programs (PMP) 49
Phase Theory 7, 8–9
phonemic awareness (PA) 12–13, 60–61, 62–63, 124–126, 133; and phonological

sensitivity in year 1 and 2 126–127; skills 131
phonemic skills 50, 60–61; automaticity in **130**, 131; time frame 62
phonics 13–16, 136–149; basic code **139–140**, 141; code charts 147; complex code **143–144**; complex code, teaching of 141–142; conducting lesson on 138; consolidating alternate spellings 145–146; explicitly and systematically teaching 63–65; fast lane learners 138; foundation and year 1 and 2, teaching in 148; handwriting 138, 141; identifying students who need teaching 137–138; magnetic letters 138, 141; and morphology instruction **28**; multisyllable words 142; pace and intensity of learning 136–137; resourcing phonics lessons 147–148; review and consolidation 142–145; sound walls 147; supported practice 145; teacher led review 145; teaching 69–70; troubleshooting 148–149
phonological awareness 12–13, 61, 132–133
phonological sensitivity: activities 62; and phonemic awareness in year 1 and 2 126–131; teachable moments for 121–124
phonological skills 60; time frame 62
picture books: as source of tier 2 vocabulary 60; use to teach vocabulary 108–109
planning and teaching 57
Powell, S. 181
pre-alphabetic phase 9
pre-reading activities 152, 153–154, **176**
Principles of Instruction (Rosenshine) 36
prosody 17, 18; skills-based assessment 185; text level reading 179

rapid automatic naming (RAN) 50
reading: assessment 72–73, 183, 186, 187, 189; comprehension 179–180; and decoding 95; intervention 49; and spelling 73–74; using a set sequence 69–70; *see also* guided reading; text-level reading
reading difficulty 40–51; advice for teachers 50–51; causes of 47; children with oral language difficulties 48; differentiation 40–42; identify students with 47; prevention of 48–50; supporting students with 42–47
Reading Rope 8, *8*, 29, **32**, *94*

'read to me' texts 156
resourcing decodable texts 155–156; *see also* decodable texts
resourcing phonics lessons 147–148
response to intervention 49; *see also* intervention
reteach and monitoring progress 71–73
review and consolidation, phonics 142–145
rhyming during transitions 123
Rice, X. 102
rich text 19, 56, 60, 95, 153, 171–172, 180
Rosenshine, B. 36–37, 63

Scarborough, H. 8, *8*, 29, **32**, *94*
secondary skills and knowledge 34
segmenting: basic phonemic awareness 12; joint construction 128; lesson sequence **130**; model and deconstruct 130; phonemic 35; supported practice 129; of syllable during transitions 122
Seidenberg, M. 47
self-teaching hypothesis 76
semantic networks 58, *58*
sentence(s): and fragments 112–113; instruction 110–112, *112*; simple 110; structure **111**; teaching about 110
sentence-level transcription 94–95; decodable texts **157**, 157–158
sequence of teaching 75–76; *see also* teaching
Share, D. 76, 171
shared reading 12, 118
shared writing 30, 62, 95, *100*, 100–101, 126, 145
Sherrington, T. 36
sight word boxes 161–162, *161*
simple sentences 110; *see also* sentence(s)
Simple View of Reading 7, *7*, 18, 55
skill development 17, 62, 126, 135
skills-based assessment 183–189; accuracy 185; assessing decoding 183–185; assessing fluency 185; assessment capable learners 187–188; automaticity 185; comprehension 185; prosody 185; reading assessment 187; text-level assessment 185–186; troubleshooting 189; *see also* assessment
Snow, P. 10, *11*, 49
sound walls 147
speaking *see* guided speaking
Speech to Print (Moats) 29
Spelling for Life (Stone) 29
Standard Australian English 24

Stewart, C. 118
Stone, L. 29
students: automaticity development in 87–88; comparison 72–73; decoding basis for 180; engagement 71–72; identification with reading difficulty 47; inferencing skills 19; needs **173–174**; reading with accuracy 18; struggles faced by 42, 47; supporting tier 3 intervention 50–51; support with reading difficulty 42–47
students with additional needs (SWAN) 50–51
supported practice 83, 145
Swanson, E. 12
Sweller, J. 34, 41
syllable blending while giving instructions 122
syllable segmenting during transitions 123, **123**
syntax 10, 11, 30, 55, 56, 95–96, 108, 186
synthetic phonics instruction 14–15
systematic synthetic phonics instruction 14–15

teachers: advice for 50–51; led review in phonics 145; supporting students and families 49–50; year 1 and 2 89
Teaching Reading: Why the 'Fab Five' should be the 'Big Six' (Konza) 10
teach/teaching 24–33; about compound sentences 113–114, **114**; about sentences 110; complex code of phonics 141–142; considerations for 60, 62–63, 65–67, 70–71, 74, 77; fiction and non-fiction texts 59; foundation and year 1 and 2, phonics in 148; high impact strategies 36–38; literacy block 29–32, *31*, multiple meanings of words 59, *58*; phonics 63–65, 69–70; preparing to 175–176; reading and spelling together 73–74; routine 165; sentence structure **111**; sequence of 75–76; vocabulary using picture books 108–109; word relationships 58; *see also* high impact teaching
text-level assessment 185–186; *see also* assessment
text level reading 168–179; accuracy 178; automaticity 178–179; decodable texts 171, 174–176, **176–177**; fluency 177–178; prosody 179; reading comprehension 179–180; student needs **173–174**; troubleshooting 181–182; *see also* reading
Thorburn, K. 50
Tomlinson, C. 40
troubleshooting 134; decodable texts 159; irregular high frequency words 169; literacy block 104–105; phonics 148–149; skills-based assessment 189; text level reading 181–182
Tunmer, W. E. 7–8

uncontrolled texts 88, 171, 172, **173–174**
Uncovering the logic of English (Eide) 24, 29
U.S. National Reading Panel 9

visuals in high impact teaching 84–87, *85*; countdown timers 86; instructional 85–86; instructional routine 86, *86*; timetable 85, *85*; *see also* high impact teaching
vocabulary 16–17; building 58; introduction lesson plan **109**; practice 60; teaching using picture books 108–109

Watson, J. 15
word relationships, teaching of 58
working memory 34, 64, 137, 163
writing exemplars 156

For Product Safety Concerns and Information please contact our EU
representative GPSR@taylorandfrancis.com
Taylor & Francis Verlag GmbH, Kaufingerstraße 24, 80331 München, Germany

www.ingramcontent.com/pod-product-compliance
Lightning Source LLC
Chambersburg PA
CBHW061714300426
44115CB00014B/2679